MUSLIMS AND THE STATE IN BRITAIN, FRANCE, AND GERMANY

More than ten million Muslims live in Western Europe. Since the early 1990s and especially after the terrorist attacks of September 11, 2001, vexing policy questions have emerged about the religious rights of native-born and immigrant Muslims. Britain has struggled over whether to give state funding to private Islamic schools. France has been convulsed over Muslim teenagers wearing the *ḥijāb* in public schools. Germany has debated whether to grant "public-corporation" status to Muslims. And each state is searching for policies to ensure the successful incorporation of practicing Muslims into liberal democratic society. This book analyzes state accommodation of Muslims' religious practices in Britain, France, and Germany, first examining three major theories: resource mobilization, political-opportunity structure, and ideology. It then proposes an additional explanation, arguing that each nation's approach to Muslims follows from its historically based church–state institutions.

Professor Joel S. Fetzer teaches European and immigration politics at Pepperdine University. His research has been funded by the German Marshall Foundation of the United States, the MacArthur Foundation, the Friedrich Ebert Foundation, and the Yale Center for International and Area Studies. He is the author of numerous articles and book chapters on comparative immigration politics and on religion and political behavior. His most recent book is *Public Attitudes toward Immigration in the United States, France, and Germany* (Cambridge University Press 2000).

J. Christopher Soper is Endowed Professor of Political Science and Chair of the Social Science Division at Pepperdine University. A graduate of both Yale Divinity School and Yale's Ph.D. program in political science, Professor Soper has written extensively on church–state relations and religion and politics in Europe and the United States. Recipient of grants from the American Political Science Association and the Society for the Scientific Study of Religion, he is author of *Evangelical Christianity in the United States and Great Britain* (1994) and coauthor of *The Challenge of Pluralism: Church and State in Five Democracies* (1997).

Cambridge Studies in Social Theory, Religion, and Politics

Editors

David C. Leege   *University of Notre Dame*
Kenneth D. Wald   *University of Florida, Gainesville*

The most enduring and illuminating bodies of late nineteenth-century social theory – by Karl Marx, Max Weber, Emile Durkheim, and others – emphasized the integration of religion, polity, and economy through time and place. Once a staple of classic social theory, however, religion gradually lost the interest of many social scientists during the twentieth century. Scholarly interest in religiously based political conflict has reawakened with the recent emergence of phenomena such as Solidarity in Poland; the dissolution of the Soviet empire; various South American, Southern African, and South Asian liberation movements; the Christian Right in the United States; and al Qaeda. At the same time, fundamental questions are once again being asked about the role of religion in stable political regimes, public policies, and constitutional orders. The series Cambridge Studies in Social Theory, Religion, and Politics will produce books that study religion and politics by drawing upon classic social theory and more recent social scientific research traditions. Books in the series offer theoretically grounded, comparative, empirical studies that raise "big" questions about a timely subject that has long engaged the best minds in social science.

Other Books in the Series

Pippa Norris and Ronald Inglehart, *Sacred and Secular: Religion and Politics Worldwide*

Muslims and the State in Britain, France, and Germany

Joel S. Fetzer
Pepperdine University

J. Christopher Soper
Pepperdine University

PUBLISHED BY THE PRESS SYNDICATE OF THE UNIVERSITY OF CAMBRIDGE
The Pitt Building, Trumpington Street, Cambridge, United Kingdom

CAMBRIDGE UNIVERSITY PRESS
The Edinburgh Building, Cambridge CB2 2RU, UK
40 West 20th Street, New York, NY 10011-4211, USA
477 Williamstown Road, Port Melbourne, VIC 3207, Australia
Ruiz de Alarcón 13, 28014 Madrid, Spain
Dock House, The Waterfront, Cape Town 8001, South Africa

http://www.cambridge.org

First published 2005

Printed in the United States of America

Typefaces Janson Text 10/13 pt. and ITC Slimbach   *System* LATEX 2$_\varepsilon$ [TB]

A catalog record for this book is available from the British Library.

Library of Congress Cataloging in Publication Data
Fetzer, Joel S.
Muslims and the state in Britain, France, and Germany / Joel S. Fetzer, J. Christopher Soper.
p.   cm. – (Cambridge studies in social theory, religion, and politics)
Includes bibliographical references (p.) and index.
ISBN 0-521-82830-9 – ISBN 0-521-53539-5 (pb.)
1. Muslims – Europe, Western.   2. Islam and state – Europe, Western.   3. Great Britain –
Politics and government – 1945–   4. France – Politics and government – 1958–
5. Germany – Politics and government – 1990–   I. Soper, J. Christopher.
II. Title.   III. Series.
D1056.2.M87F48   2004
322′.1′088297–dc22   2004045667

ISBN 0 521 82830 9 hardback
ISBN 0 521 53539 5 paperback

Dedicated to Christina 瓊華, 親愛的太太和基督徒的姐妹, *and Ansar Fayyazuddin, dear friend and ally in the quest for justice*

– JSF

Dedicated to my wife, Jane Woodwell, and children, Katharine and David

– JCS

Contents

List of Figure and Tables

Figure

Tables

Preface

This book began while we were working on separate projects in European immigration politics and church–state relations. Throughout this previous research, we continued to encounter the somewhat anomalous phenomenon of religiously practicing Muslims settling in largely secular Western Europe. Much of the xenophobic rhetoric of extreme right-wing parties in the region also seemed increasingly anti-Islamic rather than simply anti-immigrant. The way in which states responded to the religious needs of Muslims, moreover, seemed linked to the particular church–state institutions of that country. Ted Jelen of the University of Nevada provided the first impetus to present our ideas on this topic at an American Political Science Association panel in 1999. After publishing this paper, we then decided to pursue a book-length study of the issue.

In the interest of full disclosure, we should probably document our own religious commitments, which were the subject of much curiosity during our field work. The first author is an active Mennonite with likely Jewish ancestors. The second author is an ordained minister in the United Churches of Christ, currently belongs to an Episcopal congregation, and holds fairly orthodox Christian beliefs. At any rate, both writers are strongly committed to religious liberty for all, not just for those believers whose faith is shared by a national majority or is popular.

As coauthors, we each have our individual specializations and so divided the work on this book accordingly. Fetzer focuses on quantitative studies of immigration politics in France and Germany, while Soper concentrates on institutional, church–state analysis of Britain and Germany. During the actual drafting of the text, Soper was primarily responsible for the British chapter, Fetzer for the French one, and the remaining narrative was written jointly.

The extensive field work needed for this project would never have been possible without substantial financial help from several sources. Pepperdine University provided release time for writing and financial support for travel, data collection, and translation of German-language interviews via the Dean's Summer Research Fund and the Endowed Fellowship and Endowed Professorship programs. We particularly wish to thank Dean David Baird and Assistant Dean Lee Kats for generously supporting faculty scholarship at Pepperdine. Central Michigan University funded a summer of Arabic study and preliminary writing. The German Marshall Fund of the United States made possible seven months of field work in the three countries. Grants from the American Political Science Association and the Society for the Scientific Study of Religion helped pay for the addition of several questions to two waves of Roper Europe's crossnational surveys. Responsibility for the analysis and interpretations in this book, however, rests solely with the authors.

Several institutes provided office space, research support, and collegiality during our stays abroad. Klaus J. Bade's Institut für Migrationsforschung und Interkulturelle Studien (IMIS) at the Universität Osnabrück hosted Fetzer during the winter semester of 2001. Catherine Wihtol de Wenden similarly accommodated the first author at Sciences Po's Centre d'Études et de Recherches Internationales (CERI) in Paris. North of the English Channel, Pepperdine University's London Center housed both authors in the spring and summer of 2001. Finally, the Institut de Recherches et d'Études sur le Monde Arabe et Musulman (IREMAM) of the Université de Provence was the first writer's semi-official home during his month of interviewing in Aix-en-Provence and Marseille.

A number of data archivists and survey researchers greatly aided this project. Horst Weinen of the Zentralarchiv für Empirische Sozialforschung at the Universität zu Köln generously provided us many helpful German citations and relevant data sources. Danielle Hermitan of the Banque de Données Socio-Politiques at the Institut d'Études Politiques de Grenoble likewise furnished us with the equivalent French data. London's Market and Opinion Research International (MORI) allowed us to analyze its 2001 poll on faith-based schools. Finally, Dagmar Morton and Alex Lund of Roper ASW in London conducted two waves of a three-nation poll on Islam in Europe for us. As usual, neither the producers nor providers of these data are responsible for our analyses and interpretations in this book.

We would also like to thank the many European and American scholars and activists who counseled us on their particular specialities: Mohammed Salim Abdullah, Klaus J. Bade, Laurie Brand, Jocelyne Cesari, Franck Fregosi, Vincent Geisser, Thomas Lemmen, Rémy Leveau, Francis Messner, Fuad Nahdi, Simone Nasse, Jørgen Nielsen, Jean-Claude Santucci, Ataullah Siddiqui, and Catherine Wihtol de Wenden. Thanks also to David Leege, Jørgen Nielsen, Kenneth Wald, and Catherine Wihtol de Wenden for their careful and gracious comments on all or part of our manuscript. We are similarly grateful to Klaus J. Bade, David R. Cameron, Rogers M. Smith, and Ted G. Jelen for writing letters in support of our German Marshall Fund application. All previously mentioned individuals are nonetheless relieved of any responsibility for our errors of fact or judgment.

Others provided more technical assistance. Paul Heere helped transcribe our German-language interviews. Mahmoud El-Sakkary translated some relevant works from Arabic. Malía Rivera patiently faxed countless letters all over Europe for us. And Tammy Ditmore composed our extensive index.

This book owes its existence to the approximately one hundred interviewees in Europe who graciously gave of their time to help two inquiring Americans even though our informants had no reason to trust us or our motives. Often our hosts also served us delicious South Asian, North African, or Turkish meals, fringe benefits of our jobs in comparative political science. Though we are equally grateful to them, a number of the people we interviewed do not appear in the bibliography for various reasons. Some preferred to remain anonymous, others provided information confirming the accounts of cited interviewees, and others did not grant us formal permission to use their interviews in this book. To all a sincere thank you, *merci*, or *Danke*. Sadly, international understanding has deteriorated to such an extent since September 11, 2001, that we probably would not be able to conduct such interviews now. We should also note that unless otherwise indicated, the affiliations and positions of interviewees as listed in the bibliography are current as of the first half of 2001. Since we ended our field work, some of our informants have switched titles or organizations in the rapidly changing world of European Muslims.

Lewis Bateman of Cambridge University Press deserves special gratitude for guiding us through the production process and approving this manuscript in the first place. We are also thankful to his assistant, Lauren Levin, for helping out with various publication-related details, to Cambridge University Press's two anonymous reviewers for very useful suggestions for revision, and to Andy Saff for exemplary copy-editing.

Portions of this book have appeared elsewhere previously and are used with permission. A previous version of Chapter 1 formed the basis for the article "Explaining the Accommodation of Muslim Religious Practices in France, Britain, and Germany" in *French Politics* (© 2003 by Palgrave Macmillan Ltd.). Most of Chapter 5 likewise appeared as "The Roots of Public Attitudes toward State Accommodation of European Muslims' Religious Practices before and after September 11" in the *Journal for the Scientific Study of Religion* (© 2003 by *JSSR*).

Over the seven years of work on this book, both authors have enjoyed immense support from their families and close friends. Joel is especially grateful to Christina Chiung-Hua Wu, who entered his life almost immediately upon his return to the United States. Her love, toleration, and confidence in him make their life together a joy. Fetzer similarly wishes to thank Ansar Fayyazuddin of Stockholms universitet for two decades of warm friendship, intellectual exchange, interreligious dialogue, and political solidarity as well as for serving as best man when Joel and Christina married. Fetzer's ever-adventurous parents once again found time in their busy schedules to keep him company during arduous stretches of field work on the French Riviera. Isaak I-li Fetzer, who was born six hours after Joel completed the penultimate draft of this book, has tolerated his daddy's occasional bouts of proofreading-induced absent-mindedness. The Baptiste Gemeinde Osnabrück hosted Joel during the winter of 2001. And Óscar A. Chávez, Eliseo Franco, Daniel González, and the rest of Iglesia Evangélica Bethel have prayed for and nurtured Fetzer since the mid-1990s.

Chris would like to thank Jane Woodwell, his wife and his best friend. With good humor, grace, and patience, Jane has supported his efforts while forging a career of her own. Chris would also like to thank his children, Katharine and David, who patiently endured their father's extended absences for research trips to Western Europe and sometimes long hours at the office. It is always a joy to return home to such an understanding and energetic family, and to consider with them the substance of daily living, including play schedules, sports matches, youth outings, homework assignments, and chores. Soper's parents, Ralph and Rosemary, instilled in him a love of learning and an intellectual curiosity without which such a project could never have been imagined. Finally, Chris wishes to thank his "third floor" friends Mike, Steve, Jeff, and Greg, who have provided grist for his intellectual and spiritual mill for more than a decade.

Explaining the Accommodation of Muslim Religious Practices in Western Europe

The government has been telling us that we are citizens of this country, that we have equal rights. But when we ask for equal rights, for our own schools like other faiths have their own schools, the government tells us that they will be divisive, and that they will create a ghetto mentality. It is Islam that has been ghettoized by the Establishment.

K. S. Butt (2001), chair of the Islamic Resource Centre, Birmingham

Muslims have become a part of this society. More than three million Muslims live in Germany permanently. They are not going to "go home." Their home is *here*.

Nadeem Elyas (2001), chair of the Zentralrat der Muslime in Deutschland, Cologne, Germany

Today, a French person is not necessarily Catholic, Protestant, etc. Otherwise, a French person would have a beret, a baguette – those are stereotypes. Today a person is French through an act of citizenship, by sharing certain common values and by [supporting] everyone's right to find happiness. . . . But in the end a French person can be a Muslim, can be a Catholic, can be a Jew, can be a Buddhist. . . . [Muslims should enjoy religious liberty] just as other [French] citizens do.

Saïda Kada (2001), president of Femmes Françaises et Musulmanes Engagées, Lyon, France

STATE ACCOMMODATION OF Muslim religious practices is an increasingly important political issue across Western Europe. More than ten million Muslims currently live in Western Europe, which makes them the largest religious minority in the region. Islam is the third largest religion overall, and in most West European countries, it is growing much faster than the historically dominant Catholic and Protestant churches (Hollifield 1992; Nanji 1996; Nielsen 1999). In Germany, there are an estimated 2,200 mosques or Islamic prayer rooms, most of which have been organized in the past decade but which are still insufficient to meet the religious needs of Muslims in the country (Kusbah 1997; Spuler-Stegemann 1998:150). There are nearly as many religiously active Muslims as Anglicans in England and Roman Catholics in France (Brierley 2001; Caldwell 2000). Islam is a significant social and religious force in Western Europe.

The quotations at the beginning of this chapter suggest that Muslims want the state to recognize their religious status and accommodate them justly and fairly. As we will demonstrate in the pages ahead, however, what states view as equitable treatment for Muslim citizens and immigrants, what they consider to be reasonable and just in terms of accommodating Muslim religious practices, and how governments pursue the twin policies of recognizing the religious rights of Muslims while insuring their effective incorporation into the values of the host country vary widely in Western Europe. Although states face similar challenges, there is a notable cross-national divergence in policy related to how and whether Western European states recognize and accommodate Muslim religious practices. The aim of this book is to explain how three European states – Britain, France, and Germany – have accommodated the religious needs of Muslims, and to explain why there is such a difference in how they have done so.

Background

Muslims began immigrating to Europe in large numbers following the Second World War. They were part of a great wave of immigration that brought workers from the poorer countries of the Mediterranean, Eastern Europe, and the former colonies to the industrialized states of the West that were enjoying an economic boom and trying to rebuild in the war's aftermath. Private employers and governments across Western Europe actively recruited foreign workers to provide the labor necessary to continue the economic expansion (Bade 1983:59–95; Frémeaux 1991:209–75).

In the face of the economic recession of the early 1970s, however, European states gradually closed their borders to low-skilled workers but allowed for the possibility of family reunion and political asylum. Host countries assumed that immigrants were temporary workers who would want to return to their country of origin, but many foreign-born residents had no interest in doing so. Ironically, this effort to restrict immigration had the unintended consequence of encouraging a "second wave" of immigration as family members and dependents of the original postwar economic migrants joined their families in Western Europe. This policy transformed the immigrant population from single migrants to families who wanted permanent settlement (Boyer 1998:87–104; Kettani 1996; Nielsen 1999:25–35). Since many of these immigrants were Muslims, the Muslim population in Western Europe expanded rapidly.

Family settlement also changed the political calculus; immigrants became concerned not simply with their political and economic rights as workers, but also with their cultural and religious needs as permanent residents or citizens. Vexing policy questions emerged related to the religious rights of Muslim immigrants and citizens. Governments were suddenly confronted with such issues as how or whether to accommodate Muslim religious practices in state institutions such as schools, prisons, and hospitals; how or whether to develop their communities; whether to pass laws specifically designed to protect Muslims against religious discrimination; and what efforts to take to stem native discrimination against them (Cesari 1997; Morsy 1992; Nielsen 1999:36–46; Özdemir 1999:244–59).

The result in every country in the region has been political controversy around issues of Muslim religious rights. Conflict in Britain has crystallized on the question of whether the state education system will fully finance private Islamic schools under the same conditions that apply to Christian and Jewish ones. Germany has contended with the question of how or whether to grant public corporation status (*Körperschaft des öffentlichen Rechts*) to Muslims as well as to Christians and Jews. Such a status would signal that Islam is a part of the country's religious landscape and allow Muslims' social welfare organizations to receive state funds. France annually struggles with the question of whether or not Islamic girls will be allowed to wear the *ḥijāb* in public schools. Each of the states has witnessed negotiations over such contested practices as regulations on building mosques and policy regarding the religious needs of Islamic workers. Finally, there is a vibrant debate in each of these countries on what the goals of public policy toward Muslims ought to be. On the one hand, governments sometimes pursue policies that encourage Muslims to assimilate themselves to the values of Western society, even when that means abandoning some of the particular features of their religious identity. At other times, states have encouraged Muslims and others to celebrate religious diversity and for Muslims to maintain their most deeply held religious values.

These concerns became more acute in the aftermath of the attacks on the World Trade Center in September 2001 by Muslim extremists. The realization that many of the terrorists in those attacks had lived and trained among a network of coreligionists in Western Europe raised significant questions among political leaders on how best to ensure the successful incorporation of Muslims into the values of a liberal democracy. Jean-Marie Le Pen of National Front scored a surprising electoral victory in France's presidential primary election of 2002, and the British National Party won its first two victories in over a decade in city council races that same year. In both cases, these far-right parties ran on anti-immigrant and anti-Muslim political planks. Governments throughout the region passed more restrictive immigration and asylum laws. Those policies are particularly salient to Muslims, who make up the largest percentage of immigrants and asylum seekers to Western European countries. What is clear is that disputes about the Islamic religion and Muslims are increasingly prominent in Western Europe.

While European states have faced a common set of challenges in accommodating the religious needs of Muslims, they have taken substantially different approaches in their accommodation of Muslims' religious practices. Britain[1] led the way in tightening immigration controls in the early 1960s and limiting the citizenship opportunities for residents in its former colonies. In more recent years, Britain has refused to extend the law against racial discrimination in employment, housing, and education to include religious discrimination, a key concern for Muslims (Islamic Human Rights Commission 2000), and the Blair Labour government has proposed a bill that would make it more difficult for immigrants and asylum seekers to gain citizenship (Hoge 2002).

At the same time, however, the state has been fairly open to accommodating the cultural and religious needs of Muslims (Spencer 1997). Britain embraced multiculturalism in state-supported schools in the 1970s; the curriculum in required religious-education classes includes an extensive treatment of not only Christianity, but also Judaism, Islam, and Sikhism (Keene and Keene 1997). When confronted with the issue of girls wearing the *hijāb* in state-run schools, British educational authorities quickly reached a compromise that allowed girls to wear the headcovering so long as it conformed with the color requirements of the school uniform (Liederman 2000). After

---

[1] This book will consider policy regarding state accommodation of Muslims' religious practices in England, as opposed to the policy in all four regions (England, Northern Ireland, Scotland, and Wales) that make up the United Kingdom.

many years of trying to win state aid for Islamic schools under the same conditions that govern aid to Christian schools within the state system, the government in 1998 approved two independent Islamic schools (Howe 1998). A recent Green Paper on education encouraged an expansion of the faith-based school system to allow many more religious schools to receive state aid (*Schools* 2001).

France began to place greater restrictions on immigration in the 1970s; in the early 1980s, the state initiated what turned out to be a wholly ineffectual policy of subsidizing migrants' return to their country of origin (Weil 1991). Most of these laws were repealed in the late 1990s. The legislature also passed laws that made it marginally more difficult for immigrants and the children of immigrants to gain citizenship, although most Muslims in France are citizens.

In contrast to Britain, however, France has been far less accommodating to the religious needs of Muslims. France has rejected multiculturalism as an appropriate educational model in the state schools. Aside from such short lessons on the "Muslim world" as those in the *cinquième* history and geography class (Marseille and Scheibling 1997:24–39), French secondary school students learn nothing about Islam. Despite the popular impression that the *Conseil d'État*'s decision on the "Scarf Affair" resolved the issue (Cesari 1997:108–21; de Wenden and Leveau 2001:78–9; Gaspard and Khosrokhavar 1995), French Muslim leaders estimate that "hundreds" of Muslim young women have been expelled from public schools for refusing to remove the *ḥijāb* (Kabtane 2001; Merroun 2001). These young women are then forced to study by correspondence, rely on volunteer Muslim tutors, or abandon their education altogether (Kada 2001). This strict version of *laïcité* is the dominant view in the most powerful teacher unions (Berguin 2001), which is significant because teachers are public officials who implement policy in the institution where church–state conflict around Islam most consistently arises: the schools. The state has been vigorously secular and opposed to the notion that public institutions should be made to assist the religious practices of Muslims (Peach and Glebe 1995).

A third country, Germany, represents something of a hybrid of these state responses. Only a very small percentage of Muslims in Germany are citizens, and until President Gerhard Schröder's reforms of 1999, very few immigrants had the right to become German nationals. The state has also used various measures to encourage immigrants to return home, though these have largely been ineffectual. Finally, the German government has urged states in the European Union to tighten domestic immigration controls (John 2002).

On the other hand, Germany has been more willing than France to accommodate the cultural and religious needs of its Muslim population. The state has funded some Islamic social welfare and cultural organizations and established an Islamic school in Berlin (Doomernik 1995). In the state of North Rhine-Westphalia, moreover, education authorities have mandated the teaching of Islam in required religion courses in public schools, and have even gone so far as to write the required textbook. The clear intent of this decision is to encourage Muslims to learn more about their faith in the public schools, and to ensure that the version of Islam they are taught is fully compatible with liberal democracy (Gebauer 1986, 2001; Pfaff 2001).

There have been a number of fine studies of immigration into Western Europe (Castles and Miller 1993; Collinson 1993; Joppke 1999; Soysal 1994). These scholars have focused much needed attention on a phenomenon that has, in the words of one analyst, "been more transformative in [its] effect" in Western Europe than any other since 1945 (Messina 1996:134). These accounts, however, tend to focus on economic and citizenship issues and largely ignore questions of the religious identity and needs of Muslims. Social scientists, in short, have devoted very little attention to the religious aspect of Muslim policy demands, despite the fact that social and political tensions have mounted in recent years over a series of religious matters.

One reason for this silence on religious questions has been a perception among social scientists, often assumed rather than stated, that Western Europe is essentially secular and that issues of church and state are no longer relevant to public policy. According to this view, religious disputes were historically important in Europe, but those issues were largely settled, or at least minimized, in recent decades as the state became more secular and began to treat religious groups more or less equally. As we will demonstrate in the country chapters that follow, there is something to this thesis. Religion, which was at the center of political conflict in Europe a century ago, became less important politically in the middle decades of the twentieth century. However, the migration and settlement of large numbers of Muslims into Western Europe poses a new challenge to the existing church–state arrangements in countries and has resurrected somewhat dormant religious disputes.

Theories To Be Tested

How can we explain the disparate political responses to the religious concerns of Muslims in Britain, France, and Germany? What have these states done in terms of public policy to accommodate the religious needs of their Muslim populations, and just as importantly, what explains the different state reactions? There is very little literature and no consensus on this central question, but there is a very rich literature on the policy-making process as it relates to immigration and citizenship policies in Western Europe that can be applied to our primary concern. The dominant theories in the field are resource mobilization that views politics as a contest of competing actors, with the outcome affected by their relative resources. Political opportunity structure theory analyzes how political institutions shape the way that actors advance their interests and the ensuing policies. Ideological theories contend that preexisting ideas about the nature and purpose of government impact the development of public policy. We argue in this book that each of these theories sheds some light on state accommodation of Muslim religious rights in Britain, France, and Germany, but that none of them sufficiently explains important differences among the countries. We contend that the development of public policy on Muslim religious rights is mediated in significant ways by the different institutional church–state patterns within each of these countries.

Resources and Muslim Mobilization

One common approach in the literature on immigration is to focus on the origin, ethnic composition, and organizational patterns of Muslim communities within a particular nation-state (Anwar 1995; Bistolfi and Zabbal 1995; Kepel 1997; Nielsen 1995; Penninx et al. 1993). These accounts explain a state's policy on Muslim religious rights by analyzing domestic political considerations and the relative power of parties and movements that support Muslim religious rights against those that oppose them. Borrowing implicitly from resource mobilization theory, these descriptions accent the role of resources in mobilizing Muslim groups in Western Europe and stress the organizational structures that link individuals into a social movement.

Resource mobilization theory emerged in the late 1970s as a deliberate attempt to correct the psychological models of collective behavior that dominated sociology and political science in the 1960s (Gamson 1990; Zald and McCarthy 1987). This theory rejected the assumptions of the prevailing explanations that held that collective action was a spontaneous and disorganized activity and that movement participants were essentially irrational. By contrast, resource mobilization theory assumed the rationality of participants in a social movement and focused on the capacity of organized groups to acquire politically significant resources for their collective purposes (Ferree 1992).

According to this interpretation, the most important barrier to a movement's success is a lack of resources. Mayer N. Zald and John D. McCarthy (1987:11) note that the "transformation of social movement theory rests upon the recognition that the mobilization of resources (labor, materials, and money) for collective action is problematic." While people might identify with a set of social or political goals, absent political resources, there will be no effective collective action on behalf of those group goals; successful movements are those that overcome the barriers to collective action. The key features of an effective social movement are, first, a skilled cadre of leaders who can translate the amorphously held values of the group into political capital, and, second, a well-established institutional structure from which group leaders draw resources to form new organizations. It is through these internal networks that leaders are able to raise resources and recruit members for social movement organizations.

As we noted previously, a number of scholars implicitly use the insights of resource mobilization theory to explain the political outcomes of movements for Muslim religious rights in Western Europe. A common theme in these accounts is that Muslim groups have been politically ineffective because they lack the resources necessary to bargain effectively with the state. Wasif Shadid and Sjoerd van Koningsveld note, for example, that "Muslims in most Western European states have thus far been unsuccessful in creating representative organizations at national levels which can function as spokesman for the Muslim communities with the respective government" (1996:3). It is the absence of a representative organization, in their view, that explains why Western European states have failed to respond to the political demands of Muslim immigrants and citizens. Ronald Kaye (1993) echoes this theme in his comparison of the politics of Muslim and Jewish groups in Great Britain. He notes that the Muslim community is larger than its Jewish counterpart, but that Muslim groups have not been as effective as Jewish ones at winning state concessions on the policy issue of the religious slaughter of animals. Kaye contends that Jewish groups have three significant political resources that are generally absent in the Muslim community: communal unity, coherent organizational resources, and the strategic placement of communal personnel in elite positions. It is the presence of these resources among Jewish groups, and the absence of them among their Muslim counterparts, that explains the different policy outcomes.

Several analysts also note that the existence of ethnic, religious, national, and linguistic divisions within the Muslim community acts as a barrier to their political mobilization in Western European nations (Amiraux 1996;

Scantlebury 1995; Vertovek and Peach 1997). In Britain, for example, Muslims are divided by nation of origin (India, Pakistan, Bangladesh, and various Arab countries), major branches of Islam (Sunnism and Shiism), and Islamic schools of thought (Deobandis, Barlewis, and Wahhabism). Muslim groups in Britain have organized dozens of political organizations, many of which claim to speak for the Muslim community, but given the internal divisions among Muslims, it has been difficult for any one of these groups to become an effective national group. The division of Muslim groups is so great that some scholars point out that "the term Islamic community is inaccurate, and is better replaced by the plural form, religious communities" (Rath et al. 1999:67). Steven Vertovek and Ceri Peach (1997:30) correctly note that government authorities across Europe use this apparent disunity as a way of "refusing to respond to Muslims' socio-political overtures."

Muslims in Western Europe have for the most part failed to produce a native-born leadership, relying instead on religious and political leaders who are themselves immigrants or foreign born. An estimated 95 percent of all imams in France, for example, come from abroad (Le Breton 1998). The same appears to be the case for religious leaders in other West European countries as well (Cherribi 2001). The absence of native-born clergy and group leadership almost certainly means that Muslim groups lack key resources, particularly information about how best to use the political system to their advantage.

Finally, Carolyn Warner argues that there might be something endemic in "the structure and ideology of Islam itself" that limits the mobilization of the Muslim community; there is no counterpart in Islam to a Christian church, no formally instituted body to supervise the religious and political agenda for Muslims (1999:5). Warner claims that the absence of this religious hierarchy, particularly among Sunni Muslims, makes it difficult to organize the Muslim community as a whole. Individual mosques are important places of political mobilization for the Muslim immigrant community, she argues, but because they are locally controlled, often led by persons who are not themselves clerics, and frequently led by foreign-born imams, the capacity of Muslims to form a well-organized national political movement is limited.

Much can be said for using the insights of resource mobilization theory to explain the politics of state accommodation for the religious rights of Muslims in Western European nations. To the extent that there is disunity among Muslims (which is not surprising given their diverse origins), it does act as an obstacle to forming powerful organizations for collective political action. Our account of how European states have responded to the religious needs of Muslims will thus pay attention to internal dynamics within the Muslim community that have limited its capacity to form organizations and bargain effectively with the state. On the other hand, a focus on resources alone is not enough to explain why states have responded as they have to the policy demands of Muslim immigrants. As we noted previously, Britain has been more generous in accommodating Muslim religious demands than has France. According to resource mobilization theory, the reason for this difference would have to be that British Muslims have had group leaders with access to some set of significant political resources that French Muslims have lacked. A closer look at the politics of Muslim groups in the two countries, however, will reveal that this is not entirely the case. The British Muslim community is smaller than the French one, it is no better organized, it does not enjoy a unified cadre of leaders, and it has failed to establish a single national political organization to represent the interests of Muslim immigrants. While divided in some important respects, Muslims in France are organized into central political and religious organizations through the Paris Mosque, the Union of Muslim Organizations, and the National Federation of French Muslims (Kusbah 1997). Yet it is Muslims in Britain, not France, who have won key concessions from the state. The reason, we will argue, has less to do with resources than with opportunities provided, or not provided, by the existing institutional structure of church and state in each state.[2]

Political Opportunity Structures and Muslim Mobilization

A second common approach in the literature on how European states have responded to the religious policy demands of Muslims focuses less on political resources and more on political institutions. Borrowing from political opportunity structure theory, this explanation highlights the direct and indirect ways that state officials and institutions influence the capacity of groups to engage in collective action, and examines the policy outcomes that follow from that political mobilization (Evans, Rueschemeyer, and Skocpol 1985; McAdam 1982; Tarrow 1998). The theory contends that key regime characteristics – such as whether it is a unitary or federal polity; the type of electoral system; the separation of powers between the executive,

---

[2] A resource mobilization theory also has the disadvantage of lending itself to arguments that have the flavor of blaming the victims of discriminatory treatment (Muslims in this case) for their political situation. The unstated assumption of such theories is that the Muslims would be better served if they were more like Christians.

legislative, and judicial branches of government; and the position of key political elites – all channel the politics of social groups.

There are two ways in which state structures are seen as important in the politics of Muslim groups. First, inherited political institutions influence the political activism of groups in specific ways. Ruud Koopmans and Paul Statham (2000:34) point out that a state's "institutional dimensions define the available channels of access" for groups like Muslims who want to challenge the polity. Jeroen Doomernik (1995:53) argues that "there is a direct connection between the institutionalization of the immigrant culture and what the host country's legal system allows." The political concentration of power in France, for example, means that Muslims must take their case to national political institutions if they are going to be effective. Claire Dwyer and Astrid Meyer (1996) similarly conclude that the institutionalization of Islam in Europe appears to depend on the ways in which the existing legislation can be utilized by Muslim groups. In a related vein, Virginie Guiraudon notes that "the character of the institutions responsible for migrant policy is important – whether they are centralized, parapublic, unitary, politically insulated, or under judicial scrutiny – and whether consultation with interest groups is institutionalized" (1998:295). The most important of those institutional variables for immigration politics include "the immigrants' legal situation; their social and political rights; and host society citizenship laws, naturalization procedures, and policies in such areas as education, housing, the labor market, and social assistance that shape conditions and immigrants' responses" (Ireland 1994:10). Jeannette Money focuses on the electoral process to explain divergent state policies on immigration. She contends that politicians make public policy, but that they face different incentives and electoral pressures when they do so. A geographic concentration of immigrants necessarily invites local concerns about immigration policy, but "the dynamics of the political competition funneled through British political institutions catapulted immigration controls onto the national agenda much earlier there" (1999:104).

Not only are institutions important in shaping how groups are politically active, they are also significant in determining whether groups achieve their goals. The reason for this is that the political structures of some nations are more amenable than others to the policy changes sought by Muslim groups. Patrick Ireland (1994), for example, examines immigration politics in France and Switzerland, with a particular focus on the impact of France's unitary polity compared to the effect of the Swiss federal political system. He argues that the political centralization of power in the French state forces immigrants to aim for national legislation to win state concessions;

the difficulty of that prospect, however, has meant that immigrants have had little policy impact. The Swiss federal system, by contrast, allows Muslim groups to mobilize at local levels, where their power is concentrated; the result is that they have gradually been able to win more policy victories.

Romain Garbaye (2000) highlights a similar dynamic in his comparison of the politics of ethnic conflict in Birmingham, England, and Lille, France. Garbaye notes that Birmingham city officials worked closely with ethnic groups and took their demands seriously because Britain's party system and parliamentary style of government empowers organized groups at the local level. The more centralized French party structure and presidential system, by contrast, allowed city leaders in Lille effectively to ignore ethnic groups in the city. The support or opposition of key political elites to Muslim demands can also affect a movement's outcome.

To the extent that British Muslims have won policy concessions that their French or German counterparts have not, therefore, a political opportunity structure theory might well argue this is a result of the different political opportunities afforded Muslims in the two countries. To take one example, because of very different citizenship laws in the two countries, a much higher percentage of British Muslims are citizens than are German Muslims. Because they are more likely to be citizens, British Muslims have myriad political opportunities for activism at their disposal. They can, for instance, participate through conventional political channels (voting and running for elective office), and existing parties have an incentive to make direct electoral appeals to them. German Muslims, by contrast, are less likely to be citizens, they cannot as effectively participate through conventional politics, parties have limited reasons to make appeals to them, and they even face the threat of deportation if they engage in unconventional political activism (Guiraudon 1998; Nielsen 1992; Peach and Glebe 1995). Given those political opportunities, therefore, British Muslims are likely to be more effective politically than their German counterparts.

One of the chief advantages of a political opportunity structure theory is that it is inherently comparative. The question that we posed at the beginning of this chapter as the focus of our study – why states have responded differently to the religious needs of Muslims – calls for such a crossnational approach. It is apparent that Muslim citizens and permanent residents in these three countries have identical goals; they want to build mosques for public worship and establish religious schools to transmit the faith, and they want the state to make the concessions necessary so that they can practice their religion. What is different across Western European states is how states have responded to those religious concerns. There is much to be gained in using political opportunity structure theory to focus on the institutional reasons for those differences. What we will contend is that political opportunity structure theory is not wrong for our purposes, but that it is limited in two key respects. First, the theory has not yet been applied to the question that we are principally interested in answering in this book; second, the theory has not fully recognized that religious institutions are a part of the state structure and that they have been central in shaping the politics of Muslim groups.

While there are some exceptions (Nielsen 1999), few analysts of Western European immigrants have focused much on the *religious* needs of the groups in question. Instead, state structural accounts have paid attention to immigrants' political rights, citizenship claims, labor demands, and civil rights and liberties. What we will argue, however, is that Muslim religious rights and needs are a key component – perhaps *the* key component – of their political demands. Muslims care a great deal about winning public recognition for their religion, having the state accommodate their religious practices, and being able to pass on their faith to their children in what they perceive to be a hostile social and political environment. That most accounts of Muslims in Western Europe have not systematically considered the politicization of these religious issues, therefore, marks a significant hole in the existing literature.

State structure theories have also failed to consider how the inherited institutional context of church and state in Western European nations has shaped the political resolution of Muslim religious demands. While some accounts briefly note the constitutional status of religion in particular states (Zolberg and Woon 1999), few authors expand on what role this institutional context assumes for Muslim politics, particularly for how religious issues are resolved. What we will argue, by contrast, is that the constitutional and legal status of religion in each nation, along with the historical context through which the institutions of church and state have been related, are very significant in shaping how Britain, France, and Germany have accommodated the religious needs of Muslim groups. That history and those institutional structures have been key components in explaining the disparate ways in which states have accommodated the religious needs of Muslims.

Political Ideology and Muslim Mobilization

A third theoretical perspective pays more attention to ideas than to institutions, actors, or political resources. Picking up on much of the interest in recent political science literature on the connection between ideas and policies, this view contends that a nation's political ideology, particularly ideas about citizenship, nationality, and pluralism, shapes how the state resolves issues related to immigrant rights. Adrian Favell (1998) explains the divergent responses to ethnic and racial groups, particularly those of Muslim origin, in France and Britain in terms of each nation's public philosophy, or political theory. He argues that the guiding principle of political incorporation for immigrant groups in France is the republican tradition (Weil 1991) that favors a philosophy of integration rather than accommodation. The notion that France has a culturally particular idea of what it means to become a French citizen meant that French political elites and policy makers opposed separate Islamic institutions because this arrangement would violate the state's ideological commitment to integrating individual outsiders into the French political culture (Favell 1998:45). Instead of transforming immigrants into ideal citizens, the dominant ideas in Britain's political ideology place greater emphasis on managing relations among divergent populations, and allowing separate groups to retain their distinctive identities. Such an ideology has meant that British policy makers from both of the major parties have been open to recognizing Islamic immigrants through public policy. This commitment explains why the state has supported multicultural education, race relations legislation, separate Islamic schools, and the development of independent Muslim communities. Political compromise is also consistent with Britain's pragmatic political tradition, which gives greater preference to what works than to abstract theorizing.

In a similar vein, Erik Bleich (1998) describes what he calls an "ideological prior" (a preexisting set of philosophical commitments) that structures the debate among policy makers on immigrant rights within a particular country. Once these ideas about national identity are embedded within a political culture, they prove resistant to change. In a comparison of citizenship laws in Germany and France, Rogers Brubaker (1992) argues that public policy is conditioned by an entrenched "cultural idiom" that effectively determines the policy outcome. David Blatt (1995) takes the argument a step further and contends that these "institutionalized norms" also shape the collective action of immigrant groups trying to change public policy. The inherited national ideas about political membership are so powerful that they even impact outsider groups who are trying to gain access to the political system.

A number of critics have pointed out that ideological accounts alone cannot easily explain the fact that nations' citizenship laws have proven to be quite malleable in recent years. Christian Joppke notes that the literature often characterizes Germany as a country that rejects immigration, despite the fact that "a series of Constitutional Court rules obliterated the official not-a-country-of-immigration policy" (1998:284). He makes a compelling case that guestworkers had won concessions from the state well before Schröder's reforms of 1999 made it easier for them to gain German citizenship. Joppke's evaluation does not, however, fundamentally reject the premise that ideas matter in the policy process. On the issue of family reunification policy, Joppke writes "it pitted a state that would rather not see it happen against the immigrant who only sought what liberal states cannot deny – family unity" (1998:281). European states have had a more welcoming family unification policy than their immigration rhetoric might envision, Joppke argues, because liberal values demanded it. In the German case, then, it was competing ideas, specifically international norms and self-imposed moral obligations, that undermined the state's inherited not-a-country-of-immigration ideology.

The point of this discussion is that even the detractors of ideological theories understand that ideas can drive the policy process as much as institutions or resources. Analysts who have adapted the theory have made a compelling case that existing laws on citizenship, for example, follow logically from national ideas about who can and cannot be a member of the political community. Those who have countered the theory have themselves turned to different sets of ideas to explain why public policy changes over time. Ideas, in short, have had an impact on how receiving states have accommodated Muslims in the past several decades.

As with political opportunity structure theory, our claim is not so much that ideological approaches are wrong, but that they fail systematically to consider how ideas about the role of religion in public life play a dominant role in how states have accommodated Muslim religious practices. Analysts adopting an ideological theory have given much attention to national ideas about citizenship, political incorporation, and liberal political values in their accounts, but none of them has considered how a shared public philosophy on what role religion should play in public life has helped to shape the debate around Muslim religious rights. What our theory will demonstrate is that public ideas about church and state in Britain, France, and Germany have been critical factors for determining the states' policy response to the religious needs of Muslims.

Religious Institutions, Church–State History and Muslim Mobilization

The focus of our theory will be on the policy legacy left by a country's history of church–state relations. We hypothesize that public policy on state accommodation of Muslim religious practices in Britain, France, and

Germany varies based in part on the inherited relationship between church and state in each nation. We will demonstrate that this policy tradition helped to determine the types of religious demands that Muslims have proposed, the response of various actors to those needs, and the public policy that the states eventually adopted in the area of Muslim religious rights. To the extent that policy responses in West European nations have differed, we will show that these differences resulted in large measure from dissimilar opportunities provided by the inherited church–state structures in particular nations.

The Selection of Case Studies

To test our theory, we will look at public policy on the religious needs of Muslims in Britain, France, and Germany. While we recognize that this is not an exhaustive list of Western European states, there are several reasons we believe these to be the appropriate nations to compare. First, the countries in our study share a number of institutional features. In absolute numbers, more Muslims live in these three countries than in any others in Western Europe. In two of the countries, Britain and France, migrants have come primarily from the former colonies of Pakistan and Algeria, while in Germany most have arrived from Turkey as a direct consequence of treaties signed by the two countries in the 1950s and 1960s to encourage immigration. In all three states, the impetus of this first wave of immigration was economic; workers came in response to the labor shortages that Western European countries experienced in the midst of their postwar economic boom. States considered this migration to be short-lived, however, and neither encouraged, expected, or wanted workers to become permanent residents. The fact that many of these workers did eventually stay has been, in Christian Joppke's apt phrase, "a disturbing novelty" for European states that were ill prepared to receive them (1999:9). As Muslim workers settled in Britain, France, and Germany, the issue of their incorporation became particularly pronounced. In fact, as we will show in the chapters ahead, issues surrounding Muslim integration have been central to the domestic political debate in each of these three nations over the past two decades.

Second, the countries in our study are all stable democracies whose commitment to religious freedom is generally recognized. The constitutions of France and Germany require the state to remain neutral among religions and to protect citizens' individual rights of religious expression. While Britain offers no constitutional protection for religious rights, its common law tradition supports the concepts of religious pluralism and religious liberty rights, and the recently signed Human Rights Act gives additional statutory protection to religious minorities. That said, Muslim immigration poses a common challenge to those commitments. While each of the states guarantees religious freedom, none of them has had any significant experience dealing with the rights of large numbers of non-Christian religious groups. The manner in which each state has dealt with the religious rights of Muslims will tell us how deeply each state is committed to equal treatment among religions.

A third point of comparison among the states is the way in which they have responded to secularization. In many respects, Britain, France, and Germany are in the midst of a secularizing trend whose chief social characteristics are declining church membership and the retrenchment of religious belief into the private sphere. In the political arena, secularization has pushed religion more to the margins of civic life, there has been a loss of religious influence in public institutions, and the state has gradually dispossessed the church of some of its traditional political functions. To the degree that Muslims want the state to recognize and accommodate their religious values, then, they confront the secular tide of these states that have religion and state moving farther apart, not closer together.

This movement toward secularization is not, however, uniform across the states nor complete within any one of them. While each is theoretically a secular nation-state, religion continues to affect the world of politics and of public policy in Britain, France, and Germany in ways that a secular political model cannot easily explain. Britain has an officially established church and Germany has a de facto plural religious establishment. Each state extends rights and privileges to specific religious communities, usually Christian, particularly in the social service and education public policy sectors. Muslim immigration, therefore, poses a significant dilemma to current public policy. The presence of Muslims raises the questions of public recognition and incorporation: Which religious groups will the state recognize for the purpose of granting access to social rights and privileges? Will Britain, France, and Germany grant to the Muslim community the same rights currently enjoyed, in varying degrees, by the Protestant, Catholic, and Jewish communities? Muslim immigration, in short, is a test for the inherited church–state establishment in each nation.

Finally, these countries provide a good model for comparison because of the significant ways in which they differ. Despite their many institutional similarities, these nations vary in terms of the institutional patterns of religious politics found in each. The classical distinctions we have in mind are twofold. The first is among Catholic-dominated countries (France),

Protestant-dominated countries (Britain), and religiously mixed countries (Germany). The second distinction is among nations with a tradition of anticlericalism and strict church–state separation (France), those with a state church (Britain), and those where the state accommodates more than one religious tradition (Germany). What we intend to show is that these different church–state traditions have been very important in shaping the state accommodation of Muslim religious needs. These variant church–state patterns, in short, have led Britain, France, and Germany to different public policies options on how and whether to accommodate the religious needs of Islamic immigrants in public policy.

Our comparative focus, in short, is unique in that the selection of case studies is determined by a well-defined theoretical perspective: the nature of church–state relations in Britain, France, and Germany.

Applying Church–State Theory to Public Policy

The problems of state accommodation of Muslim religious practices in Britain, France, and Germany vary based on how those states have resolved church–state issues in the past. The issue of state accommodation in Britain is shaped by the fact of a formal religious establishment. In some respects, this limits what Muslims can attain from the state, but this inherited church–state model has nevertheless been an important institutional and ideological resource for Muslim activists and has opened up opportunities for Muslim political mobilization. The presence of an established church and its close link with politics and public policy in Britain has encouraged Muslim groups to look to the state for a public recognition of their religious rights and public policy needs. As we will demonstrate, Muslim activists in Britain have explicitly referenced the establishment model and contemporary church–state practices to legitimate a variety of public policy demands, including public finance of separate Islamic schools, the building of mosques, and the provision of social welfare services through Muslim agencies. British policy makers do not as a matter of principle oppose state accommodation for religious groups; in fact, they make significant allowances for it, and resources flow to religious schools and agencies as a consequence. The issue with which Muslims in Britain have had to contend has been the willingness of the state to accommodate their religious needs despite the fact that Muslims were not a part of the historical compromises that led to the inherited religious establishment.

By contrast, the French church–state model of strict separation has restricted the ability of Muslim groups to take their case for public recognition of their religious rights directly to the state. As we will note in this book, in its public policy the French state is not in fact fully committed to a strict separation of church and state; the Catholic Church won important concessions in the early part of the twentieth century in the area of public and private education. In France's political ideology, however, *laïcité* is very powerful political reality. Elite and popular support for this separation of church and state has made it very difficult for Muslims in France who wish to argue that the state should recognize their particular religious needs. France's secular republican creed, which shuns notions of special lobbies or communities, has made it particularly hard for Muslims to advocate state accommodation for their religious practices.

As both a form of public policy and an ideological tradition, *laïcité* has structured the political arguments of Muslim groups and political leaders in France. Muslims have not, for example, been able to put on the policy agenda such things as support for separate Islamic schools or state aid for Muslim social service organizations, both of which are viewed as simply unacceptable given the state's supposed commitment to church–state separation. Instead, Muslims in France find themselves contesting rearguard actions on highly symbolic, though still very significant, issues such as the right of girls to wear the *ḥijāb* in state-run schools.

The church–state policy legacy in Germany has been relatively amenable to Muslim religious policy demands. Germany has a long policy tradition of a close link between the state and the historically dominant Catholics and state-church Protestants. Churches that are recognized by the state as public corporations are eligible for a church tax *(Kirchensteuer)* that is collected by the government, and the state has run a significant portion of its social welfare services through agencies of these publicly recognized churches. As in Britain, the issue for Muslims in Germany is not whether the state should accommodate religion in public institutions; it already does. The question, instead, is whether the state is willing to expand its informal religious establishment and consider Islam as a public corporation despite the fact that Muslims were not party to the original compromise. This is not to suggest that Muslims have had an easy time gaining access to the system; it is simply to point out that the inherited patterns of church–state relations provide Muslim groups in Germany a model to which they can point in arguing for state support for their religious institutions. The church–state model legitimates their demand for public recognition and for separate cultural and social welfare institutions of their own.

Comparing the Four Theories

The dependent variable in our study is the degree of state accommodation of Muslim religious practices in Britain, France, and Germany, while the competing theories that explain this policy outcome are the independent variables. The first independent variable, for example, would be the amount of effective political resources for Muslims' mobilization in each country. Since the level of accommodation appears to be high in Britain, low in France, and medium in Germany, the amount of political resources consistent with this first theory would be correspondingly high in Britain, low in France, and medium in Germany. The predictions of the other three theories/independent variables would follow a similar logic.

It is important to note that we do not necessarily see that the four theories are fully independent in relation to each other. Our theory, in short, does not reject other causal theories of state accommodation of Muslim religious practices. In fact, we do not think it possible to understand fully Muslim political mobilization and policy outcomes in these three countries without reference to these other theories. What we suggest, instead, is that analysts who have used the existing theories (that is, resource mobilization, state structure, and political ideology) have not recognized the degree to which a focus on church–state practices and traditions in each of the countries complement those explanations. Church–state traditions shape the ideological context through which state accommodation of Muslim religious practices plays itself out. Similarly, inherited church–state structures are themselves resources that either help or hinder the capacity of Muslim groups to negotiate with state actors.

What we will demonstrate in the chapters ahead is that the outcome of the process of state accommodation for the religious needs of Muslims in Britain, France, and Germany has been affected by the institutional relationship between church and state in each nation. Some states have more easily accommodated these religious needs than others because they have well-developed relations between political and religious institutions. The church–state pattern within each state not only shapes the political opportunity structure for Muslim groups, it also affects the ideological assumptions made by political elites and the public about what is politically feasible.

The Counterargument of Race

Some critics of our approach could contend that what we attribute to religious differences in the three countries is actually a function of racial distinctions; attitudes toward Muslims in Britain, France, and Germany depend not on inherited church–state structures, but rather on differences in skin color and other physical characteristics. David C. Leege et al. (2002), for example, have shown that in recent American presidential elections, race has divided voters much more than religion has. A parallel literature exists for Western Europe (Ben Jelloun 1999; Gilroy 1991; Jansen 1999).

Muslim religious identity often coincides with non-European ethnicity or "race," and ethnicity certainly explains much of European immigration politics. German neo-Nazis probably do target their victims solely on "race" (Hasselbach 1995). Nonetheless, we do not believe that ethnicity accounts for crossnational variations in the degree to which these states have accommodated Muslim religious practices. Almost all Muslims in Britain, France, and Germany belong to one or another ethnic minority, yet these three nations differ markedly in their approach to Islam. Not only does race theory fail to explain crossnational differences, but it also has difficulties accounting for within-country differences in treatment of ethnic minorities. While *Martiniquais* Catholics have very dark skin and are a racial minority in France, they are more free to practice their religion and probably encounter slightly less public hostility than lighter-skinned *Maghrébins* Muslims. It is also ironic that European Muslims themselves vehemently reject their categorization as one race, pointing out that all followers of Allah belong to the *'ummah* regardless of their skin color.

Issues To Be Explored

To test our theory and measure the impact of the four possible causes of a government's support for Muslim rights, we will look at three public policy issues faced in each of the countries: the accommodation of Muslim religious practices and teaching in public schools (Abdullah 1981:82–94; Gaspard and Khosrokhavar 1995; Joly 1995:146–61), state funding for Islamic schools (Dwyer and Meyer 1996; Spuler-Stegemann 1998:235–40): and regulation of the building of mosques (Cohn-Bendit and Schmid 1992: 306–9; de Galambert 1994; Hoffman 1996; Kepel 1991:64–123; Kusbah 1997:167–73).

These are appropriate issues for our comparison for several reasons. First, both the Muslim and non-Muslim communities in the three countries view these issues as the most significant ones related to the Muslim population. This significance is apparent in the political conflict that has arisen around such issues and that is often reported in the popular press. In addition, interviews that we conducted with government officials and community leaders in each of the three countries suggest that these are central political concerns for the Muslim community. Second, political institutions in each of the three countries have specifically addressed some combination of these issues. As we noted previously, there has been a vigorous policy discussion in Germany on how or whether to teach about the Islamic faith in state-run schools, while Britain has wrestled considerably with whether or not the state should provide educational benefits to separate Islamic schools. A third reason for selecting these issues for comparison is that they have played themselves out through the existing church–state structures in the three countries. In other words, the key political actors themselves understand these issues to be related to religion, rather than simply related to cultural affairs or immigration politics.

Education is likely the single most important issue to Muslim immigrants and citizens in each of the countries. For many Muslims, the public education system in the West is hostile to their religious values (Modood 1994; Sarwar 1994). This hostility comes from educational systems that explicitly show a preference for the teaching of Christian religious traditions and practices in the classroom, as is the case in each of the three nations, or to an educational model that is, in their view, implicitly secular and dismissive of the role of religion in a community's life. The ability to create a school environment in which Islamic religious values and cultural traditions can be upheld, and even flourish, has therefore been a key political demand for many Muslim organizations. In public schools, this plays itself out over such issues as providing for a balanced teaching about Islam in the classroom, released-time programs for religious instruction, provision of *ḥalāl* meals, and the wearing of Islamic clothes such as the *ḥijāb*. A related policy demand for many Islamic organizations has been for state financial support for separate Islamic schools under the same conditions that apply to other religious schools. As we will note in the chapters ahead, France and Britain provide significant public money for some private religious schools. Mosque building has also become a central political concern for many Muslim organizations that have become concerned about administrative barriers to the building of new mosques and enlarging existing ones (Kusbah 1997).

Our study will base its findings on historical and contemporary secondary literature, personal interviews with religious and political leaders, and statistical analysis of national public opinion surveys. Over a six-month period in 2001, we conducted direct face-to-face interviews with more than one hundred key government officials, Muslim leaders, journalists, and relevant academics in each of the three countries. The purpose of these interviews was, in part, to gain more information about issues of state accommodation of Muslim religious needs in each of the three countries. A second intent was to determine whether persons who are involved with the issue of accommodation explicitly reference church–state practices in each nation when explaining their social and political activism. Do local government education officials in France, for example, use the language of *laïcité* when explaining why they do or do not allow the wearing of the *ḥijāb* in a public school classroom? Do Muslim activists in Britain legitimate their demand for separate Islamic schools under the terms of Britain's religious establishment? In addition, during the summer of 2001 and the spring of 2002, we added several questions to national public opinion surveys as a way of measuring support for specific policy questions such as granting state support for Islamic schools in Britain, allowing instruction about the Islamic faith in state schools in Germany, and permitting public secondary-level students to wear the *ḥijāb* in French state schools.

The three chapters (2–4) that follow will provide a thorough country-by-country analysis of how states have accommodated the religious needs of Muslims in that country. Each country chapter will give a historical overview of church–state relations, a history of immigration policy, demographic details on the size of the Muslim community, and a review of how or whether states have accommodated the religious needs of the Muslim community. To clarify this point, we want briefly to define some key terms. By "religious needs," we mean those practical devices that are necessary to practice an orthodox form of a particular religion. Most Muslims, for example, believe that the practice of their faith requires time set aside each day for prayer. Some, but not all, Muslims believe that Islam requires girls to wear the *ḥijāb* in public places. State accommodation of those religious needs means the degree to which a government, through its policies, makes it possible for those needs to be met.

Each country chapter will also test the three competing theories to ours on why states have responded as they have to Muslim religious needs and will conclude with a presentation of our theory. We will demonstrate for each country chapter that issues around state accommodation of Muslim religious practices have been shaped by the church–state history unique to each country. That history and institutional context has led to certain theories, assumptions, and mindsets and have guided how issues related to Muslim religious practices have become politicized and resolved in contemporary politics in Britain, France, and Germany.

Following this historical and descriptive analysis, Chapter 5 will use crossnational surveys from Britain, France, and Germany empirically to isolate the major determinants of Europeans' attitudes toward Muslims and their religious practices. The preceding chapters focused on political institutions and their impact on policy at an elite level. Chapter 5 will look closely at mass-level public attitudes toward state accommodation of Muslim religious practices. Specifically, the questions we designed for surveys conducted for us by Roper Europe in July 2001 and April 2002 measure support for particular religious practices (that is, wearing the *ḥijāb* in state schools, supporting private Islamic schools with public funds, or permitting the teaching of Islam in state schools) and for the major church-state institutions in the three countries (that is, French separationism, German church taxes, and the English church establishment). We will use our own polls and other surveys to estimate multivariate regression models of Europeans's support for the religious accommodation of Muslims.

Our concluding chapter will synthesize the findings of the previous chapters. In addition, Chapter 6 will confront the thorny question of what kind of public policy best protects the rights of Muslims and the religiously plural structures present in each of the three countries of our study, while at the same time encouraging those groups to embrace cultural norms that are important for social and political stability.

2

Britain: Establishment Religion and Islamic Schools

The religious establishment makes possible a recognition of a person's right to put into action what he most sincerely believes in. It is a recognition of a person's most fundamental right – the right to practice their religion. We often find that under the guise of tolerance, secular viewpoints rob people of that fundamental right. There is much good in keeping the religious establishment intact.

> Dr. Fatma Amer (2001), director of education and interfaith relations, Islamic Cultural Centre, London Central Mosque

People will contribute most strongly to our society from a strong sense of their own identity. Our society will not be enriched by people who are half themselves, and half not. Islam is not a threat to that. Islam is a reality.

> Canon John Hall (2001), general secretary, Church of England Board of Education

There is a realization by the government that Muslims are here, we are citizens, and we have to be treated equally. We are not asking for special treatment; what we want is fair treatment. You apply the same rules to us as you apply to anybody else.

> Dr. Yaqub Zaki (2001), deputy director, the Muslim Institute.

ON ITS SURFACE, nothing is particularly startling in Dr. Zaki's comment about the political and religious demands of Muslims in Britain. It is a staple for citizens of liberal political regimes to expect the state to treat like persons alike. What is unstated in his comment, however, and is particularly important in understanding how Britain has responded to the religious

needs of its Muslim citizens, is how the established rules of the game structure what Muslims such as Dr. Zaki consider to be equal and fair treatment by the government. There is, as we shall see in the country chapters
ahead, nothing given in the rules of the game, and therefore very different
concepts emerge about what Muslims can expect from the state applying
the same rules to all religious groups. To understand better how Muslims
have mobilized, we briefly review the histories of British immigration policy and church–state relations that have provided the context for Muslim
political activism.

Historical Context

Immigration History

Because of its colonial presence on the Indian subcontinent, Britain for centuries had some contact with Islam. A few Muslims settled in Britain in the
middle of the nineteenth century as companies recruited foreign workers,
some of whom were Muslims, as cheap labor for the growing industrial
and seaport cities of London, Liverpool, and Woking. With this initial
settlement came the formation of a small number of Muslim social and religious organizations and the construction of the country's first all-purpose
mosque at Woking in 1889 (Lewis 1994:10–12; Macpherson 1997:113). For
the most part, however, the Muslim presence in Britain prior to the Second
World War was invisible.

The first large wave of Muslim immigrants came to Britain after the
war, and the pattern of this immigration was rooted in British colonialism.
The largest percentage of immigrants came from Commonwealth countries, particularly from the Indian subcontinent when many people were
displaced after the partition of British India in 1947. The state had an economic incentive to encourage the migration of foreign workers to help
rebuild British cities that had been damaged during the war. This construction demanded the immigration of large numbers of unskilled and
semiskilled workers who would work for low wages and in jobs that many
British workers did not want (Siddiqui 2000:185).

Many of these early immigrants were men who, through military service or personal experience, had some connection with British colonial
administration (Vertovec 2002:19). They were the vanguard of a chain migration that would follow from India, Pakistan, and other Commonwealth
countries. Some theorists have speculated that Britain's colonial history im-
pacted the country's initial treatment of these Muslim immigrants. Jørgen
Nielsen (2001) notes that "the British inherited a positive image of Islam

because of their experiences in Muslim parts of the Empire." Of course, colonialism might have imbued the British with a paternalistic attitude toward Muslim immigrants, but at least it was a relatively benign paternalism. Moreover, this fairly positive initial impression of early Muslim immigrants was in marked contrast to that in France, where the painful memories of the Algerian War of Independence meant that the French viewed North African Muslim immigrants with a mixture of fear and apprehension (Cesari 2002b:37). In Britain, at least, Muslim immigrants had almost unrestricted right of access throughout the 1950s.

Ataullah Siddiqui (2000:185) argues that the primary goal of many of these immigrants was "to earn enough money so that they would return to Pakistan, buy a plot of land and build a house there." In describing the initial expectations of the Muslim immigrant community, Shuja Shaikh (2001), a councillor of the London borough of Hackney, deputy leader of the Conservative Party on the Council, and the town's former mayor, similarly reflects:

> Most of our people came to this country in the 1950s and '60s to work, and their concept in those days was that if we collect 2,000 pounds, that will be enough. We could take this money and go home (to Pakistan or India), set up a shop, buy a farm, and that would be enough for a livelihood because 2,000 pounds was a lot of money.

Muslim religious practice was informal, usually limited to individual daily prayers at work or in houses converted into makeshift mosques. The government gave little consideration to the religious needs of this immigrant population because it expected that this largely male, unaccompanied migrant population would eventually return to its country of origin.

For a variety of reasons, however, these migrants did not return. For many, the economic and educational opportunities in Britain encouraged them to stay, while in other cases political circumstances made a return to the country of origin less likely. The British state, however, neither anticipated a mass migration nor encouraged these foreign workers to become British citizens, but the inherited policy allowed both to occur. Under the terms of the 1948 British Nationality Act, Commonwealth immigrants had access to all the rights and privileges of British citizenship. People born in Commonwealth countries were neither subject to immigration controls nor considered aliens (Adolino 1998:25). They were, instead, citizens of the British Commonwealth who enjoyed the same civil and legal rights as persons born in Britain (Vertovec 1997:173). The intent of this very liberal policy was to allow white colonial subjects to gain automatic citizenship when they returned to Britain; the policy's unanticipated consequence was to give similar legal rights to non-white immigrants. As Christian Joppke notes, "some 80 million subjects of the Crown, inhabiting one-fourth of the earth's landmass, had the right of entry and settlement in Britain" (1998:287).

The policy did not initially elicit much popular or elite concern. While British cities witnessed a few anti-immigrant riots in the late 1940s, immigration control did not become a national political issue until after many race riots occurred in the late 1950s and early 1960s (Karapin 2000). In 1968, Enoch Powell delivered his infamous "rivers of blood" speech, in which he called for the end of non-white immigration to England and for subsidizing the repatriation of immigrants from New Commonwealth states. The Conservatives expelled Powell from the shadow cabinet because of the speech, but his populist intervention on race heightened the salience of the issue (Spencer 1997:142–3).

The Tories never adopted Powell's more vitriolic positions on race and immigration, and neither Labour nor the Conservatives explicitly supported the racist, anti-immigrant National Front Party that followed Powell in the 1970s, nor its successor, the British National Party founded in 1982. Nonetheless, beginning with the 1962 Commonwealth Immigrants Act, a series of Labour and Conservative governments passed laws that tightened citizenship laws and sharply limited the right of Commonwealth citizens to enter Britain. The result of these new policies was the virtual cessation of primary immigration; Britain became for a time as restrictive in its immigration policy as any country in Western Europe (Kepel 1997:100; Messina 1996:139–49; Money 1999:66–8).

Britain thus differed from Germany and France, where controls on immigration came later, beginning in the early 1970s and largely in response to the weakening of the European economy. In Britain, by contrast, race shaped the politics of immigration control during this period. The government was explicitly concerned with "coloured" immigration, the assumption being that racial pluralism was a problem to be avoided. The intent of the policy, as Ian Spencer notes (1997:150), was to "limit and then stop the movement into Britain of people of colour from Africa, the Caribbean and the Indian subcontinent" (1997:150). Despite this aim, hundreds of thousands of Commonwealth-born persons of color had already become citizens under the 1948 Act, and Britain was well on its way to becoming a multiracial and multireligious society when restrictions on immigration were imposed (Kepel 1997:97–9; Spencer 1997:152–3).

An ironic and wholly unanticipated consequence of the new restrictive policy was actually to increase temporarily the number of immigrants who came and settled in Britain. For while the state placed significant restrictions on primary immigration, it did not deny the legal rights of those already admitted, which included the right of family reunification. As a result, the largely male immigrant population, fearing that more restrictive resettlement legislation would eventually follow, brought their families from overseas to join them in Britain (Spencer 1997:154). The ethnic minority population expanded rapidly from the 1970s on, growing from an estimated 1 million in 1968 to 3 million in 1991. As a proportion of the total population, the non-white community grew from 1 percent in 1968, to 5.5 percent in 1991, and 7.1 percent in 2001 (Adolino 1998:27; Hoge 2002).

Recent political developments have intensified this trend toward tighter immigration controls. The media began to report on Britain's asylum law, which was said to be more liberal than its continental counterparts, and partly in response to popular pressure the Labour Party introduced the Nationality, Immigration, and Asylum Bill. The bill proposed deporting more rapidly those whose applications for asylum failed, requiring asylum seekers to learn English, and educating the children of asylum seekers in special classes in asylum centers separate from children in British schools (Lyall 2002). The bill passed the House of Commons by an overwhelming margin of 362 to 74 (Mason and Hughes 2002).

Race riots in Oldham and Burnley in May 2001 fueled some support for the anti-immigrant, far-right British National Party (BNP). While it did not win any seats in the House of Commons in the 2001 general elections, the BNP did well in constituencies near the sites of the riots and enjoyed the best performance of any far-right party since the Second World War (Crewe 2002:229). In Oldham, the BNP party leader, Nick Griffin, won 16.4 percent of the vote, and his party won its first two victories in over a decade in city council races the following year. In nearby Burnley, eight BNP councillors were elected to office in 2003 (Flinthoff 2003). While the BNP had historically focused exclusively on Britain's race policy, Griffin shifted the party's discourse from race to religion, commenting in one interview, for example, that Britain "does not have an Asian problem but a Muslim one" (quoted in McLoughlin 2002).

The Politics of Settlement

In many respects, British policy towards its immigrant population was driven by internal contradictions. Adrian Favell (1998:339) and Joppke (1999:261) have argued that at the same time that Britain placed restrictions on new immigration, it maintained a relatively liberal citizenship policy and

it even passed progressive legislation to deal with its newfound racial pluralism. As a result, most of the immigrants and their families who arrived in
the 1950s and 1960s eventually became British citizens. Many had entered
the country as citizens before the passage of the more limiting legislation,
many more gained citizenship after coming to the country, and the children
of immigrants by and large became British citizens.

With a diverse population came the political question of how best to
ensure that these immigrants, whose religious practices and cultural backgrounds were distinct from the host country, might best integrate or assimilate into British society. A number of scholars have noted that the guiding
principle for British policy was multiculturalism (Bleich 1998; Favell 1998;
Joppke 1999). Under this regime, the state encouraged cultural groups to
create their own organizational structures, to safeguard their customs and
religious practices as they saw fit, and to introduce an awareness of and
celebration for Britain's cultural pluralism into the state education system.

One tangible result of this policy was that many local schools in the
1960s began to pay greater attention to religions other than Christianity
in the required religious education classes (Rath et al. 2001:236). A high
watermark for this perspective was the 1985 government-commissioned
Swann Report on education and ethnic communities (Department of Education and Science 1985). The report recognized the need for multicultural
education in state-run schools that would expose students to the religious
pluralism in Britain. Support for multicultural education was a position
that prevailed with government education officials for the next decade. As
Favell (1998:109) concludes, "by the mid 1980s the consensus position had
evolved towards a fairly open de facto acceptance of the reality of multicultural Britain on all sides."

Britain also led the way in providing statutory protection against racial
discrimination with the passage of the 1976 Race Relations Act. The act
prohibited discrimination on "racial or ethnic grounds," and created the
Commission for Racial Equality (CRE) to take the lead on dealing with race
relations. In short, while making it much more difficult for immigrants to
come to Britain beginning in the early 1960s, the state made some positive
efforts to secure their basic civil rights once they had arrived.

The government's race relations policy was, however, curiously silent
on the issue of religion. The Race Relations Act did not specifically protect persons against discrimination on religious grounds. It was as if the
state recognized that postwar immigration introduced into Britain racial
pluralism to which the government had to respond, but the state somehow
refused to acknowledge that many of these immigrants were also Muslims,
Buddhists, and Sikhs. Absent a constitutional guarantee for religious rights,

and without specific statutory protection, the state had a positive right to discriminate on the basis of religion (Barker 1987). That immigrants themselves had not initially focused much on their religious identification helps to explain the state's silence on this issue. As we noted previously, a large percentage of the postwar immigrants were male workers who did not anticipate settling in Britain. Or as Shaikh (2001) commented about this early period, "We did not at first get used to living in this country, and so we did not prepare ourselves. We didn't bother to build a mosque; one room was enough." Many first-generation Muslim immigrants also appeared to believe that in order to avoid potential "problems" with the state, it was best to minimize the religious features of their identity (Ramadan 1999a:113). As Jan Rath et al. note, "Islam led a rather concealed existence" for this first generation of Muslim immigrants that was trying to fit in as best it could (Rath et al. 1999:53).

For Muslims, however, permanent settlement in Britain made their religious identity increasingly relevant. For many second- and third-generation Muslim immigrants, Islam provided a sense of cultural identity and pride. Muslim theologian Tariq Ramadan describes a trend among young Muslims in Western Europe toward "an affirmation of their Islamic identity and a profound revival of its spirituality and practice" (1999a:114). Many Muslims concluded that British social and cultural values were dangerously secular; only an infrastructure of Muslim organizations with a strong sense of religious identity would enable Muslims effectively to preserve their distinct values (Adolino 1998:35). Throughout the 1970s and 1980s, therefore, Muslims formed religious, social, educational, and political organizations to institutionalize the faith and to pass on its values to the younger generation.

As the values and practices of Islam became more significant to British Muslims, the absence of statutory protection against religious discrimination became more important to them. For Muslims, the government's unwillingness to include religious discrimination in race relations policy denied them their distinctive religious identity, and failed to provide the same protection that the government afforded ethnic minorities. A report of the Islamic Human Rights Commission concluded as follows:

> ... the law in the United Kingdom protects particular religious minorities (Jews and Sikhs) on the pretext that they can be defined as a race; other religions are left to suffer harassment and discrimination at the hands of xenophobes with no legal recourse (2000:8).

Muslim groups have consistently expressed concern that the CRE, the institution created by the Race Relations Act to monitor progress against discrimination, is insensitive to issues of religious discrimination. An editorial in the *Q News*, Britain's major Muslim newsmagazine, asserted that, "as much as Muslims want to confront racism, they have become disillusioned with an anti-racism movement (CRE) that refuses to combat Islamophobia and which, in many instances, is as oppressive as the establishment itself" (Khan 1999:26–7).

In practice, the Race Relations Act proved incapable of providing Muslims the same protection it provided to other minorities in British society. A 1997 report conducted for the government by the race relations think tank, the Runnymede Trust (1997), coined the term "Islamophobia" to describe the nature and the extent of anti-Muslim prejudice in Britain. The report concluded that Muslims experienced significant hostility in Britain, and recommended amending the 1976 Race Relations Act to make discrimination unlawful on religious grounds. A second study on religious discrimination, commissioned by the Home Office (the Derby Report) in 1999, similarly reported that Muslim groups experienced a consistently higher level of unfair treatment than other religious communities in "every aspect of education, employment, housing, law and order, and in all of the local government services covered in the questionnaire" (Weller, Feldman, and Purdam 2001:103). The report also recommended new legislation to protect religious minorities against such unfair treatment.

In March 2000, Lord Ahmed, the nation's first Muslim peer, introduced a bill into the House of Lords to amend the Race Relations Act to include protection against religious discrimination. The Labour government, however, opposed amending the act to include discrimination on religious grounds. The government contended that the Human Rights Act of 1998 would provide sufficient protection for Muslims, a conclusion that Muslims reject (Islamic Human Rights Commission 2000; Malik 2001).

Institutional and Social Context

The Established Church

As they began to press for political change in the 1970s, an important question Muslims had to consider was what kind of church–state regime they had inherited. To what extent would the laws on religious rights, and the existing patterns of church–state relations in Britain, enable Muslims to accommodate their religious values in public policy?

For a variety of reasons, Muslims might logically have concluded that the institutional church–state pattern in Britain would be inhospitable to their religious policy demands. England has had a formally established church since the middle of the sixteenth century, the Church of England, which on its surface would seem to represent a threat to minority faiths (Tolley 2000). The establishment of the Church of England came by way of the First and Second Acts of Supremacy in 1534 and 1559, respectively. A close relationship initially developed between the state and the Anglican Church in which the institutions worked in concert for shared political and religious goals. Legally, this cooperation came to mean a state-supported and state-enforced religion and the imposition of various restrictions on religious dissenters and nonconformists. The Corporation (1661) and Test Acts (1673), for example, effectively excluded Protestant nonconformists, Roman Catholics, and Jews from participation in political affairs.

The religious rivalry among Anglicans, Roman Catholics, and Protestant nonconformists spilled over into party politics for more than two centuries. Issues such as the religious rights for nonconformists and dissenters, church control over education, and the status of the established church divided the electorate between a Liberal Party that was committed to state neutrality among religious groups, and the Conservative Party that defended the religious establishment. The politicization of these religious disputes was intense, particularly toward the end of the nineteenth and into the early twentieth century, on the question of religion in state education. Not surprisingly, the Liberal Party consolidated support among religious dissenters while the Conservative Party attracted most Anglican votes (Wald 1983).

Despite the intensity of these conflicts, the Catholic–Protestant division in party politics became less salient throughout the twentieth century. While some voices in the Liberal, and then Labour, Party wanted a purely secular state free of any religious influence whatsoever, they were clearly in the minority. More common was the hope among Liberal and Labour Party members that the state would extend its privileges to other churches, particularly in the area of education. The Liberal Party, in short, was not deeply, philosophically an anticlerical party. Nor was the Conservative Party fundamentally committed to the political and social privileges of the Anglican Church. When the costs of imposing conformity on a religiously pluralistic country became too great, the Conservative Party lost enthusiasm for an established church with significant political power and privilege (Barker 1995; Bruce and Wright 1995).

The restrictions on religious minorities were eased through a series of reforms passed throughout the nineteenth century. The government recognized the rights of Protestant dissenters in 1828. This was followed by the passage of the Roman Catholic Relief Act in 1829 and the Jews' Relief Act in 1858 that recognized both religious groups and granted members of those faiths the right to enter Parliament and serve in government (Weller, Feldman, and Purdam 2001). Political disputes among religionists waned further in the twentieth century as the state lifted the disabilities associated with religious membership outside of the Church of England (Bebbington 1989:98; Hylson-Smith 1988:65; Monsma and Soper 1997:124–6).

While the Church's political powers and privileges have been progressively diluted since the nineteenth century, a number of ways remain in which the Church of England specifically, and Christianity more generally, are legally and politically advantaged. For example, twenty-four of the Church of England's bishops and its two archbishops sit by right in the House of Lords, the nation's blasphemy laws protect Christian doctrines, the monarchy and the Church are still linked in some respects, and the provisions made for religious chaplaincy services in public institutions such as prisons, hospitals, and the armed forces advantage clergy in the Church of England (Beckford and Gilliat 1998; McClean 1996; Weller, Feldman, and Purdam 2001).

Absent a formal constitution to mandate such arrangements, however, the state has been willing and able to modify the relationship between these institutions. Consequently, a complicated and tangled relationship has developed between the state and various religious bodies on such policy issues as education and social welfare provision (Beckford and Gilliat 1998:348). Additionally, the state has, as we noted previously, adopted a pragmatic approach to religious pluralism. While rights and privileges are not automatically extended to incoming groups, the pattern has been for the state to minimize conflict by eventually accommodating newly arrived religions. This historical precedent has proved to be an important advantage for Muslim groups, who have argued that the state should treat them as it treats other minority religious groups. This policy is also in stark contrast with France, with it strong anticlerical tradition and history of political tension among religious groups and between church and state (Weil and Crowley 1994).

A recent example of this pragmatic accommodation has been the debate on the composition of the House of Lords. The government set up a Royal Commission, chaired by Lord Wakeman, to consider the role, functions, and composition of the upper chamber. The Commission's report, titled "A House for the Future," proposed a second chamber of around 550 members, with 26 places reserved for members of British faith communities. In contrast with historical precedent, however, those places would not automatically go to bishops in the Church of England. Instead, at least five of the twenty-six would be selected to "be broadly representative of the different non-Christian faith communities" (*House for the Future* 2000: 155).

Religious Free-Exercise Rights

Unlike the other countries in our study, Britain does not have a constitution that establishes religious rights as fundamental. Religious free-exercise rights are, strictly speaking, statutory matters left to the political arena. As Jørgen Nielsen notes, "Britain has no generally applicable legal framework. The older churches operate under legal provisions particular to each church" (1992:43). No particular statute relates to the religious rights of Muslims, but they are free to practice their faith within the bounds of the law. The Human Rights Act of 1998 also incorporated the European Convention on Human Rights and provides, in theory at least, for the idea that religious freedom in Britain is a fundamental right that can be protected against state actions. Because the law creates rights only against state action and not against private individuals, however, it is not clear how far that act will go toward protecting religious free-exercise rights (Hepple and Choudhury 2001; Leckie and Pickersgill 1999; Malik 2001).

Nor have the British courts typically been willing to grant individuals exemptions from generally applicable laws on religious grounds. The leading case on religious freedom in Britain is *Mandla v. Dowell Lee* (1983). The case involved a Sikh student who wished, contrary to school rules, to wear a turban. Absent a provision for religious freedom, the Commission for Racial Equality brought suit under the Race Relations Act. The case eventually reached the House of Lords, which ruled that the ban on turbans violated the Race Relations Act, but only because Sikhs, and by extension Jews, were a racial group that the act specifically protected. The Lords did not, however, include Muslims as an ethnic or racial group in that decision. The court reaffirmed this distinction between ethnic and religious groups in the 1988 case *Nyazi v. Rymans Ltd.*, which concerned an employer's decision to refuse to allow a Muslim employee time off to celebrate *'id al-fiṭr*. In that case, the court ruled that Muslims do not constitute a racial or ethnic group that is protected under the Race Relations Act (Vertovec 2002:25)

Secularization

The other important religious factor that has affected Muslims' efforts to integrate into the existing church–state system is the growing secularism of British society. As with most other countries in Western Europe, Britain has witnessed a marked decline in religious belief and practice in recent decades. The primary features associated with this secularism include declining church attendance, the retrenchment of religious belief into the private sphere, and the loss of influence of religious institutions in public life (Hervier-Léger 1995).

While belief in God in Britain remains relatively high (71 percent), the British are increasingly an unchurched population. Weekly church attendance in England declined from 10.2 percent of the adult population in 1985 to 8.2 percent in 1995, and is estimated to fall to 6.6 percent in 2005 (Brierley 2001:2.23). Well over half of the respondents in a 1990 survey (56 percent) claim never to attend church (Davie 2000:9). It is also evident that religion has diminished in social and political significance in Britain (Bruce 1995). The religious aspirations that remain are increasingly considered a matter of individual conscience, a personal choice that should have very little influence on public policy. As a consequence, religion has become less important in British politics and less influential in shaping cultural institutions and assumptions.

At the same time that this secular ethos has become more prominent, however, the number of British Muslims has grown from an estimated 23,000 in 1951, to 369,000 in 1971, 690,000 in 1981, and over 1 million in 1991 (Lewis 1994:13–15; Nielsen 1992:41). According to the 2001 census, 1.6 million Muslims lived in England, Scotland, and Wales, representing 3 percent of the population (Office for National Statistics 2003). Not only are more Muslims living in Britain, but their religious identity is increasingly significant for them. According to one estimate (Brierley 2001:2.23, 10.6), by 2005 there will be nearly as many religiously active Muslims as practicing Anglicans in England. Muslims contend that the secularism that they have inherited is not neutral toward religion but instead discriminates against persons with deeply held religious convictions. Sallah Eddine Ben Abid argues that "secularity reduces the relationship between men and God to the private sphere and, in doing so, God is excluded from the organization of the public sphere" (2000:23). "Islam," according to Syed Ad-Darsh, former president of the United Kingdom Sharia Council, "is more than an individualized faith that can be kept in isolation. It is a faith, a social order and a legal system" (1997:24). For many Muslims, the state's secular perspective denies them the opportunity fully to practice their faith. The challenge faced by European Muslims is how "to maintain a spiritual life in a modern secular society" (Ramadan 1999a:138).

Because a secular worldview predominates in Britain, most policy makers did not think that religious issues would be important matters in the public sphere. To state officials the question of the state promoting Muslims' religious practices or encouraging them to bring their religious values to bear on public policy seemed inconsistent with the gradual depoliticization of religion that had been occurring in Britain for nearly a century. Muslims, however, dispute these secular assumptions and have brought religious concerns to politics on a variety of issues. In so doing, they have posed an implicit threat to the inherited secular ethos (Macpherson 1997:114–15).

The differences between Islamic and secular perspectives on politics played themselves out most dramatically during the Rushdie Affair and the political debate that it inspired. The portrayal of the prophet Muhammad in Salmon Rushdie's novel *The Satanic Verses* deeply offended Muslims. In response, British Muslims led a petition drive to prevent the book's publication in the United Kingdom, engaged in a series of marches to publicize their opposition to its availability once it was published, and burned copies of the novel in symbolic protest in a march in Bradford in 1989. Finally, Muslims argued that the government's blasphemy law should be extended beyond Christianity to include Islam (Nielsen 1992; O'Neill 1999).

Until the late 1970s, the blasphemy law was largely considered a relic. Philip Stevens (2001) of the Human Rights Unit of the government's Home Office wryly noted, "If the blasphemy law didn't exist, we wouldn't invent it." Nonetheless, the law was on the books, and it had been used by conservative activist Mary Whitehouse in 1977 in a successful prosecution of the magazine *Gay News* for its portrayal of Jesus. For Muslims, then, the blasphemy law was not a dead issue, but was instead something that had been used effectively to protect Christian values in the past and should consequently be a tool that Muslims could use to protect Islamic values in the future.

The ensuing debate brought an unprecedented amount of coverage – much of it negative – to the place of Muslims in British society (Lewis 1994:4–6). The issue also galvanized the Muslims, who argued that as British citizens they were "entitled to equality of treatment and respect for their customs and religion" (Anwar 1992:46). The tool that they hoped would achieve this did not require new legislation, but simply an extension of the existing blasphemy law. In the end, the state was unwilling to stretch the blasphemy law to include Muslims. Although the campaign for the amendment of the law did not succeed, Muslims have not pressed for the law's complete abolition, a position put forward by many British secular voices. In fact, the Muslim periodical *Q News* (1998:16) noted that Islamic groups supported an effort by a Christian organization to take a theater company to court for a play it produced that the group deemed blasphemous.

The blasphemy debate demonstrated that while secularism predominates at a cultural level in Britain, it does so within an institutional context that contains complex ties between church and state. Britain may be an increasingly secular culture, but it is also a state that recognizes and accommodates religion in various ways. To what extent have Muslims been affected in their political mobilization, then, by the presence of a religious establishment that benefits some churches? In interacting with the state, Muslims quickly concluded that government policy was not consistently secular nor perfectly neutral among religions. The primary point of contention was not, however, whether to have a religious establishment at all; Muslims have by and large supported this existing institutional arrangement. Far from being a political liability, Britain's established church has been an ally of Muslims, who want the state positively to recognize their religious claims. The religious establishment provided institutional access for Muslims to make their case for state recognition of their religious needs. Moreover, the religious establishment sustains a cultural assumption shared by most Muslims that religion has a public function to play and that it is appropriate for the state and religious groups to cooperate to achieve common goals.

Major Areas of Religious Accommodation

Religious Activities in State Schools

Probably no public policy issue is more important to Muslims in Britain than education. As Muhammed Anwar notes, "of all the issues faced by Muslims in Britain, education brings out the most passions and gets the strongest reaction and the widest publicity" (1992:41). As they have settled in Britain, Muslims have recognized the importance of education for their children's success in British society, and these parents are aware of the ways that education in state schools might undermine their religious values. As a result, it is no surprise that schools, and educational policy and practices, are a central point of tension and conflict between Muslims and the state.

The education policy inherited by Muslims allowed for state funding of private religious schools and required religious instruction and worship in state-run schools. The Education Act of 1944 stipulated that all state-run schools provide religious education and that each school day begin with collective worship. Because Britain contained so little religious diversity at the time, the 1944 Act did not state that the religious education and worship be Christian; it was simply assumed that nondenominational Christianity would prevail.

The Education Act of 1988 formalized this provision by specifying that a majority of the acts of collective worship in state-run schools were to be "wholly or mainly of a broadly Christian character," and that in religious education the content "devoted to Christianity in the syllabus should predominate" (Department for Education 1994:16). Parents retained the right to withdraw their children from the religious education classes and the daily collective worship. On its surface, the act affirmed a religiously particularistic vision for the schools. To supporters, the religious education curriculum prior to the 1988 act gave too much emphasis to Britain's religious and cultural minorities. In their view, the 1988 act properly reaffirmed Britain's Christian tradition in religious education and collective worship.

Despite the language of the 1988 act, however, schools have not sought to impose the Christian faith on non-Christian students. In practice, schools have a good deal of flexibility in how they interpret the requirements of the act. Detailed arrangements for the provision of religious education and collective worship are a local responsibility, under the auspices of a Local Education Authority (LEA) and a Standing Advisory Committee on Religious Education (SACRE). Moreover, the LEA and the SACRE are encouraged to take the religious makeup of the school population into account when drawing up the syllabus for religious education and worship. In considering the balance between teaching about Christianity and about other religions, a circular from the Department for Education reminds schools that "account should be taken of the local school population and the wishes of local parents, with a view to minimizing the number who might exercise the right of withdrawal from Religious Education lessons" (1994:16).

In practice, this directive has fostered considerable diversity in how schools meet the religious education requirements of the national curriculum. In exceptional circumstances, such as when a majority of the school population is not Christian, schools can even petition to be exempt from the requirement that the worship and religious education preference the Christian faith (Gold 1999). Other schools take the Christian requirements of the legislation much more seriously. In some cases, Muslims and other religious minorities have complained about unfair and discriminatory practices in the schools. A Home Office study on religious discrimination noted that respondents from Muslim organizations were more likely to report unfair treatment in education than Christian, Jewish, or Buddhist ones (Weller, Feldman, and Purdam 2001:23).

What is most common, however, is that schools work fairly closely with local religious leaders, including Muslims, to ensure that the content of religious education takes account of the religious background of the school population. A number of Muslims confirm that school officials have generally been helpful on issues related to religious education and collective worship. Muhammad Khoirul (2001), project director of the School Links Project, noted that "some schools have invited us in. A number of schools have recognized us as a valuable source to produce the link between the Muslim student and the school." Dr. Fatma Amer (2001), head of education and interfaith relations at the London Central Mosque, similarly notes that "we have a good relationship with the government's Department for Education, and other organizations at both the national and local level. We have good relations with SACREs in most boroughs."

It is also apparent from looking at the religious education curriculum and from talking with officials from the Department for Education that a deep commitment remains to multicultural approaches to religious education and collective worship. One popular religious education text provides an extensive introduction to the practices and beliefs of Christianity, Judaism, Islam, and Sikhism (Keene and Keene 1997). Anne Barlow (2001) of the Department for Education and Skills sees a broad purpose to the religious education requirement: "[Religious education] has an important role to play in people's spiritual, moral, and cultural development." The Runnymede Trust Commission on the future of multi-ethnic Britain, which was chaired by Bhiku Parekh, similarly concluded that the integration of Britain's diverse populations was best achieved by educational policies that would recognize and accommodate group differences (Runnymede Trust 2000).

Nor has the daily act of collective worship proved, in most cases, to be overtly Christian. Gill Griffiths (2001), deputy headteacher of a predominantly Muslim primary school in Birmingham, described the collective worship requirement in her school in this way: "By law, the daily assembly must be of a broadly Christian character. I think we, as most schools, get around this by focusing on the moral aspect that is shared among religions."

Muslims and other religionists have sometimes complained that this multicultural approach glosses over the very real differences among religious traditions, and that it reinforces the secular idea that religious values are a matter of an inherited culture, rather than of a religious choice (Chapman 1998:153; Nielsen 1992:56). *The Muslim Parent's Handbook*

(Akhtar 1993:6), while not rejecting a multicultural emphasis, nonetheless notes the following:

> ...we do insist that these policies be formulated and implemented after due consultation and negotiation between the majority and the minorities. Otherwise, multiculturalism in education is simply an imposed doctrine that might well be harmful to the interests of Muslims and other faith groups.

Muslims have been quite adept, in short, at pointing to the unstated secular assumptions that often accompany a focus on multiculturalism.

While it is certainly appropriate to question the ideological presuppositions of multiculturalism, we would argue that these concerns are, comparatively speaking, luxurious ones to debate. This seems to be confirmed in the interviews we conducted with Muslims involved on the education issue. While many Muslims opposed the 1988 Education Bill because they believed that their children would be required to participate in Christian worship services, there is currently no strong opposition among Muslims to religious education and no thought that the practice should be abandoned in state-run schools.

Issues other than religious education do exist that could cause conflict between school policy and Muslim religious practices. One question that has caused considerable political controversy in France is the wearing the *ḥijāb* by Muslim schoolgirls. This has been a nonissue in Britain. Muslim girls who wish to wear the *ḥijāb* in state-run schools are allowed to do so. In describing the policy at the predominantly Islamic school in which she works, Griffiths (2001) notes:

> We have many students who wear the *ḥijāb*. It is just considered part of their uniform. It is not worth commenting on. People see it as, "that is just what they wear." No non-Muslim parent has mentioned the wearing of the *ḥijāb* as a problem.

In a detailed comparison of France and Britain on policy regarding wearing the *ḥijāb* in state-run schools, Lina Liederman (2000) notes that in one instance a British school official did refuse entry to Muslim girls wearing Islamic headscarves in a classroom in Manchester, but that the issue was quickly resolved; Muslim schoolgirls could henceforth wear the *ḥijāb* so long as the headscarves conformed to the color requirements of the school uniform. Dr. Zahoor Anwar Chaudhary (2001), of the Birminghman Local Education Authority, similarly confirmed that "we have not heard of any incident where a child was expelled from school because she wanted to wear a *ḥijāb*."

Muslims have also raised some questions about school dress codes for girls participating in physical education classes, the provision of *ḥalāl* meat in state-run schools, and time off for religious holidays. As a rule, however, school officials have been flexible and have accommodated Muslim needs. The Muslim Liaison Committee, a Muslim community consultation group in the City of Birmingham, concludes a report on school policy, "This authority believes that with goodwill and sensitivity it can work with schools to develop responses to ensure pupils will participate wholeheartedly in the curriculum" (n.d.: 4–5). While none of this is to deny that Muslims continue to face "some kinds of discrimination" in the schools, according to Chaudhary (2001) "if we look at the basic issues like prayer time, *ḥijāb*, and understanding religious needs, the policy is as good as possible."

Grace Davie claims that the British "escaped" the problems of incorporating Muslim students that have beset state-run schools in France "more by luck than good judgement" (2000:133). However, this conclusion fails to consider that British educational policy toward Muslims has shown a consistent tendency toward understanding Muslims' needs, accommodating existing policy to allow for their religious practices, and pragmatically bending the requirements to avoid political controversy.

One concern consistently expressed by Muslims was about the quality of education in state-run schools. While some Muslim parents are, in Chaudhary's view (2001), satisfied with the religious practices that state-run schools allow:

> ...they are not satisfied with how Muslim children are doing in schools. Muslim children are not doing well. They are at the bottom of the achievement ladder, but there are a number of factors to explain this that have nothing to do with religion.

The data generally confirm this perception. As a whole, ethnic minority students fare less well than white students on standardized tests. Pakistani and Bangladeshi pupils, most of whom are Muslim, perform below the national average. Black students fare the worst among all racial groups on measurements of educational achievement. Indian students, on the other hand, actually do better than whites. Finally, girls outperform boys. All of this suggests, as Chaudhary notes, that educational success is a function of a combination of factors, including race, social class, culture, gender, and possibly religion (Cassidy 2003; Office for National Statistics 2002). The rising popularity of religious schools among Muslim parents is, nonetheless, partly a function of their conviction that the state-run schools are failing to train their children adequately.

Public Funding of Islamic Schools

State funding of Muslim schools has been a contentious political issue in Britain. For well over a decade, Muslims pressed the government to provide state aid to their schools under the same conditions that it grants money to Anglican, Catholic, and Jewish ones. For most of that time, the secretary of state for education turned down Muslim applications. The issue of state funding became a powerfully symbolic one for Muslims, who wanted the state to recognize the legitimacy of their demands as a religious community. As one Muslim active in the education field put it, "It [state funding for Islamic schools] seemed not so much a matter of educational choice for Muslim parents but a matter of civil rights for the community" (Hewitt 1998:14). It was also an issue that was very much shaped by the historical context of Britain's educational and church–state system.

When the state began to provide education in the middle decades of the nineteenth century, it came into a field dominated by the churches. Education, along with social welfare provision more generally, had been part of the churches' domain for well over a century. Because neither of the major political parties, nor the state, had a strong anticlerical bent, there was no reason for state officials not to work closely with the churches in policy formation and planning when the state entered the education field. The 1944 Education Act solidified a partnership between the churches and the state in education by creating state-run and religious schools that shared the responsibility for educating British schoolchildren.

County or community schools are controlled by an LEA, which hires the school's staff, owns the school's land and buildings, and has primary responsibility for arrangements for admitting pupils. A church education trust owns church schools (voluntary aided and voluntary controlled), by contrast, and a board of governors employs the schools staff and exercises full control over admissions policy, religious education, school buildings, and staff appointments.[1] Church schools are required to follow the National Curriculum, but they are allowed to give preference in hiring to persons whose religious views are in accordance with the tenets of the religious denomination, and to admit coreligionists if they choose (Gold 1999:76–7). In a detailed study of Church of England schools, Bernadette O'Keefe found that the primary admissions criterion for most Church of England schools

---

[1] The text describes policy at voluntary-aided schools. Voluntary-controlled schools are similar, though the LEA employs the school's staff and has primary responsibility for admission arrangements. A majority of religious schools are voluntary-aided.

is the Christian faith of the student's family (1986:152). Finally, the state finances most of the running costs for church schools and 85 percent of capital expenditures.

Church schools are very popular in Britain, both because they generally outperform county schools and because parents very much want their children to have a religious education. As a result, church schools are far more likely than county schools to be oversubscribed. Church schools in Britain currently educate nearly a third of all primary school children (29 percent) and 15 percent of all secondary pupils. Thirty-five percent of all primary schools and 15 percent of all secondary schools are church-related (Statistics of Education 2001).

Anglicans and Roman Catholics were the only churches with a large stake in education in 1944, and they quickly became partners with the government in education policy. Both churches have powerful education boards that negotiate with the government on issues of funding, curriculum, and school governance (Waddington 1985). The state determines which new church schools to finance, and while the state has funded new church schools, often in consultation with Catholic and Anglican educational authorities, until recently Jewish schools were the only religious newcomer to the denominational system since the passage of the 1944 Education Act.

Muslims began forming their own schools in the late 1970s and the early 1980s. By 2000, the *Muslim Directory* listed sixty-six Muslim schools, and by 2003 the Salaam portal database had ninety-eight (*Muslim Directory* 2000; Salaam Portal 2003). For some Muslim parents, the primary motivation for separate schools is to get out of a state system that they have concluded has failed their children. As we noted previously, Muslim children in mainstream British schools generally perform less well on standardized tests than do other children. An independent Muslim girls' school in Bradford, on the other hand, achieved the city's highest average test scores in 2002 (Buaras 2003).

The leadership of the Muslim community, however, argues that separate Muslim schools are also necessary to promote an Islamic way of life in a secular environment. Iqbal Siddiqui asserted that Muslims' first concern was to "survive and prosper as a community based on their common faith, a common value system and a common morality." For the education of children, this goal requires "that we create an environment in which being Muslim is the most natural and comfortable path, rather than a difficult or even dangerous one" (2000:13). Muslim schools challenge the liberal, secular presuppositions of the state school system and make education within the context of a Muslim worldview the central feature of the curriculum.

A syllabus on Islamic education published by the Muslim Educational Trust states:

> Islamic education is a total and complete system which does not separate the mundane affairs of life from the moral and spiritual aspects.... The objective is to educate young people in Islam and to make them conscious and practicing Muslims and to prepare them for life (1984:1).

Beginning in the early 1980s, a number of Muslim schools, most notably Islamia Primary School, submitted applications with the Department for Education to receive state funding. On three separate occasions, the government turned down applications from Muslim schools. In each case, the secretary of state claimed that the refusal had nothing to do with the school being Islamic. Muslims, however, were understandably frustrated with a system where Christian and Jewish schools were fully financed by the government but their own schools were not.

Some opponents of separate schools argued that state schools would better serve Muslims because they would more effectively integrate ethnic minorities into mainstream British culture. The 1985 Swann Report that had promoted multicultural education, for example, concluded that government funding for separate religious schools "would not be in the long term interest of ethnic minority communities" (O'Keefe 1988:ch. 1). This argument raised the thorny question about what "integration" into British society ought to mean for the Muslim community. For Muslims who wanted to retain their distinctive religious and cultural values, assimilating the values of a liberal, secular society was not necessarily attractive.

To the extent that Muslims perceive state schools as promoting an ideology that makes it more difficult for them to sustain their faith in British society, many concluded "that only with some form of separate schooling does the Muslim community have a chance of withstanding inexorable pressures toward assimilation" (Nielsen 1999:63). When asked to describe the primary benefit of an Islamic school for Muslim children, Ibrahim Hewitt (2001), headmaster of the Al-Aqsa School and former director of the Association of Muslim Schools in the UK and Eire, noted the following:

> The value added of Muslim schools is that the children do not have to apologize for being Muslim. They do not have to make a special effort to pray. It is a shift in emphasis that makes the faith a living faith. It is a more balanced development of their spirituality, of their whole human development. In a Muslim school you start the day with prayers [and] Arabic studies, and Islam goes into other studies as well. Islam is the ethos of the school, not just a religious education lesson half an hour a week.

In 1997, the Labour government approved the first Muslim state primary schools. Prime Minister Tony Blair reinforced state support for a pluralistic faith school system when he pushed the government to expand the number of church schools that the state would finance. "Church schools," Blair argued, "are a true partnership between the churches and the government. Since 1997 we have been glad to form partnerships with other faith groups to provide state-funded schools" (Blair 2000). The Blair government followed this proposal up with a Green Paper on education that proposed expanding both the number of "church" schools and their diversity: "...we welcome more schools provided by the churches and other major faith groups" (*Schools: Building on Success* 2001:48). Teachers' unions opposed the proposal, and forty-five Labour Members of Parliament (MPs) defied the government and voted against the bill (Morris 2002). Despite the backbench rebellion against the government's policy, the Education Bill passed the House by 405 to 87, a government majority of 318 (James 2002).

By 2001, the two Muslim schools were joined by the first publicly financed Sikh, Seventh-Day Adventist, Greek Orthodox, and Hindu state schools (Statistics of Education 2001:53). While these few schools paled in number to the more than forty-seven hundred Church of England and two thousand Roman Catholic schools, it was nevertheless apparent that a watershed moment had occurred and that the state education system would be more religiously pluralistic in the future. Given the popularity of church schools, the historical pattern of state accommodation of new religious groups, and the patent unfairness of excluding Muslim schools from the state system, it was only a matter of time before the state recognized the legitimacy of Muslim claims. As one Muslim leader put it (El Essawy 2001):

> The fact that there were no government-funded Muslim schools was a ridiculous anomaly that had to go. The Anglicans had their schools, Roman Catholics had their schools, Jews had their schools. It was only right that we got our schools.

In the end, then, Muslims in Britain were able to use the existing pattern of gradual accommodation of newly arrived religious groups to gain state funding for their own schools.

Mosque Building

As they settled in Britain, Muslims who initially worshiped in makeshift prayer rooms began to construct formal mosques. The number of mosques has expanded rapidly over the past several decades, from an estimated ten in 1945, to 329 in 1989, and 1,493 in 2003 (Étienne 1989:97; Foreign and Commonwealth Office 1995; Salaam Portal 2003). Given an estimated 1.6 million Muslims living in Great Britain, there is one mosque or prayer room for every 1,071 Muslims in England, Wales, and Scotland.

In contrast with the other countries in our study, mosque building in Britain has not been particularly controversial (Dassetto 2000). As a matter of public policy, the decision to grant permission for the construction of a mosque rests with local political officials. Some observers have noted that the planning process is sometimes delayed because of questions raised about parking spaces and the impact that the mosque might have on traffic in the area, but no one we interviewed asserted that a mosque-building project had been blocked on illegitimate or religious grounds. The moulana of the Old Trafford Muslim Society in Manchester, Mohammed Kassim Diwan (2001), described a typical situation:

> We have a converted warehouse that we use for our mosque, but we have just received permission to construct a purpose-built mosque. It took us two to three years to get the permission to build the mosque. Because our mosque is in a residential area, they [the government] required certain parking regulations to be met, but we came to a compromise and we have started the building of the mosque. The City Council, however, did help us by giving us first preference on a piece of land.

Muhammad Afzal (2001), a member of the Birmingham City Council, similarly noted that "there is no controversy on mosque building now. The City Council uses the Birmingham Central Mosque in its advertising material. The Council is keen to portray the mosque as part of the city's diversity."

The closest thing to a mosque controversy in recent years involved the planning for the construction of the Oxford Centre for Islamic Studies. Opened in temporary quarters in 1985 as an independent research institute affiliated with the famous university, the Centre secured a £20 million grant from King Fahd of Saudi Arabia to build a permanent structure. The architectural plans that were submitted to the city for approval included lecture halls, dining facilities, a prayer hall, a seventy-five-foot-high dome, and a one-hundred-foot-high minaret. Some academics and residents of Oxford opposed the project, allegedly because it would take up valuable open space and disrupt the city's historic skyline. Project supporters, including the Prince of Wales, accused some of their opponents of Islamophobia. As

David Browning (2001), registrar of the Centre, puts it:

> The project attracted a lot of attention, which is completely understandable. During the long process of consultation, we had very strong support from the majority of people. There were those who opposed the Centre for less worthy reasons, and there was undeniably a degree of straight prejudice. I wouldn't, however, overemphasize that. It was a very small, a very vocal minority, that opposed the project.

In 2000, the Oxford City Council approved the plans, and later that year the High Court rejected appeals to have the Council's decision blocked (Aston 2000; Dennis and Ungoed-Thomas 2000).

For the most part, gaining permission to build a mosque or Islamic center in Britain is no more difficult than securing permission for any other similar building. Akhtar Raja (2001), founding partner of Quist (a firm of lawyers) and a governor of the Islamia Primary School, echoes this view: "Generally speaking, it is as easy to build a mosque [in Britain] as it is to build any other kind of house of worship."

Testing the Theories

What explains the way in which the British state has accommodated the religious needs of its Muslim population? The policy review of our three dependent variables – religious instruction in state schools, state aid to Muslim schools, and policy on mosque building – suggests that British Muslims have done relatively well. While he noted that British Muslims had a long way to go in achieving their goals, community activist Nadim Malik (2001) concluded, "We (Muslims) are hugely privileged here. It is horrific in other countries. England has a much better sense of tolerance and multiculturalism." While we do not want to suggest that British Muslims face no significant obstacles, on the variables that we analyzed the state has been relatively accommodating to Muslim religious needs and practices. What, however, explains such generosity?

Resource Mobilization

One theory that tries to account for state policy is resource mobilization. According to this explanation, Muslims have generated concessions from the state because of the political resources that they possess. If, as we suggest, British Muslims have won policy victories from the state, it is a function of some key political resource at their disposal. To take the argument a step further, if British Muslims are comparatively advantaged, a resource theory would suggest that they have significant political resources that Muslims in Germany and France lack.

One indication of resource strength is the formation of organizations to represent a group's interests. At one level, British Muslims are very well organized. According to Steven Vertovek, there are more than 950 Muslim organizations in Britain (1997:175). The number of mosques, Muslim charities, schools, and social organizations has certainly increased since that estimate. While the majority of these groups are not specifically political, that many Muslims are associated with some organization lowers the costs for those group leaders who want to mobilize Muslims for political purposes. From a resource perspective, leaders can recruit Muslims through sympathetic mosques, schools, and other groups that they have joined.

Some evidence does suggest that Muslims are joining forces for politics. With the encouragement of the Labour government, Muslim leaders came together to form an umbrella organization, the Muslim Council of Britain (MCB), to be a unified voice for the British Muslim community. Taking as its model Britain's Jewish community, which is politically well represented by the Board of Deputies of British Jews (Kaye 1993), the MCB hopes to provide a similarly cohesive voice for Muslim concerns.

Philip Lewis also notes that Muslim communities in Britain are geographically concentrated, which enables them to "generate and sustain a separate institutional and economic infrastructure which embodies and perpetuates religious and cultural norms" (1994:19). Taking as his case study Bradford, England, where 16 percent of the population is Muslim (Office for National Statistics 2003), Lewis demonstrates that the large and well-integrated Muslim community in that city forged an effective movement that successfully negotiated with local government officials on various social and political issues. Muslim theology champions this unified perspective by encouraging Muslims to see themselves as a united community (*'ummah*) that transcends national, ethnic, and social class identities (Sanneh 1998:57). To the extent that British Muslims are socially and politically unified, as Muslim theology suggests that they ought to be, such organization would clearly increase their political clout.

Muslim groups may likewise be borrowing the political tactics of other well-organized movements in British politics. Muslim associations entered the electoral arena in the 1997 elections with a document providing information to help guide Muslim voters at the general election (Vallely 1997). The point of the guide was to educate Muslim voters about the issues and to encourage them to vote for candidates most sympathetic to Muslims' interests. According to a *Q News* analysis of that election, all forty-three constituencies with significant Muslim minorities returned a Labour MP, and four out of five Muslims surveyed said that they voted for a Labour candidate (Azam 1997:16). It is possible that the Labour Party's commitment to state funding of Muslim schools, which followed that election, came as a result of the electoral pressure from Muslim voters.

Finally, a key resource is people in positions of political authority. There are two Muslim MPs, 217 Muslim councillors were elected in the May 2000 local elections (out of a total of 25,000 councillors UK-wide), and the government appointed its first two Muslim members of the House of Lords (Chapman and Versi 2001). As we noted previously, Lord Ahmed has used his position in the House of Lords to press for an expansion of the Race Relations Act to include protection against religious discrimination, a central political concern for Muslims.

The organizational presence of Muslims, their political mobilization, and the election of Muslims to elected positions are all resources that mobilization theory would use to explain why British Muslims have won policy victories on our dependent variables of religious instruction in state schools, public financing of Muslim schools, and policy on mosque construction.

The problem with a resource hypothesis, however, is that British Muslims are not, in fact, well organized at the national level, and crossnationally, they are no better mobilized than Muslims in Germany and France. To the extent that British Muslims have won concessions from the state on the variables we analyzed, it is *despite* their organizational strength, not because of it. Lewis is correct to note that British Muslims are frequently well mobilized at the local level, but they remain deeply divided in national politics. At the local level, Muslims are often united by religion, language, race, and country, or even village, of origin. At the national level, by contrast, Muslims are frequently divided linguistically, racially, theologically, and by national origin. A large percentage of the 950 Muslim groups in Britain reflect those divisions. According to the *Muslim Directory* (2000), those organizations include the Council of British Pakistanis, the Bangladesh Welfare Association, the Kashmir Welfare Action Committee, the Quranic Arabic Foundation, the Iraqi Welfare Association, the Moroccan Community Welfare Group, and the Muslim Association of Nigeria, to name a few. Even the proliferation of mosques, which is at one level a sign of effective mobilization by Muslims, also indicates a fragmented religious community (Scantlebury 1995:427).

Muslims have made various efforts to form a single national organization to represent Islamic interests before the government. In the early 1990s, the Muslim Parliament under the leadership of the controversial Kalim

Siddiqui unsuccessfully tried to unify the disparate Muslim community. The most successful umbrella Muslim organization thus far is the MCB, which represents over three hundred national, regional, and local groups (Muslim Council of Britain 2003). Along with many other West European states, the British government was instrumental in pressing for the formation of the MCB so that it could more effectively communicate with a single group on issues of importance to the Muslim community (Dassetto 2000:41). Nonetheless, the MCB has failed in significant ways to unify the disparate British Muslim community. Many British Muslims perceive the MCB as having been created by the government as a "friendly Muslim party" (Faraz 1998:288). According to a lead article in the *Q News* (2002), the Muslim Council of Britain

> ...has not made a name for itself as either an imaginative or innovative organization.... Insofar as the majority of British Muslims are concerned the MCB has not only failed to deliver but has continued to be unrepresentative and irrelevant.

We asked each of our British interviewees to name the three most politically significant Muslim groups in the country. A committee member of the Islamic Resource Centre of Birmingham, Ahmed Parwez (2001), simply replied: "None. There are some significant Islamic organizations within the local community, but there are none that are politically significant within the system." While not everyone with whom we spoke shared his dismal assessment of national Muslim groups, there was no single group cited by all of the persons we interviewed. We suspect that were a similar poll conducted of leaders of the Jewish community, all of them would mention the Board of Deputies of British Jews. Despite the *qur'ānic* teaching on unity, diverse and conflicting loyalties among British Muslims limit the community's ability to create a cohesive political movement. Muslims are not, in short, resource-rich in Britain.

The socioeconomic status of Muslims in Britain further weakens a resource-based argument. As a rule, the Muslim community does not command the kind of resources that are so important to political mobilization. Muslims are, on the whole, economically deprived and educationally disadvantaged, even relative to other ethnic groups (Islamic Human Rights Commission 2001). According to government statistics, Pakistani Muslims were three times as likely as Pakistani Hindus to be unemployed, while Indian Muslims were twice as likely as Indian Hindus to be jobless (Walker 2002:3).

This resource weakness hampers Muslims' political efforts. As we noted previously, Muslims typically vote Labour, and Muslim organizations lobby the party for positions sympathetic to their cause. The Labour Party, however, hardly feels bound by this pressure and frequently takes positions at odds with Muslim voters. In commenting on the 2001 elections, Anthony McRoy sarcastically notes the following:

> The likelihood is that in this election the Labour leadership will merely make some compliments to the community, promise to consider their concerns, and then ignore them, secure in the knowledge that when push comes to shove, Muslims will vote Labour (2001:12).

Muslim disaffection with the Labour Party's position on relations with India reached such a critical point that Muslim voters in Birmingham ran candidates for city council positions under the newly created Justice for Kashmir Party. The party's national coordinator, Shafaq Hussain (2001), described his party's founding: "[Because] we were not getting any real support from Labour MPs, we needed to organize our own party and get people to stand in elections." While it has virtually no national support among Muslims, the party has done relatively well among the large Pakistani population in Birmingham, winning eight city council seats (Luck 2000:5).

It would, in short, be wrong to conclude that the recent Labour Party support for Muslim schools has anything to do with the resource strength of the Muslim community. In making the case for separate Islamic schools, Shabbir Akhtar argues that "only a mobilized Muslim community, united in its goals...can succeed against all odds" (1993:50). Muslim political unity would certainly increase their political power as an organized interest group, but thus far British Muslims have secured policy victories from the state despite their lack of resources and political cohesiveness.

Political Opportunity Structures

If resources alone fail to explain state accommodation of Muslim religious practices, perhaps a focus on political institutions can. Political opportunity structure theory contends that a regime's political institutions influence the capacity of groups to engage in collective action. Rath et al., for example, argue that the key variable in state recognition of Muslim religious needs is "the institutional context of the society in question. Some institutions seem to fit in relatively easily...and others seem to be more difficult" (1999:54). This theory predicts that Muslims will win policy concessions from the state where existing institutions support their efforts or encourage grass-roots political mobilization. A political opportunity structure theory can focus on various institutions, including political parties, the legal system, the media, and interest groups, but the most common state structure analyzed when looking at Muslim political mobilization is federalism.

Britain is not, of course, a federal polity. However, on many of issues of state accommodation of Muslims' religious practices, local political authorities do have significant autonomy from the national state. In explaining educational policy, for example, Gilles Kepel (1997:112) contends that Muslim demands "found conditions in Britain particularly propitious because of the decentralized nature of the educational system." In a similar vein, Erik Bleich contrasts Britain's decentralized educational polity with France's unitary system to explain why Britain, but not France, adopted multiculturalism in the schools. Bleich argues that:

> ...because decisions [in Britain] could be taken at local levels, more gatekeepers allowed more possible paths to multiculturalism to enter educational policy. France's education system, by contrast, is highly centralized (1998:91–92).

Whether or not a polity is centralized is particularly important for a community, such as Muslims, which is numerically small but geographically concentrated. As we noted in our review of British educational practice, British policy grants significant autonomy to local schools to go their own way on religious instruction and collective worship in state schools. Muslims have used this political opportunity to help shape educational policy. Britain's polity, in short, empowered Muslims. In France, by contrast, Muslims are geographically concentrated, but it matters little because France's unitary polity provides fewer opportunities for local activism and decision making. Absent the opportunity to affect school policy at the local level, French Muslims have effectively been shut out of the process. "Different institutional arrangements," Jocelyne Cesari writes, "tend to shape the agendas of Islamic mobilization and claims in different countries" (2000:3).

The local control over policy matters that federalism entails also empowers Muslims to become active in local politics. Lewis (1994:203) discusses in great detail how Muslims in Bradford "developed an understanding of local government" to ensure that political officials were "responsive to their needs." Christian Joppke similarly notes that British Muslims have "been hugely successful at the local government level" (1999:250). The mobilization of Muslims in Bradford succeeded because local politicians and government bureaucrats had political control over education policy. Even on an education issue where the national government has traditionally dominated – state funding for Islamic school – British MPs, because they represent parliamentary constituencies, are encouraged to be more responsive to pressure from local constituents. It is no surprise that MPs whose constituencies included a large Muslim population supported the expansion of the church school system to include Muslim schools.

A focus on political institutions, particularly decentralized politics, has much to commend it. As the theory predicts, the institutional context in which Muslim mobilization has occurred affects the political outcome on the dependent variables that we analyze. Nevertheless, the theory has some limitations. First, while institutional theorists are correct to point to the importance of inherited political structures, with several exceptions (Beckford and Gilliat 1998; Cesari 2000; Nielsen 1999; Zolberg and Litt 1999), they fail to note that one of the most important state structures shaping the politics of state accommodation of Muslims' religious needs is the existing pattern of church–state relations.

Britain's religious establishment facilitated institutional ties between church and state on a variety of issues, particularly related to education. This institutional model proved to be significant in shaping how Muslims mobilized on religious issues. On education, the Anglican Church has not aggressively defended its political advantage against other churches for the past several decades. Catholics, Methodists, and Baptists were part of the original compromise on state funding for church schools, and Jews were later incorporated as well. This twentieth-century pattern of accommodation created the expectation that religious newcomers would eventually be included in the system. Because of the popularity of church schools, the abolition of state aid was politically unviable, while a system that provided funding for the schools of some faiths but not others seemed overtly discriminatory. When Muslims began to advocate for their own schools, therefore, it was within a church–state context where such arrangements had become ordinary and expected. Because of this church–state institutional precedent, it was only a matter of time before the state would acquiesce to funding for Muslim schools.

The same is true on religious instruction and worship in state schools. Given the close institutional ties between church and state, it is no surprise that religious worship and instruction were part of the curriculum for all schools under the Education Act of 1944. The purpose of religious instruction was to represent the nation's shared moral and cultural norms and to counterbalance an increasingly secular society. What was provided in schools was never particularly Anglican, but instead recognized Britain's religious pluralism. These practices greatly affected Muslims as they immigrated in large numbers to Britain. Because the state provided religious worship and instruction in schools, and recognized religions other than

Christianity in the curriculum, Muslims could more easily press their case for state accommodation of their religious tradition. With little controversy, state schools accommodated Muslims on such matters as wearing of the *ḥijāb* and providing instruction about Islam. Church–state practices, in short, mattered a great deal in shaping how Britain recognized Muslims' religious needs.

A second limitation of most institutional analyses is that they fail to note that British Muslims, while "rich" in institutional opportunities in some respects, are not uniformly advantaged. Several key political institutions are consistently hostile to Muslim efforts. The Derby Report concluded that Muslims organizations were more likely than other religious groups to report unfair treatment in the criminal justice system, education, employment, housing, social services, and the media (Weller, Feldman, and Purdam 2001). In most of these institutions, particularly the media, a majority of Muslim organizations reported that the situation had worsened in recent years. Political parties at the local level have periodically been responsive to Muslim needs, but at the national level they have largely ignored Muslims' political demands. Mahmooda Qureshi (2001), vice president of the Sister Section of the Young Muslims of the UK, is not far off the mark in commenting that "in mainstream British politics today we [Muslims] have lost hope of any particular party championing our causes or sympathizing with us, even though they make the right noises."

Institutional analyses predict that differential outcomes on the state accommodation of Muslim religious needs result from variant opportunities provided by the state for political success. This theory, however, comes up short by failing to recognize consistently the significance of church–state structures in determining the policy outcome and in implying that the relative success of British Muslims must solely be a function of institutional support and political opportunities.

Ideology

Ideological theories accent the ways in which national ideas about citizenship, nationhood, and assimilation, rather than political structures, have determined state responses to Muslims' political demands. Such accounts have been used to explain public policy on citizenship and educational policies. Rogers Brubaker (1992), for example, argues that different citizenship traditions are particularly important in contemporary debates over immigration policy. Bleich contends that Britain's "liberal priors" contributed to the state adopting a multiculturalist educational policy (1998:82). Favell (1998) asserts that Britain's liberal political tradition makes policy makers open to recognizing the needs of Muslim immigrants. And the state accommodated Muslim demands, Vertovek argues, because "it is apparent they are for the most part only asking for an exercise of liberal rights according to wholly British procedures and standards" (1997:173). These comments suggest, as Virginie Guiraudon notes, that "governments do not operate from a 'tabula rasa' perspective and [that] the shadow of the past looms large" (1998:278).

While no ideological theory has specifically focused on how or why states have recognized Muslims' religious needs, such an account could be used to explain Britain's relative accommodation on the variables we analyzed. Political pragmatism and ideological liberalism characterize British political culture. On issues related to church and state, for example, the state, at least in the last half century, has not demonstrated a strong commitment to the established Anglican Church, but has instead compromised with religious newcomers. The recent incorporation of Muslim schools into the state system can also be interpreted as consistent with the state's norms and as a pragmatic response to an increasingly divisive political debate.

A limitation of ideological theories is in their claim that Britain's political liberalism can fully explain the state's church–state policy. To the extent that a liberal state presumes to treat its citizens as individuals, rather than as members of social groups, the British state's recognition and accommodation of religious groups is not fully consistent with ideological liberalism. Britain is arguably illiberal in preserving a public role for religion.

As with state structural accounts, our evaluation of ideological theories stems primarily from our view that such models have failed to consider systematically how church–state structures are themselves "ideological priors" that fundamentally shape the resolution of policy issues related to Muslims' religious needs. The historically close ties between the Church of England and the British state forged an expectation that the institutions would work closely together for common purposes. As the state gradually recognized and accommodated the needs of religious nonconformists, Catholics, and Jews, an assumption formed that religious newcomers would eventually receive similar recognition and benefits from the state. Inherited traditions and practices sustained an ideology that the state should recognize and accommodate group differences as they were expressed in religion. This ideology also legitimated a particular course of action for Muslim activists in Britain, who understood not only what the state provided other religious groups, but also that elite and public opinion generally shared those ideological assumptions.

Church–State Institutions

Our critique of structural and ideological theories suggests how our church–state theory can account for state accommodation of Muslim religious needs in Britain. In our review of existing explanations, we have already noted why a focus on church–state practices expands both institutional and ideological accounts of group action. Our claim is that these theories do not give adequate attention to how church–state structures and practices are key institutional and ideological variables that help to explain how and why the state accommodates Muslims' religious practices. This final section expands that argument with a closer analysis of how this process has occurred in Britain.

First and foremost, the close alliance between church and state in Britain shapes the political agenda. State aid to Muslim schools is an issue in Britain only because the state was already financing Christian and Jewish schools, and the state was doing so because church–state practices allowed and even encouraged it. Absent an institutional arrangement where the state worked with various churches, particularly Anglicans and Roman Catholics on education issues, it is impossible to imagine Muslims being able to make the case that the state similarly ought to work with them on the needs of Muslim pupils. Indeed, the issue of state finance for Muslim schools is simply not on the political agenda in France, which lacks the same history of close cooperation between the churches and the state on educational issues.

Moreover, the established church is an ally, sometimes explicitly and sometimes implicitly, in Muslim efforts to gain state accommodation of their religious practices. For the most part, the leadership of the Churches in the 1960s and 1970s advocated policies of immigration for Commonwealth residents – many of whom were Muslims – and the elimination of discrimination against them (Deakin 1984:101; Machen 1998:209). More recently, the established Church of England has supported Muslim political efforts. On religious instruction in state schools, for example, Canon John Hall (2001) commented, "It is important for people in schools to know and respect other faiths in our community. There is no question about this." Hall also indicated that the Church supported state aid to Muslim schools.

This help is significant because the Anglican and Catholic churches, in particular, act as brokers between religious groups and the secular polity on various issues. On education, Anglican and Catholic officials are key players in working out arrangements for religious instruction in state schools and in advising and lobbying the government on behalf of religious schools. Anne Barlow (2001) of the Department for Education and Skills affirmed that "the Church of England and the Roman Catholic Church are considered important partners in the education process." The support of influential insiders, then, has been a significant factor in explaining why the British state has generally accommodated Muslims on education issues, a circumstance not lost on Muslim leaders. Dr. Yaqub Zaki (2001), deputy director of the Muslim Institute, commented, "We see the religious establishment as an ally.... There is within the Muslim community the realization that we have to have friends in the wider religious society."

These "friends" are particularly significant when some members of the elite or general public oppose expanding the system to include Muslims. In 2001, the Home Office commissioned the Cantle Report on the causes of the 2001 race riots in Oldham and Burnley. As a way of overcoming the religious and racial segregation that was seen as the primary cause of the riots, the report recommended that all religious schools voluntarily offer 25 percent of all places to students of other faiths or no faith. Such a practice would "be more inclusive and create better representation of all cultures and ethnicities" (Home Office 2001:50).

Many Muslim leaders viewed this recommendation as an implicit criticism of their schools, which had only recently won public funding. Ibrahim Hewitt wryly noted the following:

> ... recent criticism of faith schools is not a new phenomenon, but neither is it historically based. Education for centuries had a religious foundation. Until Muslim schools came on the scene, though, faith schools weren't described as "separate" schools, nor were they criticized as they are today (2002:16).

Britain's church–state structures and close political alliances between religious and political leaders, however, aided Muslims. Catholic and Anglican educational leaders blasted the recommendation of the Cantle Report. Oona Stannard, director of Catholic Education Service, said, "We see no need to oblige new faith schools to take a certain percentage of pupils of other faiths." The government's education secretary, Estelle Morris, also backed away from the report's recommendation: "It is wrong to land on the head of faith schools all of society's concerns about segregated communities" (MORI 2001b). In the end, the government never adopted the recommendations of the report on religious schools.

Not only are secular and religious education officials closely allied in Britain, but an infrastructure is also in place for new schools that want to receive state aid. The Department for Education has copious documents giving detailed descriptions of how promoters of new religious schools can bring a successful application before the Department for Education (Department for Education n.d.). In light of the government's commitment to approve more "church" schools, Barlow (2001) noted that "we are looking at creating an environment where we can encourage people from various religious traditions to make successful applications." Various Muslim organizations use this institutional framework to their advantage. The Muslim Education Trust, for instance, specializes in working with schools to provide Islamic instruction, while the IQRA Trust publishes a manual advising Muslims on how they can participate in SACREs, the local committees responsible for religious education in state schools (Akhtar 1993; IQRA Trust 1991; Sarwar 1994). None of this would have been possible absent the church–state structure in Britain that made such an arrangement both feasible and necessary.

Insider influence and support have been important on other issues as well. We noted previously that the Royal Commission on the Reform of the House of Lords recommended that religious leaders outside of the established Anglican Church have permanent representation in the reconstituted House. One of the twelve members of that commission, who no doubt took a lead on the question of religious representation, was Richard Harries, bishop of Oxford. From the standpoint of the Church of England, which has a dwindling membership, the proposed change to the religious membership of the House of Lords has two advantages. First, by providing seats in the Lords for members of other religious communities, the Church is acknowledging that Britain has become a multifaith society. On the other hand, the preservation of assigned seats for religious leaders in the House secures the idea that the *secular* polity should make formal space for *religious* voices. Moreover, the Church of England would, under the proposed plan, retain a majority of the assigned religious seats in the Lords, meaning that it would strategically maintain its role as the leading voice on religious matters in both the upper house and the country as a whole.

This does not mean, of course, that the state has automatically accorded Muslims the same benefits it grants to the Church of England. The state has, for example, consistently refused to extend the blasphemy law to apply to all religious communities, nor have Conservative or Labour governments supported an extension of the Race Relations Act to protect persons against discrimination on religious grounds. Finally, it took the state decades to agree to finance the first Islamic schools. Despite these setbacks, Muslims have not argued that equal treatment demands the abolition of the blasphemy law or the removal of state aid to all religious schools. As a rule, Muslims have little in common with secular, liberal arguments in favor of disestablishment that, in their view, dismiss the public, political role of religion (Chapman 1998:182; Siddiqui 2000:192). Daoud Rosser-Owen (2001:2) of the Association of British Muslims succinctly notes, "For us there must be a church–state link, or rather a religion–state link."

Even when the Church of England fails to provide explicit political support to Muslim efforts, the existence of a religious establishment implicitly aids Muslims. Such an arrangement creates opportunities that other churches and faith communities can successfully exploit, particularly when they are excluded from state benefits. Ataullah Siddiqui (2001), head of the Interfaith Unit of the Islamic Foundation, commented, "One benefit of the religious establishment is that it allows a back door to other religions to have access to the government." An officially recognized church, even if it is a Christian church, makes it easier for Muslims to make the case for state accommodation of their community's religious needs.

Conclusion

On our dependent variables – religious instruction in state schools, state aid to religious schools, and mosque building – Britain has been remarkably accommodating to Muslims. While state recognition of Muslims has certainly taken some time and some noticeable lapses remain, as a rule the state has both recognized Muslim religious needs and adapted existing policy to accommodate the Muslim population. The reason for this, we conclude, is the interaction between religious institutions, on the one hand, and political ideology and state actors, on the other. The inherited church–state structures provided a context through which issues of religious accommodation were successfully negotiated. Moreover, long-established practices in these policy areas forged ideological expectations about what Muslims could reasonably expect from the state. As both an institution and a set of ideas about the proper relationship between religion and politics, the established church provided Muslims with an important resource in their efforts.

What is somewhat ironic is that it took the arrival of Muslims, religious newcomers and a community that took its faith very seriously, to expose the degree to which the established church in Britain remained vital to the politics of various issues. The gradual secularization of British society led many to conclude that religion would and should be less important politically in the future, and that whatever vestiges of an alliance between church and state in public policy remained would gradually disappear. The arrival of Muslims, however, disclosed the intimate ties between church and state on such issues as state financing of religious schools and religious instruction in state-run schools. In the process, Muslims have gradually won for themselves state recognition for their religious practices.

3

France: *Laïcité* and the *Ḥijāb*

It is *laïcité* that has allowed the public school to be the melting pot in which, through the alchemy of education, differences vanish so the nation can emerge.

> Ernest Chenière, principal of a public junior high school in Creil, explaining why he suspended three Muslim girls for wearing the *ḥijāb* (Gonod 1989)

The position of the Catholic Church is to say that, in this landscape which until now has been filled with . . . churches or synagogues, it is completely normal for Muslims also to be able to build mosques. That is, for them to have the freedom to live out their religion. I think that in a society which claims to be *laïque*, it is extremely important for all religions to have freedom of expression and so for Muslims to be able to set up places of worship.

> Bernard Panafieu (2001), archbishop of Marseille

If we integrate them, if all the Arabs and Berbers of Algeria were considered French, how could they be prevented from settling in France, where the living standard is so much higher? My village would no longer be called Colombey-les-Deux-Églises [Colombey-the-Two-Churches] but Colombey-les-Deux-Mosquées [Colombey-the-Two-Mosques].

> Charles de Gaulle, discussing why France should grant independence to Algeria (Shatz 2002:54)

IN CONTRAST TO the situation in Britain, the societal and political environment in France is surprisingly hostile to public accommodation of Muslims' religious practices. Guided above all by the separationist concept of *laïcité*, the French state permits less religious expression in the public schools, funds not a single private Islamic school in metropolitan France, and has often impeded Muslims' efforts to construct mosques. As in the previous chapter, we begin with the historical and political background for these policies.

Historical Context

Immigration History

Metropolitan France's contacts with Islam and Muslims are probably even more ancient than Britain's. As early as 716 A.D., a group of North African soldiers entered what is today France and, several years later, established a Muslim protectorate and mosque in Narbonne. Various Muslim invasions and expulsions continued in southern France throughout the Middle Ages and early Modern Period, sometimes leaving behind a few mosques and Muslim settlers (Clément 1990; Poly 1992; Poly and Riché 1992). With the French conquest of Algeria in 1830, however, France gained the first of several Mediterranean and Sub-Saharan African colonies with large Muslim populations. The first significant migration of these Muslim colonial subjects to European France occurred during World War I, bringing a few hundred thousand *Maghrébins* and smaller numbers of such other African Muslims as the Comorians to serve in the army and replace ethnic French workers in the fields and munitions factories (Frémeaux 1991:55–157; Toihiri 2001). In gratitude for these Muslims' wartime efforts, the French state built the large Mosque of Paris in 1926 (Boyer 1998:53–8; Kepel 1991:65–76).

Muslim immigration to the *métropole* began in earnest, however, in response to the severe post-World War II labor shortage. During the three decades following the end of the war, French employers and officials especially recruited or "regularized" workers from such predominantly Muslim countries as Algeria (independent after 1962), Morocco, Tunisia, and Turkey (Boyer 1998:77–9; Le Moigne 1986:7–11; Tapinos 1975; Wihtol de Wenden 1988:85–185). North Africans often found employment in construction or heavy industry, while Turkish immigrants were likely to work in mining, the building trades, or forestry. By 1975, over one million such Muslim immigrants were living in metropolitan France (Noiriel 1988:409, 412–13; Sunay 2001).

One cannot overemphasize the searing effects of the Algerian War of Independence on the psyches of both ethnic European and ethnic Arab or Berber residents of France and Algeria. Beginning in the mid-1950s with a series of street assassinations of French police officers and allegedly pro-French Algerians, the war rapidly degenerated into a gruesome, civil-war-style conflict of indiscriminate, merciless terrorism pitted against horrific, systematic torture and counterterror (Branche 2001; Droz and Lever 1982:57–180). Since the leading Algerian guerrilla group, the Front de libération nationale (FLN), drew much of its rhetoric and at least some of its motivation from Islam, many French colonists in Algeria and citizens of European France soon developed a tremendous fear of this religion. Resentment toward North African Muslims seemed especially great among the many *pieds-noirs* colonists, who were traumatized by the terrorist bombings and massacres of the war and ultimately forced, along with their ethnic Algerian allies, the *harkis*, to flee to France after Algeria's victory in 1962 (Barrette 2001; Droz and Lever 1982:334–54; Frémeaux 1991:248–51; Gadant 1988:21–33; Martinez 2001).

Many first-generation, nonrefugee Muslim immigrants initially viewed their stay in France as temporary. At first heavily male, these Muslim workers would often leave their wife and children in the country of origin, live as inexpensively as possible, and send remittances back home to support their families. After several years' sojourn in France, some would indeed return to their country of birth (Hargreaves 1995:11–17; INED 1977:10–13). Under such conditions, Muslims in France practiced their faith with little fanfare in often makeshift facilities. As Évry imam Khalil Merroun (2001) notes:

> ...during the 1960s and on into the '70s, this Islam [of the Muslim immigrants to France] was not out in the open. And where [Muslims did attempt to] express it, it was completely suppressed. [The French] sensed that there was a big elephant pushing against them with its trunk, but they didn't know where the elephant came from.... So Islam was relegated to the cellars.

Such hidden, "cellar Islam" remained more or less the norm through the early 1970s (Kepel 1991:125–32; see also Leveau and Schnapper 1988).

In 1974, however, the oil crisis–induced recession and jump in unemployment spurred the French government to stop recruiting and, at least in theory, admitting any more foreign-born workers. Though President Valéry Giscard d'Estaing also tried to ban family reunification, the Conseil d'État ultimately nullified his efforts. As in Britain, the ironic result of these restrictive measures was that many supposedly "temporary" immigrants decided to stay permanently and so brought their family members to France as well. Sociologically, this transformation from the immigration of individual workers to that of complete families meant that France suddenly needed to concern itself with integrating Muslims of all ages and backgrounds into what was hitherto a predominantly Catholic Christian nation (Hargreaves 1995:17–20; Tribalat 1995:27–33; Weil 1991:112–57; Wihtol de Wenden 1988:189–208; Wihtol de Wenden and Leveau 2001:15–22).

In the intervening years, French governments attempted to reduce immigration further and to tighten the requirements for becoming a French citizen. In 1977, Immigration Minister Lionel Stoléru tried to bribe North African immigrants to return home by offering them ten thousand francs each for leaving the country. Very few took up the offer. Beginning in 1978, Stoléru next tried a more coercive approach, attempting to deport hundreds of thousands of foreign-born Muslim workers and their families. This second initiative also largely failed, mainly for lack of legislative support (Hargreaves 1995:19–20; Wihtol de Wenden 1988:224–51; Weil 1991:158–211). A similar, ultimately unsuccessful effort to cut back on the number of ethnic North Africans obtaining French nationality at birth occurred with the Gaullist-led passage of the 1993 revisions to the French Code of Nationality. Once the Socialists regained power, however, their 1998 reforms changed France's citizenship laws back to the relatively liberal status quo ante (Hargreaves 1995:24; Marchand 1997; Marlowe 1998; *Migration News* 1998; Philippe and Herzberg 1997; Wihtol de Wenden and Leveau 2001:63–71, 124–7).

Despite the many efforts to exclude or deport immigrants, post-World War II France has become one of the most multi-ethnic societies on the continent. The proportion of foreign-born residents of metropolitan France has remained more-or-less constant since 1975 at around 10 percent, which now corresponds to about 5.9 million people. The official census of 1999 reported that among the universe of first-generation immigrants[1] in metropolitan France, 55 percent come from outside Europe, 30 percent from North Africa, 9 percent from Sub-Saharan Africa, 4 percent from Turkey, and 9 percent from the rest of Asia. To the almost 6 million foreign-born residents of France must be added approximately 6 million more

---

[1] These statistics for the national origin of "immigrants" use the more restrictive definition of "immigrant" favored by the French Haut Conseil à l'Intégration. Thus, while the actual number of foreign-born residents equals 5.9 million according to the 1999 census, the Haut Conseil counts only 4.3 million "immigrants." The difference appears to be the 1.6 million "French citizens by birth" who were nonetheless "born abroad," or in former French colonies outside Europe (Lebon 2000:5–9). Many of these "natives born abroad" are probably not ethnically French, and all are sociologically immigrants to the *métropole*.

"natives" who descended from twentieth-century immigrants. In the end, then, almost one in five residents of France is foreign-born or comes from recent-immigrant stock (Boëldieu and Borrel 2000; Lebon 2000:7–13; Tribalat 1991:257).

Beginning in the early 1980s, moderate politicians from both the Gaullist and Socialist camps found in the growing popularity of Jean-Marie Le Pen's Front National Party another reason to harden their positions on this growing number of immigrants. Benefiting from a poor economy and mainstream political leaders' increasing willingness to scapegoat immigrants, Le Pen's vehemently anti-immigration and anti-Muslim party first achieved significant public notice in the 1983 municipal elections in Dreux, a depressed suburb of Paris (Hargreaves 1995:182–7; Schain 1987; Tribalat 1999). Despite its racist, neo-Nazi rhetoric and ties (Camus 1996; Tristan 1987), the Front has continued to garner substantial electoral support in the years since. A few southern French cities such as Marignane now have National Front mayors (Fındık 2001), and the party's share of the national vote typically ranges from 10 percent to 15 percent (Hargreaves 1995:183). But Le Pen's most spectacular coup occurred during the first round of the 2002 presidential elections, when he outpolled even the Socialist Prime Minister Lionel Jospin. Though he ultimately lost to the Gaullist incumbent Jacques Chirac in the second round, Le Pen did receive the votes of 18 percent of the French electorate (Daley 2002b; Ysmal 2002).

Finally, a wave of Islamist terror in 1995 and the inexorable rise of France's crime rate[2] – blamed largely on immigrants – further exacerbated the already tense relations between ethnic French "Français de souche" and residents of North African heritage. Led by Khaled Kelkal, a Muslim immigrant from the Lyon ghetto, terrorists affiliated with the Armed Islamic Group (GIA) blew up a Paris RER train in July 1995, killing seven people and wounding over eighty. Several weeks later, French security forces tracked down Kelkal and shot him to death (Debeusscher 1995; Gattegno and Inciyan 1996; Loch 1995). The rate of "ordinary" crime has likewise

---

[2] Joel Fetzer, for example, was offered the choice of being "cut open [couper]" with a knife or donating "something of value" to a fellow passenger in a suburban Paris RER train one Sunday afternoon in the summer of 2001. To make matters worse, the gendarme to whom Fetzer tried to report the mugging refused even to take his statement. "Things like this happen so often that we don't even report them," he claimed. "Just be glad he didn't really stab you." When Fetzer finally reached his destination, moreover, the French grandmother he was visiting told him that she had herself just been released from the hospital after having been slammed against a concrete floor during another successful mugging in the Paris Métro.

risen dramatically since the mid-1990s, especially in the working-class, heavily immigrant suburbs surrounding major French cities. Random violence committed by teenagers carrying knives and even guns has become disturbingly common, leading the French electorate to rank crime as its top concern. In 2002, even Paris Mayor Bertrand Delanoë nearly lost his life when a suburban attacker allegedly targeting politicians and gays stabbed him in the chest (Chevènement 1998; Daley 2002a; Jeffries 2000; Ray 2002; Sung 2002).

The Politics of Settlement

Especially beginning in the 1970s, Muslim immigrants gradually brought their relatives to France or married and started families in the country. Particularly among the French-born children, integration into mainstream society became an ever more pressing concern (Gildea 1997:137–8). French public policy thus shifted from simply policing immigration flows into much more of a socioculturally based effort to help the migrants and their children settle in France (Le Carpentier 2001).

Unfortunately, however, North African and Sub-Saharan Muslims do not, on the whole, appear to have been welcomed as warmly as most European immigrants have been (Fetzer 2000:48–62, 110–22; Gildea 1997:230). Not only have African-origin Muslims become the *bête noir* of Le Pen's all-too-successful Front National Party (Hargreaves 1995:183–7), but many French citizens also view them as fundamentally "unassimilable." Echoing what even many relatively mainstream *français de souche* privately believe (Ben Jelloun 1999), former French Algeria leader Jacques Soustelle claimed the following in 1990:

> Islam is not only a religion, a metaphysics and ethics, but a determining and constrictive framework of all aspects of life. Consequently, to speak of integration, that is to say assimilation, is dangerously utopian. You can only assimilate what can be assimilated (Gildea 1997:21, 142).

Finally, even more virulent hostility may underlie much of the violence directed at French Muslims by the police and private citizens. Chronicling a host of "Arabicides" from 1970 to 1991, for example, journalist Fausto Giudice (1992:362) concludes that "one may, in post-'68 France, kill Arabs with impunity" (see also Webster 1993).

Reacting against such rejection and abuse, many young working-class Muslims have created an alternative counterculture of protest, embraced fundamentalist Islam, or engaged in violent insurrections against the French state. Mathieu Kassovitz's Spike Lee–like film *La haine* [Hate] (1996) portrays disenfranchised Muslim and Jewish teenagers from the Paris ghetto who try to resist police oppression through graffiti, rap music, and counterviolence. And Kassovitz's vision of despair is firmly rooted in French reality (Colio 1998; Pyslarou 2000; Xinhua News Agency 1997). Following in the footsteps of their "martyred" hero, Khaled Kelkal, other young *beurs* seek salvation in militant Islamist movements (Aziz 1996:111–17; Delorme 1998:171–2). More dramatically, France has witnessed a long series of ethnic rebellions in its large cities (Bachmann and Le Guennec 1996:341–448). During perhaps the most noted such "riot," police involvement in the death of a motorcyclist sparked four nights of stone throwing and firebombing by angry youths in the Lyon suburb of Vaulx-en-Velin. Authorities estimated the damages from the October 1990 disturbance at 25 million francs (Associated Press 1990; Bachmann and Le Guennec 1996:441–3; United Press International 1990).

To combat such "problems of the suburbs," the French state has increased funding for education and social service organizations in such poor Zones à Urbaniser en Priorité (ZUP). Under the Zones d'Éducation Prioritaire (ZEP) program, public schools with 30 percent or more immigrant students are more likely to receive extra money for more teachers and better facilities (Hargreaves 1995:71, 201–2). The Education Ministry likewise directs additional resources toward "sensitive," or particularly violence-prone, schools (OECD 1995:46). A third program, the FAS (Fonds d'Action Sociale pour les Travailleurs Immigrés et leurs Familles [Social Action Fund for Immigrant Workers and their Families]), targets poorly qualified immigrant-origin residents for additional vocational training and also assists integration-oriented ethnic associations (Hargreaves 1995:201, 204–5).

At a more general level, the French government has tried to foster immigrants' incorporation by establishing specialized agencies and by enforcing antidiscrimination laws. Each focusing on a particular aspect of migration, such state entities as the Haut Conseil à l'Intégration [High Council for Integration], Institut National d'Études Démographiques [National Institute for Demographic Studies], and Office National d'Immigration [National Immigration Office] have all contributed toward making immigrants part of mainstream French society by recommending new policies, conducting immigration-related research, and managing migratory flows (Hargreaves 1995:11, 33, 39–40; Haut Conseil à l'Intégration 1998; Tribalat 1991). The French state has also endeavored to end ethnic and religious discrimination in employment by enforcing such civil rights legislation as the Pleven Law of July 1, 1972 (Haut Conseil à l'Intégration 1998:94–6).

Institutional and Social Context

Laïcité

French policy on state accommodation of religious practices is governed above all else by *laïcité*, or a certain version of separationism between religion and state. Today, a century after its enactment into French law, *laïcité* continues to structure public debate over the proper place of religion in French politics and society. Not only secularists but even most practicing Christians, Jews, and Muslims still justify their respective positions by appealing to some version of this particularly French concept.

What eventually became *laïcité* first originated in political opposition to the monarchist Catholic Church. Rejecting not only King Louis XVI's absolutist regime but also his powerful religious supporters, French revolutionaries disestablished the Church, deported or murdered thousands of Catholic priests, seized most ecclesiastical property, and outlawed most Catholic religious orders (Baubérot 2000:11–17). The revolutionaries even went so far as to abolish the Christian calendar and institute a "religion of the Republic." This new civil religion included such ceremonies as the "Festival for the Goddess Reason," which took place in Notre Dame Cathedral on November 10, 1793, and the adoration of French revolutionary "martyrs" instead of Catholic saints (Baubérot 2000:15–17; Frigulietti 1991; Haarscher 1998:13). After the fall of Maximilien Robespierre, more pragmatic leaders established an uncomfortable separation of church and state in 1795. Citizens were once again allowed to celebrate mass or their religion's equivalent, but the state refused to pay clergy's salaries and maintained police surveillance over religious activities (Baubérot 2000:17–18; Le Tourneau 2000:74–5).

This strict-separationist regime ended abruptly in 1801, when the new French ruler, Napoleon Bonaparte, signed a Concordat with Pope Pius VII. Under this new arrangement, Catholicism became the "religion of the great majority of French people," not the established religion. The Pope gave up his claims to former church property, but the state in turn paid the salaries of Catholic (as well as Lutheran and Calvinist) clergy, appointed Catholic bishops, and required Catholic priests to swear allegiance to the French government (Haarscher 1998:14–15; Le Tourneau 2000:78–86). With a few brief exceptions, some version of this church-state arrangement remained intact until 1905 (Jézéquel 1999:49–51; Le Tourneau 2000:86–97).

In the late 1800s, nonetheless, the divide between supporters and opponents of the Catholic Church – and its favorite political institution, the monarchy – became so sharp in French society and politics that scholars speak of "two Frances": one clerical and monarchist, and the other anticlerical and republican. Once the partisans of anticlericalism gained parliamentary power in 1881, they wasted no time transforming public policy in the arena perhaps dearest to their hearts: the school. The result was the law of March 28, 1882, known as the "Ferry Law" after Minister of Public Instruction Jules Ferry, which effectively *laïcized* public education. Perhaps the most important provision stripped clergy of their right to "inspect" public schools and fire those teachers who displeased them. Public schools were nonetheless obligated under the 1882 law to close one day per week so students could attend catechism classes elsewhere if they wished (Baubérot 2000:43–55; Jézéquel 1999:50).

But more *laïcization* was yet to come. Partly as a reaction to Catholic antisemitism and militarism during the Dreyfus Affair (Rémond 1999:205–6), anticlerical forces mobilized to pass their defining piece of legislation, the Separation Law of December 9, 1905 (Le Tourneau 2000:96–7). Breaking forever with the Concordat of 1801,[3] the French government would henceforth "neither recognize nor pay salaries or other expenses for any form of worship [*culte*]." The state would nonetheless continue to fund chaplaincies in "such public establishments as . . . schools, hospices, asylums, and prisons." The freedom to worship was only to be restricted in the interest of "public order," but the placing of any "religious sign or emblem on public monuments" was forbidden. Except during the Vichy regime, this relatively thoroughgoing separation of religion and state has remained in place since 1905 (Baubérot 2000:76–124; Jézéquel 1999:51–3, 87; Le Tourneau 2000:98–108).

From the beginning, some more religiously oriented citizens have rejected French *laïcité* outright, seeing it primarily as a Trojan horse for anticlerical militants' campaign to rid French society of all vestiges of traditional religion. In 1886, Roman Catholic authorities denounced the "atheisation"

---

[3] The three eastern *départements* of Bas-Rhin, Haut-Rhin, and Moselle, being part of Germany from 1871 to 1918, remain to this day under the Concordat of 1801 (Jézéquel 1999:58–9; Le Tourneau 2000:109). The situation of Muslims in these *départements* is typically better than in the rest of France, more closely resembling the arrangements in Germany (Fregosi 1997; see also Messner 2000). The public University of Strasbourg, for example, even attempted to create an Islamic seminary to train future French imams (Messner 1998).

unleashed by the 1882 law (Baubérot 2000:58), and in 1925 a group of cardinals and bishops publicly declared *laïcité* "intrinsically perverse" (Jézéquel 1999:51). Today, *pied-noir* novelist and literary critic Louis Martinez (2001; see also Barrette 2001) does not view French

> secularism or *laïcité* [as] *laïcité* in the highest meaning of the word because *laïcité* in France is related to powerful atheistic or anti-Christian propaganda. . . . Pure *laïcité* does not exist. There's always a polemical position behind it . . . in general, an anti-Christian [one].

Abdellatif Hmito (2001), a French Muslim who teaches mathematics in a public school in Le Havre, likewise contends that many *laïcards*, "on the pretext that they want to defend the Republic, defend *laïcité*, actually defend the fact that they are, most of the time, atheists or agnostics or the people who won the battle against the Catholic Church."

Some isolated statements by a few of the original advocates of *laïcité* certainly do lend credence to such opponents' views. Even the relatively moderate Jules Ferry once explained his project of *laïcizing* the public schools as a way to "organize humanity without God and without a king" (Le Tourneau 2000:96). But dismissing *laïcité* as nothing more than a tactic of militant atheists is not completely accurate because its original formulators held various metaphysical views and did not agree on what role traditional religion should be allowed to play in French political and social life.

Some "founders" of *laïcité* such as Edgar Quinet were indeed unabashed atheists (Jézéquel 1999:91). Yet Ferry appears to have tended toward agnosticism (Loeffel 1999:44), and Émile Combes had studied at a Catholic seminary before becoming a "fervent spiritualist" (Baubérot 2000:79). Félix Pécaut and Jules Steeg were former Protestant pastors, though extremely liberal in their theology. Ferdinand Buisson had been raised in an evangelical Protestant home but eventually embraced a form of rationalist Protestantism similar to that of Pécaut and Steeg (Loeffel 1999:11–13). In short, the principal advocates of *laïcité* were hardly devout Roman Catholics or even orthodox Christians, yet many seem to have held some kind of religious or semireligious worldview.

The "framers" of *laïcité* likewise disagreed over what role religion may legitimately play in French life. At one extreme, Combes praised "society's emancipation from its former subjection to religious dogma." Free of religion, humans could now think freely. As head of the government from 1902 to 1905, Combes proposed a draconian church–state bill that contained no guarantee of liberty of conscience and that would have given political authorities the power to manage and even confiscate church buildings. During the so-called "File Affair" *(affaire des fiches)*, he even presided over the secret surveillance of military officers' religious activities. Officers who were observed attending mass were then to be passed over for promotion in favor of nonreligious ones (Baubérot 2000:80–6; Le Tourneau 2000:96–7).

In contrast, the much more accommodationist Buisson argued in 1903 – two years *before* the passage of the Separation Law – that the continued anticlerical campaign was becoming illegitimate:

> What is left of the [Catholic] Church? A single role, one that cannot reasonably be taken away from her: religion, religion alone. For even morality, joined for so long to religion, has been separated from her. Our laws, our regulations, even our schools no longer know anything but *laïque* morality.
>
> [Our opponents say,] "Since the Church no longer acts outside the realm of the soul, leave her alone, if it's true that you only wanted to wage war on the omnipresence of the now-beaten clergy. But you continue to attack her. So admit that it wasn't clericalism that was the enemy, but religion."...All the defenders of Catholicism agree that this deathly hatred of religion is the only motive that they can find for our conduct.

Though Buisson's 1903 essay did call for the abrogation of the 1801 Concordat, he described his colleagues' "anticlerical fury [*acharnement*]" as a "kind of fanaticism." This excessively aggressive attack on the Church, he warned, might have even become counterproductive:

> The Church...in France today occupies a position that it has never had before: she has developed welfare, charitable, and philanthropic activities; through her "works" of all kinds, today she enjoys a level of popularity never before achieved as well as an even greater degree of respectability (Rémond 1999:220–3).

Ferry appears to have had similar doubts about an overweening, persecutorial version of anticlericalism and insisted repeatedly, "My struggle is the anticlerical struggle, but the antireligious struggle[?...] Never! Never!" (Baubérot 2000:51–3).[4] In his famous circular of November 17, 1883, furthermore, Ferry emphasized that "the teacher must avoid anything in his or her words or attitudes that would offend the religious beliefs of the children in his or her care" (Haarscher 1998:28).

---

[4] A generation later, the moderate anticlerical politician Édouard Herriot likewise distinguished between the "Christianity of the bankers and that of the Catacombs." While Herriot wished to restrict the former version of Christianity, he defended the latter's right to exist: "When religion limits itself to its spiritual resources, when it is no longer clerical, between me and you, it will not have any more respectful defenders than us" (Rémond 1999:35).

Today, one might divide the various interpretations of *laïcité* into two broad categories: "strict" (also called "militant" or "closed") and "soft" ("pluralist" or "open"). Each of these broad versions in turn contains numerous subcategories and is embraced by various sectors of French society.

"Strict" *laïcité* finds most of its vocal supporters among feminists, the "Republican" left, and major teachers' unions in France (Berguin 2001; Gastaut 2000:576–83). Under most formulations of this first version of *laïcité*, French citizens may, in their private life, believe what they will about religion:

> Whether a person believes in God or is an atheist is his or her personal or private business. The state is not to concern itself with such matters. It is not an arbitrator of beliefs: it is neither to impose nor to forbid a [religious] creed (Pena-Ruiz 2001:22).

In public, however, religious individuals face more restrictions. If they are employed by the state or find themselves in a public services setting (such as in a public school), believers are not to engage in any "exterior manifestation" of their particular religion. Praying in public, refusing to eat certain kinds of food in a school cafeteria, and wearing religiously distinctive clothing or jewelry outside the home, for example, all violate the first type of *laïcité* (Jézéquel 1999:38–9). This version is thus least likely to make "special exceptions" for religious practices that conflict with secularly based laws or regulations:

> [*Laïcité*] is made of general, impersonal rules and principles that are equally applicable to everyone and that are the foundation of the public order to which each individual as well as each group must submit so long as these [rules and principles] were produced democratically and allow the possibility for individual convictions to be expressed perfectly freely.... As Claude Nicolet correctly writes, "*laïcité*... is the rule for everyone" (Ducomte 2000:85; see also Martino 2001).

Since the government is above all not to favor or support any religion (Pena-Ruiz 2001:22–8), "bending" the rules for a particular faith community or funding their private schools would thus violate the state's obligation to be neutral (Jézéquel 1999:39).

Within teachers' unions such as the powerful Syndicat National des Enseignements de Second degré (SNES), a few individual members may advocate an antireligious form of strict *laïcité*. Atheists or agnostics, they wish to use the public schools to promote their secular values in society. Other teachers may present secularism in the classroom for more pedagogical reasons, simply to show students that the antireligious perspective exists. SNES National Secretary Francis Berguin (2001) affirms, however, that his union as a whole is not antireligious but "neutralist." He notes that SNES supports freedom of conscience as well as the complete neutrality of the state on religious questions. In the public space (including public employment), the individual must "leave his or her religious concepts behind," however. Public school teachers, for example, have no "liberty to propagandize" religiously in the classroom.

In contrast to the various strands of "strict" *laïcité*, the "soft" version of this concept includes among its adherents members of the "multi-cultural left" (*gauche plurielle*), some Christian and Jewish leaders, most French Muslims, and many human rights advocates (Ben Jelloun 2002: 66–7; Gastaut 2000:576–8, 583–7; Seksig 1999). According to this second interpretation, the state should respect all religious beliefs but also foster the free exercise of religion by, for example, funding private religious schools. Far from wanting to confine religion to the private sphere, advocates of "open" *laïcité* wish to encourage interreligious understanding and public dialogue among different religious groups, even in the public schools. As the Conseil d'État noted in its famous decision of November 27, 1989, students' religious liberty "includes their right to express and indicate [*manifester*] their religious beliefs within educational institutions," so long as pupils "respect pluralism and the liberty of others" (Jézéquel 1999:39–40).

Many supporters of "soft" *laïcité* accuse proponents of the "strict" form of trying to make secularist *laïcité* the "state religion" in France (Gastaut 2000:583). French Muslims are especially likely to make this argument. The director of the Grande Mosquée de Lyon, Kamel Kabtane (2001), thus complains of "extreme secularists who want to impose *laïcité* as a new religion . . . as in [Soviet] Russia." Muslim public school teacher Youcef Mammeri (2001) likewise believes that some militant *laïcards* are trying to "impose *laïcité* as a religion, which is rather paradoxical."

Advocates of the "open" version next contend that "true" *laïcité* is not necessarily hostile to faith. Catholic Archbishop Bernard Panafieu (2001) sees no inherent contradiction between traditional religion and *laïcité*, and Muslim activist Saïda Kada (2001) tries to rebut the "cliché" that *laïcité* is "irreligious." Instead, *laïcité* "permits each philosophical current, et cetera., to have a space where it is not disturbed by a dogma which considers itself superior." The Separation Law of 1905, she notes, itself provides for "chaplains in [public] educational institutions." Even junior high school

Principal Alberto Bendelac (2001) sees no reason to ban religion per se from his *collège*:

> In theory, *laïcité* is equally accepting of all religious and philosophical beliefs. What we try to get the students to understand here is that whatever their national or religious origins, for us they are all members of the junior high school in the same way. *Laïcité* doesn't mean that religion is forbidden, simply that all religions are allowed, but not one more than another.

Larbi Kechat (2001) of the Mosquée Ada'wa in Paris similarly rejects the notion that *laïcité* is "antireligious." Rather, it is the "neutrality that guarantees to each religion a tranquil existence and a healthy, intelligent practice."

A few defenders of "soft" *laïcité* also lament that the "strict" version tends to sterilize society of all cultural diversity and to strip public school students of all individuality.[5] Educational activist Nicole Granier (2001), for instance, supports religious differences in state schools and argues that such cultural distinctiveness actually helps prepare students for the outside world:

> People are mistaken about *laïcité*. *Laïcité* doesn't mean making a gadget that lacks fragrance, flavor . . . and anything that could give an individual personality. It's about each person remaining as he or she is and about learning to live with other people. In everyday life, when you aren't at school, you meet people who are wearing a [Muslim] veil. Why shouldn't it be the same at school? It would be learning to live the kind of life you are going to lead in the society. If you respect other people, it means accepting them with their differences and respecting those differences. . . . You have to learn to live together beginning at school.

Kechat (2001) echoes Granier's call for the tolerance of religious differences in the state schools:

> The *laïque* school must permit . . . the diversity of the students while respecting unity. It's not in the name of *laïcité* that one prevents a Muslim from being a Muslim, a Jew from being a Jew, a Catholic from being a Catholic, or a Buddhist from being Buddhist. . . . One must respect the general framework of the *laïque* school, which does not have any particular religious orientation, but at the same time permit all cultures and all religions to coexist.

---

[5] This argument for allowing greater religious diversity in the public school has some parallels with the justification for what the SNES's Berguin (2001) calls "societal *laïcité*." According to this Jaurèsian view of *laïcité*, conflicts in society should be allowed to be fought in such public institutions as the schools. While the SNES in general is "neutralist" on religious concerns in public schools, the union is more "societalist" for social or economic questions.

Teachers may not, according to Kechat, favor a particular religion, but nor should they "force . . . students to be something other than themselves."

A final complaint that advocates of "soft" *laïcité* make is that the strict form violates international law and peoples' human rights. Legal scholar Dominique Le Tourneau warns that some antireligious versions of *laïcité* might lead to a conflict with "France's international commitments" (2000:119). He further contends that "today, *laïque* solutions are no longer at all compatible with the politics of human rights, which recognize above all else freedom of conscience and religious liberty." The human rights group MRAP (Mouvement contre le racisme et pour l'amitié entre les peuples) accused a *laïcard* principal of violating Muslim students' "civil liberties" (Gastaut 2000:585). Imam Khalil Merroun (2001) likewise notes that "Muslims in France are the most important defenders of *laïcité* . . . on the condition that this *laïcité* doesn't violate people's human rights."

Religious Free-Exercise Rights

At least within certain boundaries, France's foundational legal documents guarantee French citizens' freedom of religion. Article 10 of the Revolutionary *Déclaration des droits de l'homme et du citoyen* of 1789 reads, "No one may be troubled on account of his or her opinions, even religious ones, provided that their manifestation does not disturb the public order established by law" (Ministère de l'intérieur 1999:5). Article 1 of the 1958 Constitution of the Fifth Republic also declares:

> France is an indivisible, *laïque*, democratic, and social Republic. She ensures the equality of all citizens before the law without regard for [their] origin, race, or religion. She respects all beliefs (Ministère de l'intérieur 1999:3).

On paper at least, religious liberty thus appears to be assured. It is nonetheless ironic that Muslims in France, where religious freedom is in theory protected by the Constitution, are more likely to complain about violations of this liberty than are Muslims in Britain, which lacks a written constitutional guarantee of freedom of conscience. Lyon's Saïda Kada (2001), for example, does not feel that French Muslims enjoy "true religious freedom." Hmito (2001) of Le Havre contends that France's approach to women who wear the traditional Muslim headcovering is "a poor lesson in what liberty is all about." And Marignane's Hicabi Fındık (2001) complains that "in France they talk about liberty," but French treatment of Muslims is too often "contrary to liberty."

Secularization

Even in the largely "post-Christian" Western Europe, France stands out in the extent to which it has become thoroughly secularized. From 1973 to 1994, the proportion of French people who claimed in European Community/European Union polls to have "no religion" rose from about 11 percent to almost 34 percent. In this same period, French respondents reporting at least weekly church attendance halved from 14 percent to 7 percent (Soper and Fetzer 2002). According to the 1990 European Values Survey, 59 percent of French respondents claimed never to attend church. Only 57 percent claimed a belief in God, the lowest percentage of all West European countries save Norway (Davie 2000; Willaime 1998).

At the same time, however, France has witnessed dramatic growth in the number of Muslims. In 1964, the Muslim population in metropolitan France might have constituted as few as one hundred thousand people, but by the mid-1970s the figure had probably risen to around one million (Ramadan 1999b:5; see also Krieger-Krynicki 1985:27–8). Historian Jacques Frémeaux (1991:272) spoke of "two to three million" French Muslims in 1991 (see also Kepel 1991:13). And although French law forbids census takers from asking about one's religion or ethnicity, the Interior Ministry estimated the Muslim population at around 5 million in 2000 (ADRI 2000:20–1).

All of these 5 million are not necessarily theologically orthodox or regular mosque attenders, however. The younger generation is especially likely to have loosened its strictly religious, as opposed to cultural, ties to Islam. In a 1989 survey of ethnic Algerians from Roubaix, for example, around 30 percent of those under twenty-six years of age claimed neither to fast during *ramadān* nor to pray. Among respondents over age fifty, however, these practices were almost universal. Secularization of young North African ethnics has proceeded so far that some *beurs* now even label themselves "Muslim atheists" (Hargreaves 1995:120–1; Tribalat 1995:96–8).

Nevertheless, French Muslims as a whole appear more likely to practice their religion than are French Catholics, the nominal religious majority (Tribalat 1995:104–6). In its summary of the relevant research, the French Interior Ministry puts the proportion of Muslims regularly attending mosque for Friday prayers at 11 percent to 34 percent (ADRI 2000:22). Michèle Tribalat (1995:94) likewise estimates that 29 percent of Algerian immigrants, 40 percent of Moroccan-origin migrants, and 36 percent of Turkish immigrants regularly practice their religion.

In this highly secular country, Muslim parents are thus especially concerned that their children will eventually stop practicing Islam. Turkish-origin Muslim Fındık (2001) worries that if he and his wife "don't teach our three children about Islam [ourselves], one of these days they're not going to be Muslims anymore." Some practicing Muslims are also scandalized by the extent to which mainstream French society has become "extremely eroticized" (Mammeri 2001) and tolerant of pornography (Amalou 2001).

Major Areas of Religious Accommodation

Religious Activities in State Schools

By far the most controversial issue in French public schools is whether Muslim schoolgirls may wear the *ḥijāb*, also known in France as the *foulard* ("scarf"), *voile* ("veil"), or even *tchador* as in the Iranian Revolution. The first major battle in what has become a continuing politico-cultural war was the "Scarf Affair" *(affaire du foulard)* of October, 1989. As chronicled in the definitive study on the affair by Françoise Gaspard and Farhad Khosrokhaver (1995:12–16, 19; see also Koulberg 1991), the incident began when the principal of a public junior high school *(collège)* in Creil, a Paris suburb, suspended three Muslim students for refusing to remove their *ḥijāb*s upon entering the school building. According to principal Ernest Chenière and many of the school's teachers, allowing the *ḥijāb* would violate *laïcité*. Instantly the focus of intense scrutiny by the national media, the Antillean Chenière and the students' families reached a compromise after a week of negotiations. The Muslim girls would be allowed to wear the *ḥijāb* everywhere in the school except for in the classroom itself; upon entering a classroom, they would have to slip off the *ḥijāb* and place it around their shoulders. This compromise held for ten days. But perhaps encouraged by the support of several human rights groups and the Catholic cardinal of Paris (Révillion 1989a), the students then refused to remove their *ḥijāb*s even in the classroom and were once again expelled. The entry of the Catholic Church into the debate in turn alarmed the defenders of strict *laïcité*, who remembered all too well the previous century's struggles between the Church and advocates of *l'école laïque*. The battle lines between the anti-*ḥijāb*, "strict" *laïcité* forces and their pro-*ḥijāb*, "soft" *laïcité* opponents were thus drawn.

The beginnings of an official, national policy on the *ḥijāb* appeared a few days later. Perhaps responding to the controversy over "first lady" Danielle

Mitterrand's public call to "accept all [religious] traditions" and thus reinstate the *ḥijāb*-wearing girls, Socialist Education Minster Lionel Jospin instructed public school principals to engage in dialogue with Muslim students and their parents but in any case not to expel Muslim girls who persist in wearing the *ḥijāb*: "The school cannot exclude [students], for it is designed *[faite]* to welcome [them]." Immediately, Jospin's pronouncement was denounced not only by most teachers' unions and his Gaullist political opponents, but also by many leaders within his own party. In a widely read "open letter" to the education minister, five French philosophers urged teachers to disobey Jospin's orders and even called his statement the "Munich of the Republican school" (Gaspard and Khosrokhavar 1995:21–2).

Politically besieged, the minister of education called on the Conseil d'État to decide the matter (Gaspard and Khosrokhaver 1995:28). In its resulting *avis* of November 27, 1989, the Conseil appeared to side more with Jospin than with his opponents:

> In educational institutions, students' wearing of symbols *[signes]* by which they intend to indicate their belonging to a [particular] religion is not in itself incompatible with the principle of *laïcité* since [this display] constitutes one's exercise of the liberty of expression and the right to indicate one's religious beliefs; but this liberty does not permit students to display symbols of religious membership that, by their nature, by the conditions under which they are individually or collectively worn, or by their ostentatious or protesting character . . . disturb the order or normal functioning of public services (Jézéquel 1999:89–90).

In short, the Conseil seemed to say that the *ḥijāb* was allowed so long as public schools otherwise functioned as usual. Five years later, in the so-called "Bayrou circular," the new minister of education more or less confirmed this policy of not banning religious symbols per se but nonetheless proscribing "ostentatious symbols that in themselves constitute agents *[éléments]* of proselytism or discrimination" (Jézéquel 1999:90).

Because of the passions surrounding the issue and given the ambiguous guidance of the Conseil d'État and education ministers, the current situation on the ground varies dramatically. The most important determinant of whether Muslim students are allowed to wear the *ḥijāb* is often the orientation of the particular principal (Martino 2001; Sicard 2001). At the one extreme, principals in cities such as Montpellier seem to have no objection to the *ḥijāb* (Monin 1989). In the heavily Muslim L'Estaque district of Marseille, *collège* Principal Alberto Bendelac (2001) likewise appears to follow the spirit of the 1989 Conseil d'État decision:

> If a girl from a Muslim background wants to cover her head, well, that's her
> concern. But on the other hand, the law requires her to attend all the classes.
> If she covers her head and attends all the classes, there's no reason to stop her
> [from wearing the *ḥijāb*].

Perhaps out of sight of the national media, an unknown number of *ḥijāb*-wearing Muslim girls have the good fortune to attend public schools run by such tolerant headmasters.

At the opposite extreme are other principals who, either independently or under pressure from their teachers, approve the expulsion of Muslim students for refusing to remove the *ḥijāb*. At the Lycée Ronsard in Vendôme, for example, the *proviseur* expelled two Turkish-origin Muslim girls in 1993 for wearing the *ḥijāb* but was forced to reinstate them a year later after the Tribunal Administratif d'Orléans overturned his decision (Abdullah 1995: 101–31). Elsewhere teachers sometimes go so far as to strike rather than teach a *ḥijāb*-wearing student (Bacque 2003; Bronner 2002; Olivier 2003). In an all-too-typical incident at one public school in France,[6] the principal confirmed the academic disciplinary committee's recommendation to expel a Muslim girl for wearing the *ḥijāb*. According to our well-placed informants, however, the girl had made no effort to proselytize Islam. To convince the principal to remove the student, the school's teachers – many of whom belonged to a prominent French teachers' union – staged anti-*ḥijāb* protests and went on strike. A mediator was eventually brought in to try to reconcile the parties. But each time the Muslim girl accepted a compromise solution negotiated by the mediator, the teachers added yet another demand. Though the student tried to convince higher educational authorities to have her reinstated, her appeal was ultimately rejected (Durand 2001; Muslimah 2001).

The overall result of such opposition to the *ḥijāb* is that since 1989 many Muslim girls and young women in France have been deprived of a normal public education. Although the SNES estimates that "dozens" of *ḥijāb*-wearing Muslims have been expelled (Berguin 2001), French Muslims (Hmito 2001; Kada 2001; Kechat 2001; Merroun 2001) and some of the media (*Migration News* 2003) generally speak of "hundreds" of such expulsions. In what Larbi Kechat (2001) describes as "a continuation of the class war in another form," some Muslim parents with the necessary resources

---

[6] We have omitted from this example specific details of time and place in order to protect our informants from retaliation.

have secured lawyers and challenged their daughters' expulsion in court
(Merroun 2001). Away from the passionate media and political debates,
perhaps half of the judges in these cases have overruled the principal and
reinstated the student. Especially since the Conseil d'État ruled in 1997
that the *ḥijāb* is not in itself "ostentatious," courts have often sided with
students accused of nothing more than simply wearing the headcovering in
class (Abdullah 1995; Gaspard and Khosrokhavar 1995:188; Rotman 2002;
Venel 1999).[7] From 1992 to 1999, the Conseil d'État itself overturned
forty-one of the forty-nine expulsion cases that reached it (Haut Conseil
à l'Intégration 2001:66). In one atypical case, a sympathetic administrative
judge in Nancy even awarded the parents of an improperly suspended girl
52,000 francs in damages (Zouari 2002:141).

Expelled Muslim students whose parents are not affluent enough to af-
ford a lawyer – unfortunately the vast majority – usually have to choose between taking classes via correspondence ("Centre National d'Enseignement
à Distance") or abandoning their education entirely. Private schools are
usually too expensive for working-class parents and in any case might not
allow the *ḥijāb* either (Abdullah 1995:113; Kada 2001). Even when these
young women are able to complete their secondary-level classes by correspondence, however, they sometimes encounter difficulties taking the *bac*,
the French university entrance exam, while wearing the *ḥijāb* (Aïnouche
2001). As a way to compensate for these girls' educational disadvantages,
some Muslim organizations such as the Femmes Françaises et Musulmanes
Engagées of Lyon have set up special tutoring services staffed largely by
university student volunteers. The costs of correspondence school (around
600 francs for a student in *sixième*) can nonetheless represent a financial
hardship for a poor family (Bourg 2000; Kada 2001), and some Muslims
view such "distance education" as academically and socially "inferior" to
normal public schooling (Muslimah 2001).

Relying on a strict interpretation of *laïcité*, advocates of banning the *ḥijāb*
from public schools argue that this policy is the only way to maintain the
integrity of the *école laïque* and the dignity of each student regardless of his
or her religious background. One of the most eloquent defenders of this
policy, attorney and SNES National Secretary Francis Berguin (2001), rec-
ommends that school authorities first try to persuade a Muslim girl to cease

---

[7] In the standard legal textbook on French educational law, attorneys Yann Buttner, André
Maurin, and Blaise Thouveny (2002:100) lament that school authorities "sometimes continue illegally to forbid the simple wearing of the scarf, without taking into account the
jurisprudential contributions" to the debate.

wearing the *ḥijāb* while on school property. If dialogue fails, however, she should be "shown the door.... After all, there are correspondence courses. There are private schools."

Calling the *ḥijāb* "only the Trojan horse for other things," Berguin (2001) takes a hard line on the Muslim headcovering because he sees it as part of a slippery slope that would destroy French public education:

> You start with the scarf. And then, after the scarf, it's, "I refuse to go to physical education class, especially to the pool."... "I refuse to go to music class because Allah doesn't want us to play music." "I refuse to go to sculpture class because we're not supposed to make images of living things."... And *everywhere* where there have been penetrations of this sort, there has been this downward spiral.... And the result is what happens in the United States in certain states, where you read, "Darwin's theory [of evolution] is one of several [theories of the origins of life]."

Elaborating on his slippery-slope argument, Berguin says he knows of no case from SNES archives where a Muslim student simply wanted to wear the *ḥijāb*. In all such cases, he contends, the *ḥijāb* request was accompanied by other, more problematic demands.

Finally, Berguin (2001) argues that allowing some Muslim students to wear the "scarf" will compromise other Muslim girls' ability to choose not to wear it. Discussing a *collège* whose principal does allow the *ḥijāb*, the SNES leader says he is "certain that there are [Muslim] students [in this school] who are called 'whores' because they refuse to wear the *ḥijāb*." In the early 1990s, moreover, a Muslim teenager in a public school where he was teaching came up to him and said, "Sir, above all, never give in [to the students wanting to wear the *ḥijāb*], because if not, I will be forced [by the other Muslim students] to wear it too, and I don't want to."[8]

In a similar vein, many French feminists oppose the *ḥijāb* in public schools not only on *laïcité* grounds but perhaps even more because these opponents see it as a form of the oppression of women. Paris public school teacher Elizabeth Altschull, for example, explains her decision to order a thirteen-year-old Muslim student to remove her *ḥijāb* as "more feminist than *laïque*.... To veil a kid that young struck me as obviously unacceptable" (1995:11). According to Altschull, the "injunction to wear the *ḥijāb* is not so evident" from the letter of the *qur'ān*. Arguing that Islam is inherently

---

[8] At the almost exclusively Muslim *Collège* Edgar Quinet in Marseille, the assistant principal similarly reports that during *ramadān*, fasting Muslim students sometimes "make the throat-slitting gesture" to a Muslim teenager who violates the fast by eating at school (Haut Conseil à l'Intégration 2001:68).

sexist, she writes that "the veil is a way to 'hide' the female body" and represents an "extremely archaic [male] 'obsession' with womens' hair" (ibid., 13). In the *qur'ān*, the woman is little more than "a walking temptation to sin" (ibid., 200–3). Similarly, French immigration scholar Michèle Tribalat (2001) denies that French school authorities are obliged to take into consideration the theological belief that failing to wear the *ḥijāb* will condemn a Muslim woman to hell. Tribalat and her coauthor Jeanne-Hélène Kaltenbach further argue that giving in to the Muslim community's demand to permit the *ḥijāb* amounts to

> . . . acquiesc[ing . . .] in a conception of feminine modesty that rejects the slightest glance and that is supposed to protect the man from his own concupiscence. If complete covering of the female body represents the height of modesty, it doesn't take a genius to figure out how a young Muslim man might view a pretty girl *[une jeune fille coquette]* wearing a skirt and high heels (Kaltenbach and Tribalat 2002:330).

Kaltenbach and Tribalat also wonder "if it is by chance that games of seduction, which are a form of civility, are becoming more rare in our suburbs while organized gang rapes in the cellars of [public housing] projects are becoming more common" (2002:530).

Sharply disagreeing with many French teachers' unions and feminists, supporters of Muslim girls' right to wear the *ḥijāb* in public institutions usually base their arguments on the more pluralist, "soft" form of *laïcité* and on broader notions of pragmatism, human rights, and/or religious freedom. First, supporters contend that expelling vulnerable Muslim girls from public schools hardly increases their chances of ultimately becoming "liberated" adult women. Parents' representative Nicole Granier (2001) explains:

> The people [who are opposed to a girl wearing a *ḥijāb* in the public school] start out with the idea of defending women's rights. In defense of women's rights, they don't accept the veil. So, what do they do? They defend women's rights and send her [a *ḥijāb*-wearing girl] home. And then, at home, she no longer has any rights at all. But in school, if they allow her to keep her veil so long as she does not proselytize . . . she has contact with other people, which will permit her to express something else [besides just what she learns at home], . . . So [the result] is really the opposite of what they desired – even for her.

Marseille teacher Youcef Mammeri (2001) likewise contends that "by expelling certain girls because they wear the *ḥijāb*, one is at the same time preventing them from receiving an education that will allow them to take up professional careers and so become emancipated."

Opponents of expulsion next point to the psychological damage that such official ostracism can cause. Saïda Kada (2001) reports that one Muslim girl from the Paris region was so upset over being expelled that she had a nervous breakdown and needed to be treated by a psychologist. Even more serious is the case of a fourteen- or fifteen-year-old student from central Marseille who, because she "didn't want to cause an uproar," would take off her *ḥijāb* upon entering the grounds of her *collège*. One day a teacher of French observed her removing the *ḥijāb* and severely reprimanded her even for wearing it outside of class. The girl then became so distraught that she ended up attempting suicide (Mammeri 2001).

Third, such *ḥijāb*-wearing French Muslim women as Kada (2001) find many arguments against the headcovering arrogant, neocolonialist, and out of touch with reality. Responding to feminist Elizabeth Altschull, Kada comments:

> What's funny is who's saying that [the *ḥijāb* is a symbol of the oppression of women]. It's the non-Muslims. [But] it's not their place to say [whether not wearing the *ḥijāb* is a serious sin]. . . . The logic is that one has the right to interfere in the choices of people who are not adults.

Kada thus implies that many ethnic French feminists do not believe an ethnic North African Muslim woman can think for herself or make her own decision about what is oppressive or not. She likewise disputes Berguin's concern that *ḥijāb* wearers will force the headcovering on all Muslim women:

> The problem is always the same. They try to justify political, official injustice by using fear and fantasy. . . . On the pretext that there could possibly, eventually be a problem, they expel [Muslim girls].

In her own personal interactions, however, Kada (2001) reports that she has always seen mutual respect demonstrated between Muslim women who wear the *ḥijāb* and those who do not.

Although controversy over the *ḥijāb* dwarfs that surrounding other issues, practicing Muslims also face other problems in the French public schools. Unlike that in Britain, the national French curriculum does not include religious education as a formal subject. Islam itself only appears in one unit of the *cinqième* history and geography class (Marseille and Scheibling 1997:24–39) and, for some Arabic- or Turkish-speaking children, in special Language and Culture of Origin (LCO) courses (Lorcerie 1994). Muslim parents sometimes feel obliged to use pretexts in letters asking instructors to excuse their children from overnight field trips where boys and girls sleep in the same room. Some parents likewise resent their teenaged daughters being forced to change into a bathing suit and to swim with boys during physical education class (Fındık 2001; Haut Conseil à l'Intégration 2001:68). Though most schools provide substitute non-pork meals for Muslims and Jews, virtually none accommodates Muslims' increasingly frequent requests for *ḥalāl* meat (Aïnouche 2001; Haut Conseil à l'Intégration 2001:64–65; Hmito 2001). Fatima Muslimah (2001) reports that a few Muslim girls refuse to attend music, art, biology, or sexual education classes because these subjects are seen as contrary to Islam. She opposes such behavior, however, since she believes that even sex education is good because it teaches young Muslims what to do after they marry. Since more and more Muslim students fast during *ramaḍān*, many school administrators are pragmatically allowing single-day absences for *ʿid* and recommending that instructors avoid scheduling exams during this month. The academic performance of many fasting Muslim students nevertheless tends to suffer (Buttner, Maurin and Thouveny 2002:114–17; Haut Conseil à l'Intégration 2001:67–8; Maurin 2001; Toihiri 2001).

Public Funding for Islamic Schools

In contrast with Britain and, as we will see, Germany, metropolitan France contains not a single state-funded Islamic school (Aïnouche 2001; Martino 2001). In theory, Muslims are eligible to receive state funding for their private schools just as the many Catholic and Jewish parochial schools do (*Le Monde* 1989a; Maurin 2001; Révillion 1989b). Under the governing Debré Law of December 31, 1959 (Buttner 2001), Muslims seeking public funding would need to demonstrate the following: 1) that their school has already been functioning for five years; 2) that their teachers are well qualified; 3) that the "number of students" is relatively large; and 4) that the school facilities are "clean" (Monchambert 1993:53–64). A state-supported Islamic school would also have to accept students from any religious background, make in-school religious instruction and practices voluntary, and follow a general curriculum similar to that used in public schools (Bozonnet 1989; *Le Monde* 1989a; Monchambert 1993:95–105).

Despite this theoretical possibility, French educational authorities have thus far failed to approve any of the admittedly very few applications for public funding of an Islamic school. Robert Chapuis, secretary of state for technical education, argued in 1989 that French Muslims had not yet formed a sufficiently representative organization capable of negotiating with the state for such funding (Révillion 1989b), and *collège* principal Bendelac (2001) echoed this concern as late as 2001. Mosquée de Paris affiliate Eddin Sari's 1982 application for an Islamic high school (*lycée*) was summarily rejected, apparently because his establishment had not already been functioning for the requisite five years (*Le Monde* 1989a). Muslims further point to a lack of financial resources and suitable instructors (Fındık 2001; Kechat 2001; *Le Monde* 1989a; Toihiri 2001). And both Muslims and non-Muslims candidly acknowledge that the current political climate in France makes approval of such an Islamic school very unlikely (Douai 2001; Kabtane 2001; Kechat 2001; Maurin 2001).

European France does contain a handful of privately funded Islamic schools, however. The Mosquée de Strasbourg, for example, hosts an elementary-level Islamic boarding school. This French- and Arabic-language primary school funds itself via parents' tuition payments (Douai 2001). The Montesquieu Private School (*cours privé Montesquieu*) in the Paris suburb Joinville-le-Pont similarly provides a religiously oriented general education to its 130 largely Muslim students but receives no public moneys (*Le Monde* 1989a). Mammeri (2001) is familiar with a few tentative plans to start Islamic schools in greater Marseille, and Kamel Dallali (2001) believes the Paris region contains at least two parent-funded Muslim schools.

The only Islamic *école* in France that the government has approved as a "private school under contract with the state" is the Medersa ta'lim oul-islam/École Franco-Musulmane on the French island of Réunion (Achi 2001; Boyer 1993:79 n. 3), off the Eastern coast of Africa. Founded in 1947, the school operated independently until 1970, when it received "simple contract" status and hence funding from the French government. Under the school's related "association contract" (El Ghissassi 2001), the state currently pays the salaries of teachers of the standard French curriculum, but the Muslims themselves finance the separate classes in Islam. According to Osman Molla, president of the affiliated Grande Mosquée de Saint-Denis, this arrangement "works well" and "would be possible in [European] France." Though French educational officials regularly inspect the general studies portion of the 150-student school, students and even teachers may of course choose to wear the *ḥijāb* (Bozonnet 1989; Molla 2001).

Perhaps another reason for the lack of such a school in metropolitan France is that French Muslims themselves are divided on the question. Turkish-French Muslim leader Fındık (2001) and Lyon imam Kabtane (2001) support Islamic schools, yet Paris-based imam Kechat (2001) worries about thereby "ghettoizing" Muslim students. Just before the 2002 presidential elections, the Muslim political coalition Forum Citoyen de Cultures Musulmanes (FCCM 2002:26) called for "the creation of Muslim-oriented

French private schools recognized and sanctioned by the National Education Ministry." At the height of the Scarf Affair in 1989, however, the plurality of Muslims with French citizenship opposed such institutions (*Le Monde* 1989b).

As one would expect, non-Muslims are even less supportive. Parent-representative Granier (2001) opposes private Islamic schools, arguing that the best way for children of different religious and ethnic backgrounds to avoid becoming racist is to learn together in the public schools. Marseille Front National leader Jackie Blanc (2001) also believes that Islamic schools would hinder Muslims' ultimate integration into mainstream French society. "If you really want to integrate yourself when you arrive in a country," Blanc contends, "you embrace the customs of the country, without [necessarily] becoming Catholic."

Mosque Building

With the increased permanence of the largely North African immigrant population since the 1970s, the demand for suitable Muslim prayer facilities has risen dramatically. Local political opposition has sometimes hindered Muslim's efforts to construct large, specially built mosques from scratch or to convert existing buildings into places of worship (Douai 2001; Kechat 2001; Le Carpentier 2001). Yet despite this opposition, France saw a proliferation of mosques and prayer halls in the last two decades of the twentieth century. From around 265 such buildings in 1980 (Krieger-Krynicki 1985:115), the total number of Muslim houses of worship grew to at least 1,500 by 1999 (ADRI 2000:29). Assuming a Muslim population of 5 million (ADRI 2000:21), France has one mosque or prayer room for every 3,333 Muslims. French followers of Islam are thus much less likely to be able to find prayer facilities than are their coreligionists in Britain.

The mosque-building project that comes closest to being a success is probably that of the Grande Mosquée de Lyon. The origins of this traditionally styled, 2,500-person mosque (Depagneux 1994) date back to the 1970s, when a group of local Muslims began worshiping in various rented Catholic churches. Eventually Catholic leaders asked city officials to help the Muslims obtain their own mosque, noting that it was psychologically damaging for Lyon Catholics to convert their churches into mosques (Kabtane 2001).

Around 1979, the Muslims thus formed an association to work with local politicians on the project. Though political leaders were initially helpful, the Iranian Revolution of the early 1980s and growing opposition from potential neighbors of the mosque eventually eroded official support (Kabtane 2001). In the ensuing years, the mosque project was the object of six administrative lawsuits, two appeals to the Conseil d'État, and three applications for a building permit (Depagneux 1994). Local opponents staged several large antimosque demonstrations and circulated petitions to stop its construction. The Front National likewise took up the cause during its electoral campaigns (Kabtane 2001).

Thanks to the political skills of Lyon Mayor Michel Noir, a 19.5 million franc grant from King Fahd of Saudi Arabia, and the *sang froid* of project leader Kabtane, however, the mosque finally opened its doors in 1994. As a *fait accompli*, the mosque had suddenly become popular, drawing to its inauguration a broad range of religious and political leaders. Even Charles Pasqua, the anti-immigration minister of the interior, gave a speech in which he called for "Islam to find its place in France" (Depagneux 1994; *Le Monde* 1994). Rector Kabtane (2001) reports that most of the neighbors are now "happy" with the mosque. In the mid-1990s, however, an unknown vandal shot live bullets into its windows and doors, and in 1999 another unapprehended assailant threw a Molotov cocktail through a window. During the night of December 27–8, 2002, moreover, someone hurled bottles filled with paint in the French national colors of blue, white, and red against the mosque's facade (Cornevin 2002).

If the Lyon mosque can be seen as a tempered success, competition among candidates for the title of "most abject failure" is keen. Perhaps the most dramatic debacle in mosque building in France occurred in Charvieu-Chavagneux, a small town half an hour away from Lyon (Didier 2000). The approximately eight hundred Muslims of Charvieu originally had access to a makeshift prayer hall that had formerly been a factory cafeteria. After the 1983 election of right-wing Mayor Gérard Dezempte, however, their situation deteriorated rapidly. Dezempte first announced an urban renewal project for the neighborhood where the improvised mosque was located. Faced with expulsion, Imam Mohamed Mizjaldi offered to return the Muslims' facilities back to the city[9] in exchange for a new place to pray. When the city declined, the Muslims in 1987 bought a modest piece of property nearby and applied for permission to construct a small mosque there. By now campaigning for reelection on a platform of "de-Islamization,"

---

[9] It is unclear exactly who owned the mosque. Michel Friedman (1990) speaks of the Muslims proposing that the city "buy back" *(rachat)* the building from them, but the perhaps less-than-objective Kaltenbach and Tribalat (2002:142) claim the facilities were being "put at the disposition of the [Muslim] association by city hall."

however, the mayor refused to sign the necessary building permit. The town's Muslims thus had no option but to continue meeting for prayers in their converted cafeteria. But at dawn on August 16, 1989 – apparently on Dezempte's orders and as police officers watched – a bulldozer began demolishing the building where the Muslims prayed. Of the three people still inside that morning, one sleeping adolescent was slightly injured during the operation (Friedman 1990; Le Hir 1991).

This bulldozing of the Charvieu mosque caused outrage among French Muslims and their supporters throughout France and led to something close to political civil war between the mayor and the Muslim community. The now dispossessed congregation of Charvieu conducted prayers in front of the mayor's office in protest, while unknown arsonists firebombed city hall shortly thereafter (Gastaut 2000:500; *Le Monde* 1991; Renard 1999). With the aid of Évry's Merroun (2001), Grenoble Mayor Alain Carignon arranged for provincial authorities to deliver a temporary, prefabricated "mosque" to the Muslims of Charvieu. Two years later, Dezempte ordered the congregation out of even these "temporary" quarters and then cut off water to the building after they refused to leave. A week after the cutoff, the Muslims also discovered an unexploded Molotov cocktail inside the main prayer room on Monday morning (Le Hir 1991; *Le Monde* 1991). The mayor, for his part, appears to have benefited politically from his actions against the Muslims (Didier 2000; Friedman 1990), though in 1992 a Grenoble appeals court made him pay 6,000 francs for having "incited racial and religious hatred" in his campaign literature. The tract in question asserted that "mosques [and] Islam represent a true danger for our society and have no place in our country" (*Le Monde* 1992).

French Muslims in other localities have faced similar roadblocks in their efforts to build mosques. In Marseille, the de facto Muslim "capital" of France, proposals for a "Grande Mosquée de Marseille" date to as far back as 1839 (Guillaume 2001; *Le Messager de Marseille* 1839). Partly because of local political opposition and Muslims' lack of unity on the question, however, as of 2003 the city still lacked a large, specially constructed "cathedral mosque" such as those found in Lyon, Paris, or Évry (Aïnouche 2001; Blanc 2001; Cesari 1994:116–121; Falanga and Trouvé 1992; Mammeri 2001; Samson 2002). In nearby Marignane, the roughly 2,500 largely Turkish-origin Muslims have outgrown their current, five hundred–person facilities. They nonetheless found their efforts to buy public land for a larger mosque blocked by the new mayor, a member of the anti-immigration Front National Party (Fındık 2001). An even worse fate awaited the Muslims of Romans-sur-Isère; following a racism-tinged electoral campaign against the local mosque and its supporters, vandals used plastic explosives to blow up the building during the night of May 2–3, 1982. Though the mosque was eventually rebuilt, the perpetrators were never apprehended (Gastaut 2000:499; Kepel 1991:298–300; Krieger-Krynicki 1985:117).

After the events of September 11, 2001, some French Muslims report that French politicians are now so eager to "integrate" them into French society that officials "practically run up to you and ask, 'Are you sure you don't want a mosque?'" (Power 2003). When a city government itself pays for and supervises the construction of a mosque, however, new problems can arise.[10] In Montpellier, for example, Mayor Georges Frêche spent 4 million francs of public money to build a 2,300-person "multipurpose auditorium" that nonetheless contains inside such features of a traditional mosque as Muslim prayer rugs, a *minbar*, a *miḥrāb*, and a ritual foot-washing fountain (Boyer 1998:298). The city then leases these facilities to the "Association pour la culture arabe du Langedoc-Roussillon" (Kaltenbach and Tribalat 2002:148). Some local Muslims complain, however, that this association does not represent them and that the mayor tries to interfere in the religious life of the mosque. Rejecting such "colonial Islam," a number of the city's Muslims have decided to conduct their prayers elsewhere (Djoufelkit 2001).

Testing the Theories

In stark contrast to Britain, France not only has done precious little positively to accommodate Muslims' religious practices but has also exerted all too much effort to make Muslims' life even more difficult than it already is for this largely immigrant-origin, working-class population. On all three dependent variables that we explore in this chapter – wearing religiously motivated dress in public schools, publicly funding private Islamic schools, and building mosques – France ranks dramatically below Britain and, as we will show in the next chapter, even significantly below Germany. As with

---

[10] Some advocates of "strict" *laïcité* contend that such public financing of a house of worship violates the Separation Law of 1905 (Kaltenbach and Tribalat 2002:148–54). The Conseil d'État seems to have adopted an extremely generous view of this law, however, approving even the mayor of Rennes' construction of an "Islamic cultural center" that housed a prayer hall. Perhaps French courts allow such publicly owned mosques out of a sense of equity; in general, the many Catholic churches built before 1906 also belong to the localities or the French state and are maintained with public funds (Boyé 1994:8–10).

Britain in the previous chapter, we conclude our analysis by examining the validity of four possible explanations for France's policy toward Muslims.

Resource Mobilization

The first theory focuses on a group's politically relevant resources. If French Muslims have had greater difficulty obtaining state accommodation for their religious practices, this theory would argue, it is because these believers lack the political resources available to their coreligionists in Britain.

Of course, one of the most important resources for a group trying to influence public policy is effective organizations. To the extent that Muslims are organizationally unified, the resource mobilization theory would hold, they should succeed in winning policy concessions from the state. Yet contrary to this explanation's expectations, it is Muslims in France who are relatively well organized, not those in Britain.

Even before their ultimate consolidation into a single, nationally representative council in 2003, French Muslims appear to have been at least as organizationally mobilized and unified as British Muslims (Cesari 2002a). Catherine Wihtol de Wenden and Rémy Leveau (2001) document the rise of a host of "*beur*" associations created by the children of North African, Muslim immigrants. At least 1,400 specifically Muslim groups also exist in France (Ramadan 1999b:35), most of which are primarily local (Boyer 1998:281; Cesari 1994:180–5). Yet two years before the election of the Conseil Français du Culte Musulman, activist Mammeri (2001) could already point to several panregional, "effective" Muslim organizations: the Union des Organisations Islamiques de France (UOIF), Jeunes Musulmans de France (JMF), Union de Jeunes Musulmans (UJM), and the Collectif des Musulmans de France. The very large UOIF and its affiliated youth wing, the JMF, represent over two hundred local Muslim organizations (Boyer 1998:289–90; Cesari 2002b), and the UOIF's yearly meeting of tens of thousands of Muslims in Paris is the "most important annual assembly of Muslims anywhere in Europe" (Ramadan 1999b:38). The Lyon-based UJM has a membership of Muslim youth from various French regions (Ramadan 1999b:34–5). The Collectif, inspired by the French-speaking Swiss scholar Tariq Ramadan, is especially active among young Muslims in France's universities and working-class neighborhoods (Aït-Hamadouche 2003; *Le Monde* 2003). In addition, the Fédération nationale des musulmans de France (FNMF) serves as an umbrella organization for around sixty Muslim associations (Ramadan 1999b:34–5), and the Mosquée de

Paris for decades has been the organizational point of reference for many Algerian-origin Muslims (Boyer 1998:282–9; Boyer 1992; von Krosigk 2000:227–236).

With the organization beginning in 1999 of what became the Conseil Français du culte musulman (CFCM), however, French Muslims achieved one of the highest levels of formal, national unity in Europe. State efforts to organize French Muslims date back at least as far as Interior Minister Pierre Joxe's creation of the Conseil de réflexion sur l'islam en France (CORIF) in 1990. But it was Interior Minister Jean-Pierre Chevènement's "Consulta-tion" with French Muslim leaders in 1999 that led directly to the formation of the CFCM (El Ghissassi 2003; Haut Conseil à l'Intégration 2001:88). According to Philippe Le Carpentier (2001), head of the Interior Ministry's Central Office for Religions, Chevènement first tried to invite people from all major Muslim entities to the Consultation, including important Muslim personalities, representatives of the principal Muslim organizations and federations, and leaders of the large mosques. After discussing relevant ju-dicial principles and the framework for organizing and holding elections for what became the CFCM (Le Carpentier 2001), members of the Con-sultation signed a memorandum of understandings on January 28, 2000 (*al istichara* 2000; Haut Conseil à l'Intégration 2001:89). This memoran-dum in turn guided the April 2003 elections of the CFCM's representatives. French Muslim groups from a wide range of ethnicities and theological perspectives competed for CFCM seats. Voters from about 80 percent of France's Muslim places of worship ultimately chose to take part, electing the forty-one council members who will negotiate with the French gov-ernment on Islam-related public policy (Mammeri 2002; Sciolino 2003a, 2003b; Ternisien 2003).

French Muslims also appear to be at least as politically mobilized as their British counterparts. Among France's roughly 3 million ethnic North Africans (Filali 2002), almost all of whom are Muslims, as many as 1.5 million are registered to vote (Geisser 2002). Most of the remaining Maghrebi-origin Muslims are probably noncitizens (see Couvreur 1998: 9–15; Ramadan 1999b:6). Since their formation in the mid-1980s, the ethnic minority organizations SOS-Racisme and France-Plus have brought many Muslims into the political system and agitated for the rights of immigrant-origin French citizens (Wihtol de Wenden and Leveau 2001:48–59). For the 2002 presidential elections, the Muslim activist group Forum Citoyen de Cultures Musulmanes (FCCM) likewise helped around seventeen thou-sand young Muslims register to vote in forty-five different cities, con-ducted a grass-roots survey of French Muslims to ascertain their policy preferences, and published and distributed a summary of these policy demands to voters and the presidential candidates (FCCM 2002; Nekkaz 2002). So seriously did French politicians take the Muslim vote that candidates Jacques Chirac and Lionel Jospin both tried to appeal to French Muslims by granting long interviews to the principal Muslim newsmagazine, *La Médina* (Chirac 2002; Jospin 2002).

One of the most important political disadvantages, on the other hand, is a lack of prominent Muslim officials in France. Perhaps partly because an indigenous French-Muslim elite has yet to develop (Leveau and Schnapper 1988), the country has no equivalent to Britain's Lord Ahmed or Germany's Cem Özemir. Apparently not a single member of the National Assembly is a Muslim, and neither are any of the *ministres* followers of Islam (Sciolino 2003c). Perhaps the most visible Muslim in the French government is Hanifa Chérifi, the appointed "*ḥijāb* czar." One of her main functions, however, is to persuade French Muslims *not* to wear the *ḥijāb* in public schools (Kaltenbach and Tribalat 2002:227–31). For most practicing Muslims, then, she is far from a hero.

Despite this lack of Muslim officials, Muslims in France are much more organizationally unified and significantly more politically mobilized than are British Muslims. As we have demonstrated, however, it is Muslims north of the English Channel who have been much more successful in obtaining their preferred policies. Of course, some advocates of resource theory might contend that it is still to soon to see what effect the unification of French Muslims into the CFCM will have on Islam-related policy. We do hesitate to predict the future of the always-effervescent French political scene. But a year after the CFCM election in 2003, the French legislature passed a law banning the wearing of the *ḥijāb* (Associated Press 2004) – hardly a goal of practicing Muslims. In short, resource mobilization does not seem to go very far in explaining French Muslims' policy failures.

Political Opportunity Structures

A second theory focuses on such political institutions as the legal system, governmental structure, party system, media, and interest groups. French Muslims would thus have difficulties achieving their goals not because this religious minority is poorly organized or lacks relevant resources, but instead because the institutionalized political rules disadvantage followers of Islam (Garbaye 2000; Ireland 1994; Koopmans and Statham 2000).

As Bleich (1998:91–2) suggests, the highly unitary structure of French government certainly does hinder French Muslims' efforts to change local

educational policies. Since public schools use the same curriculum throughout France (Lewis 1985), Muslim parents in Marseille or Lille have no
chance of persuading a *collège* principal to drop the section on Darwinism
from a junior high biology course; a local principal has no control over the
content of the national curriculum.

On some issues important to French Muslims, however, Paris-based
educational and governmental authorities have de facto allowed considerable local autonomy. Especially on the highly contested *ḥijāb* question, the
Education Ministry has failed consistently to articulate a clear standard.
The Conseil d'État's original 1989 *ḥijāb* decision also lacked clarity, seem-
ing almost to invite case-by-case decisions by individual principals. Taking
advantage of this pseudo federal system, Muslims in cities such as Évry do
appear to have been able to avert new Scarf Affairs by negotiating with local
politicians and school officials (Merroun 2001).

On the other hand, some national authorities such as the Conseil d'État
and former Education Minister Jospin have probably been more willing to
permit the *ḥijāb* in public schools than have local principals and teachers. On
what the French public most likely views as the premier "Muslim issue,"
then, France's unitary system does not appear to have particularly hurt
Muslims' cause. If anything, Muslims would be better off if local school
authorities strictly followed Jospin's early, pro-*ḥijāb* policy as well as the
Conseil d'État's post-1989 series of mainly pro-*ḥijāb* rulings, instead of deciding each case individually or even willfully disregarding national French
jurisprudence on the wearing of religious emblems in public schools. Or in
other words, standard state-structure theory does not seem to explain very
well France's systematic unwillingness to accommodate Muslims' religious
practices, at least in the school.

Those political institutions that do a better job making sense of the
French policy toward Muslims are instead products of France's long and
contentious church-state history: the laws, regulations, and constitutional
jurisprudence upholding and expanding *laïcité*. While state-structure theory
is not necessarily wrong, then, we contend that it has too often overlooked
the specifically religious aspects of France's political institutions.

Ideology

A third theory understands policy outcomes as a function of the dominant
immigration-related ideology in a particular country. How the political
culture views citizenship, the nation, and the integration of immigrants ultimately guides a state's approach to Muslims. France, in contrast to Britain,

embraces an assimilationist, "Republican" model of immigrant incorporation (Weil 1991). Under this paradigm, immigrants become part of the French nation as individuals, not as groups having a common ethnicity or religion. Rogers Brubaker notes, "Since the Revolution, the self-styled '*nation une et indivisible*' has been violently intolerant of anything that could be interpreted as a 'nation within a nation'" (1992:106). That "France has an integrationist tradition... not a communitarian one," French jurist Philippe Le Carpentier (2001) similarly contends, is the "origin of the [immigration-related] tensions created in France – tensions much less present in Anglo-Saxon countries." An ideological theory might also contend that French policy toward Muslims arises from a particularly ethnocentric reading of the Republican tradition. Some supporters of Le Pen, for example, might oppose the very idea that practicing Muslims could ever become true French citizens because all authentic French people are (Catholic) Christians.

In such an ideological context, Muslims should theoretically find it difficult to obtain benefits or "special exceptions" from the state for their particular religious community (see Gildea 1997:230). Such issues as the *ḥijāb* do seem to support an ideological theory. Other French policies, however, appear to contradict such an approach. For example, simply by negotiating with a group billing itself as "Muslim" (for example the Conseil Français du Culte Musulman), the French state appears to be violating the Republican ideal. Moreover, some local French officials jettison Republican principles against recognizing ethnic or religious communities when the city government builds Muslims a mosque (as in Montpellier).

Yet even where ideological theory explains French policy toward Muslims, it is the specifically religious aspects of that ideology that are particularly salient. On most issues, we believe, French Muslims find their policy demands impeded more often by appeals to the intrinsically religion-oriented *laïcité* than by arguments based on the much more general Republican ideal. Ideological theory thus is not simply wrong in the French case, just not narrowly enough focused on that portion of the prevailing ideology that is directly relevant to church–state relations.

Church–State Institutions

Our examination of the three previous theories suggests that something critical is lacking from each account: the church–state institutions developed over decades or centuries. In France, we conclude that the crucial missing piece to the puzzle of Muslim-related public policy is *laïcité* (see also Cesari 2000). Throughout our many interviews in France, Muslim and non-Muslim respondents time and again pointed to this separationist concept when explaining the French state's policy toward Islam. Muslim activist Mammeri (2001), for example, believes as follows:

> It is necessary to look into more-or-less recent history for the reasons why, here in France, [Muslims' relations with the state are] unique in Europe. First, [one needs to look] at the history of *laïcité*, which is really specific to France.

Catholic Archbishop Panafieu (2001) likewise points to *laïcité*'s role in accentuating political conflict over Islam: "We French in particular – given the French Revolution [and] our system of separation of church and state – have great difficulty understanding the place of religion in the national structure." Finally, Strasbourg Muslim leader Fouad Douai (2001) observes:

> In France you have this notion of *laïcité* which is completely different from [religion–state arrangements] in other European countries. . . . France was once the "eldest daughter of the Church." To stop being the "eldest daughter of the Church," it was necessary to spill blood, which made . . . the French allergic to everything religious. It's not the same in Germany, in England, in Belgium, where there was not this fracture, this confrontation with the religious orders. Now it's the same thing with Islam. . . . It's this conception of *laïcité* which makes France difficult [for Muslims].

Arising out of the many battles between Catholics and anticlericals since the French Revolution, *laïcité* thus remains firmly in place in French political rhetoric and law. In particular, our discussion of the treatment of Muslims in the schools suggests that *laïcité* continues to shape much Islam-related public policy in France.

Of course, some observers outside the *métropole* might wonder why France does not simply abandon *laïcité* in favor of a more pragmatic, flexible, or "workable" approach to religion–state relations. In response, defenders of *laïcité* argue that it is neither easy nor prudent to destroy overnight a political institution that took centuries to create and that has served France well throughout the years. Legal scholar Berguin (2001) explains:

> I remember an English colleague, a law professor, telling me . . . "Oh no, not *laïcité* again! You're not going to keep making trouble for yourself with that?" [But] each [country] does what [it] wants. England is a land of tolerance. The United States is in a certain way too – even for Scientologists. Each society manages the religious question in its own way. But those are complicated questions about which it has taken centuries to reach a *modus vivendi*. These are complex mechanisms that one should not suddenly eliminate.

For better or worse, then, "the [religious] conflicts have left their traces in generation after generation" of French *citoyens* (Berguin 2001) and in the way the French state has approached Islam.

Conclusion

As this chapter demonstrates, France is far less likely to accommodate Muslim religious practices than is Britain. The following chapter will also argue that France ranks even below its archrival Germany in its treatment of Muslims. French followers of Islam have spent so much time fighting battles over the *ḥijāb* that they have precious few resources left to devote to such equally important causes as private Islamic schools. In many ways, French Muslims seem to be trying simply to obtain a modicum of religious free exercise rather than to create a flourishing spiritual and cultural life for themselves. Indeed, the situation for Muslims in some parts of France appears so bleak that one wonders why more do not emigrate to a more hospitable country such as Britain or Canada.

But perhaps more strongly than for either of our other two nations, France's policy towards Islam appears tied to its dominant church–state institution, *laïcité*. Virtually everyone we interviewed in France evoked some version of this concept to justify her or his position on Muslim-related issues. And the French-language scholarly, religious, and polemical literature is overflowing with explications of this term. The French case therefore seems to provide stronger evidence for our church–state interpretation than for the usual formulations of the resource-mobilization, state-structure, and ideological theories.

4

Germany: Multiple Establishment and Public Corporation Status

In the past, religious instruction was provided by the Protestant and Catholic churches. Then Muslims came in and said, "Hey, if they can have it, why can't we have it as well?" The question is not if, but the question is how.

Halima Krausen (2001), German Muslim convert and theologian

One of the greatest difficulties for Islam in Germany is that [Muslim] organizations...have not been viewed as representative. For this reason, recognition as a public corporation has thus far not been granted....It is nonetheless important that the Islamic religious community, to which so many people in our country belong, obtain a respected position in society.

Official statement of the German Evangelische churches (VELKD and EKD 2001:133)

I see that Islam can represent an enrichment for social life. I think it could represent an even greater enrichment if people approached it with a more open mind....People just want to have their prejudices confirmed. No one is ready, really to listen or in any way to think a little differently....Especially on the topic "Women and Islam," Islam is reduced to the ḥijāb, polygamy, and inheritance law.

Maryam, a thirty-seven-year-old German convert to Islam (Biehl and Kabak 1999:108)

OUR THIRD COUNTRY, Germany, represents a middle ground between Britain's relatively generous accommodation of Muslims' religious practices and France's much greater reluctance to make room for Islam. In Germany, such key church–state institutions as public corporation status and the constitutional guarantee of religious instruction in public schools play an important role in determining not only Muslims' policy aims but also the outcome of their efforts.

Historical Context

Immigration History

Germany has a long history of interactions with Muslims, especially those from the Ottoman Empire. As early as 1732, King Friedrich Wilhelm I of Prussia set up an Islamic prayer room in Potsdam for twenty Turkish mercenaries in his employ. His successor, Friedrich II, also established formal diplomatic relations with Sultan Mohammed II of Istanbul in 1740, opening a centuries-long precedent of political and cultural ties between the two countries. Commenting on the possibility of Turkish Muslim laborers arriving in Prussia, he reportedly said, "If Turks come to Berlin, mosques must be built for them." This statement also suggests the second precedent from this period: the degree to which German policy toward Muslims was determined by the elite rather than the masses (Abdullah 1981:13–15; Abdullah 2001; Totakhyl 2001).

Though Muslims continued to reside temporarily off and on in Germany for the next two centuries, it was not until 1925 that enough Muslims had settled in the country to warrant the construction of Berlin's first large, specially constructed mosque. As a sign of the prevalence of Turks within the German Muslim population, the mosque was dedicated by, among other dignitaries, the Turkish ambassador general. Even during the Second World War, the Nazi regime helped train imams to lead prayers for the tens of thousands of foreign Muslims who found themselves fighting for Germany in Wehrmacht or SS units (Abdullah 1981:16–36).

After the war, Germany faced a severe labor shortage that required the influx of significant numbers of immigrant workers. At first, Germany needed labor to rebuild from the devastation of the war. Beginning in the late 1940s, the *Wirtschaftswunder* (German economic miracle) similarly required more workers than the domestic labor market could provide (Bade 1983:59–72). In contrast with Britain and France, Germany did not have the same opportunity to recruit workers from its former colonies because German decolonization had come earlier in the century, before this post–World War II labor shortage (Holborn 1969:563).

As we have seen in the previous chapters, that many immigrants came to Britain and France from their former colonies colored the initial relationship and expectations between immigrants and the host country. Germany was somewhat distinct in that it signed recruitment treaties with a number of states beginning in the 1950s to recruit foreign workers actively. Germany signed treaties with, among others, Italy, Spain, Greece, Portugal, Morocco, and Yugoslavia, but it was from Turkey that Germany would eventually receive the largest percentage of its immigrant worker population. This high proportion of Turks is not surprising given the close military and cultural ties between the two countries (Bade 1992; Peach and Glebe 1995:35; Stowasser 2002:54).

Never seriously considering the issues of possible settlement and citizenship for these migrants, Germany promoted this policy as a short-term, temporary solution to its labor shortages. The idea was that these guestworkers *(Gastarbeiter)* were foreigners, not immigrants, who would help enhance Germany's economic growth but would return to their country of origin when the nation's labor needs had been met. In fact, early regulations stipulated that foreign workers had to return home after one year in Germany unless they obtained special permission from the German government (Herbert 1990:214). The policy initially envisioned a rotation system by which different sets of workers would circulate into and out of Germany. While this system proved unworkable, the expectation remained that this influx of workers was temporary. As Christian Joppke notes "the logic of a guest worker regime . . . did not envisage the permanent stay of migrant workers, stipulating instead the priority of German state interests over the interest of migrants" (1999:98). That the early contract workers were predominantly male and often lived in makeshift, cramped hostels rather than permanent apartments or houses further bolstered the idea that they were temporary workers who would eventually go back to Turkey (Bade 1992; Herbert 1990:193–254; Münz and Ulrich 1995).

The guestworker regime also reinforced the ideology that Germany – even as it was admitting more and more foreign workers – was not a country of immigration. The German conception of citizenship, based as it was on ethnic descent *(jus sanguinis)* as opposed to place of birth *(jus soli)*, discouraged foreigners from trying to become citizens (Brubaker 1992; Peach and Glebe 1995:42). The inherited policy reinforced this perception, presenting nearly insurmountable hurdles for non-ethnic German foreigners who wished to gain German citizenship. In stark contrast with Britain, which initially had a very liberal citizenship policy for residents of its former colonies, foreign workers in Germany could apply for citizenship only

under certain very specific conditions. Among the less byzantine requirements were at least ten years of residence in Germany, German language
proficiency, the ability to work, good moral character, a stable residence,
economic self-sufficiency for themselves and their families, and a willingness to renounce their original citizenship (Kugler 1993:77–86; Stowasser
2002:62). Many Turks, especially, were unwilling to give up their original
passports because these migrants did not feel at all accepted in Germany
and were often unwilling to lose their right to inherit property in Turkey
(*Migration News* 2000a; Wallraff 1985). Thus, relatively few non-European
foreigners obtained German citizenship.

Because it was not officially a country of immigration, the German
state also did very little to recognize, let alone meet, the educational,
cultural, or religious needs of this largely male Muslim population. The
establishment of places of worship, for example, was not part of the employment treaties signed between Germany and Turkey (Karakasoğlu and
Nonnemann 1996:243). Most of the migrant workers also believed that
their stay in the country was temporary and so had little reason to consider constructing a permanent presence for Islam in Germany. So long as
Germany and Turkey had treaties that allowed workers ease of movement
between the two countries, it was possible for the German and Turkish
governments to maintain the fiction that these workers were not actually
settling in Germany. While some workers did return to Turkey as the policy envisioned, however, many others did not, choosing instead a de facto
permanent settlement in Germany (Kolinsky 1996).

The economic decline brought on by the oil embargo of 1973 exposed the
inherent tensions within this system. In the face of rising unemployment,
Germany suspended its recruitment of foreign workers (*Anwerbestopp*). The
implied assumption of this new labor policy was that the now-superfluous
foreign workers would simply return to their country of origin. This expectation flew in the face of the reality that many of the workers – particularly
Turks – had been living in Germany for more than a decade and that many
more had little or no interest in returning "home." Moreover, this policy
had the ironic and unintended consequence of encouraging chain migration
by the families of guestworkers coming to Germany, a form of immigration
constitutionally protected by the German Basic Law *(Grundgesetz)* of 1949
(Doomernik 1995:47; Guiraudon 1998; Herbert 1990:203).

The result was a significant increase in the number of foreigners living
in Germany. In 1973, 6.4 percent of the German population, or 3.5 million
people, were "foreigners" according to German law (Thränhardt 2000:164).
This proportion had increased to 9 percent by 2001 (Cohen 2001). The

largest percentage of those foreigners, more than one-third of the total foreigner population or nearly 2 million people, was Turkish (Stowasser 2002:54). Because most Turkish migrants subscribed to some form of Islam, the Muslim percentage of the German population also rose dramatically during this period. An estimated 6,500 Muslims were living in Germany in 1961; by 1989 the Muslim population had grown to 1.8 million, and by 2002 there were approximately 3.4 million Muslims living in united Germany. At present, Islam is the third largest religion in the country after Catholicism and *Evangelische* Protestantism (Abdullah 2002; Karakosuğlu 1996:159; Nanji 1996:131; Tibi 2000:13).

The recruitment halt of 1973 also marked a decisive break in the policy needs of the immigrant population. Instead of perceiving themselves as short-term workers who primarily had an economic interest in being in Germany, the growing population of migrant workers and their families became de facto residents who had housing, educational, social welfare, and religious needs that had to be met, needs that had essentially been ignored under the guestworker regime. As Islamrat General Secretary Ghulam Totakhyl (2001) notes:

> At the beginning [the guestworkers] were just going to come for a short time. . . . The employers thought, "they'll come for five, ten, or at most fifteen years to work, earn some money, and then go back." But it wasn't simply a labor force that arrived, but rather real people, with their own religion and culture. And then their families came, with their attendant social needs.

As entire Muslim families settled in Germany, migrants became increasingly concerned about finding appropriate places to worship and providing opportunities for the religious education of their newly arrived children. If one looks at Turkish immigrants alone, for example, in the mid-1970s 60 percent of new migrants were under the age of eighteen (Heine 1997; Kolinsky 1996).

The Politics of Settlement

Because Islam was effectively treated as a "guest religion" that the state had no obligation to accommodate under the law, Germany was ill prepared to meet the religious needs of its growing Muslim population. Instead of understanding those issues as domestic political matters, Germany considered the religious needs of its *Ausländische* ("foreign") population as part of the nation's foreign affairs. Because the vast majority of German Muslims came from Turkey, the government assumed that the bilateral agreements

signed between Germany and Turkey meant that the Turkish government
would provide for workers' religious needs. There were, however, myriad
problems with this assumption.

First, it was only in 1972 that the Turkish prime minister formed a separate division of the official religious affairs office (Diyanet İşleri Başkanliği)
to handle the religious needs of Turks abroad, and it was a decade later that
even one German region had a representative of DİTİB (Diyanet İşleri
Türk-İslam Birliği, or Turkish-Islamic Association for Religious Affairs).
Thus, DİTİB was not sufficiently organized early enough to provide for
the religious needs of at least the first generation of Turkish *Gastarbeiter* (Heine 1997:118; Spuler-Stegemann 1998:111–13; see also DİTİB
1987). In its absence, Muslims in Germany formed their own organizations to respond to the religious, cultural, and political interests of the
Muslim population. Already in 1980, for example, the Verband Islamischer
Kulturzentren (VIKZ, or Union of Islamic Cultural Centers, part of the
Süleyman movement) claimed around eighteen thousand members, and
the Milli Görüş–affiliated Islamische Union Deutschlands reported twenty
thousand (Abdullah 1981:95–103, 120–4).

Even when DİTİB became more active in Germany, its ideological
laicism limited its appeal among many German Muslims. Kemal Atatürk
had formed the Diyanet early in the twentieth century to monopolize and
control religious activities in the Turkish state and to keep Islam out of politics (Karakasoğlu 1996; Sahinoglu 1986). DİTİB imposed a similar model
on the emigŕe community in Germany, requiring, for example, that only
imams and religious teachers approved by Ankara could serve the Turkish
community abroad. The Turkish state likewise tried to maintain control
over DİTİB imams in Germany by paying their salaries and requiring
that they return "home" after five years' service abroad (Bundesregierung
2000:15; Nielsen 1995:30). As Henning von Schroeter (2001), a former se-
nior advisor to the governor of North-Rhine Westphalia, puts it, "We have
a special situation in that the Turkish government doesn't want its nationals
in Germany to lose their connection to their homeland." Unfortunately for
the Turkish government, however, this effort to dominate Muslim religious
life in Germany ultimately failed.

The counterorganizations that formed often advocated a version of Islam
quite different from that of the laicist Diyanet. By the 1970s, the Diyanet's
Presidium in Turkey had declared the Süleyman movement "heretical,"
meaning that DİTİB also condemned the growing Süleyman organization
in Germany, the VIKZ (Gür 1993:49–62; Spuler-Stegemann 1998:138–41).
After a long struggle, in 1998 the secularist Turkish government similarly

banned the *Refah Partisi* (Welfare Party), the Islamist political party with which the Turkish-German Milli Görüş organization is closely linked (Heitmeyer et al. 1997:132–42; Spuler-Stegemann 1998:118–23; *Turkish Daily News* 1998). In the end, Ankara could not direct Muslims' religious life in Germany. Even Turkish-born Muslims increasingly had a mind of their own, which undermined Turkey's efforts to maintain the loyalty of its diaspora. As Jeroen Doomernik notes, "the Diyanet only seemed to recognize at a very late stage that the unbridled proliferation of religious institutions which did not subscribe to its ideology could pose a threat to the stability of the Turkish state" (1995:51). German officials were similarly tardy in realizing that Turkey did not effectively "control" the myriad Islamic organizations that had formed, including such notorious "Islamists" as the "Kaplan group" of Cologne (Gür 1993:62–79; Schiffauer 2000).

In a parallel development, the related issues of immigration and settlement became increasingly politicized. As early as 1982, two-thirds of German respondents wanted to see the *Gastarbeiter* leave the country, and by 1989 three-quarters of the interviewees agreed that there were "too many foreigners" in Germany (Leggewie 1992). But the "foreigner" question leapt to the top of the political agenda in the early 1990s after a wave of xenophobic violence. The German Office for the Protection of the Constitution reported 2,283 acts of antiforeigner violence for 1992, many of which targeted asylum-seekers (Bundesverfassungsschutz 1993:77–8). In response, German legislators significantly stiffened the previously liberal constitutional requirements for asylum (Bade 2000).

Half a decade later, the Christian Democrats (CDU/CSU) worked against the 1999 naturalization law that eased the process for foreigners seeking German citizenship by reducing the residency requirement of new citizens to eight years. The party warned of the potential dangers of naturalizing so large a percentage of the German population. A year after the law had been passed, party leaders recommended for the first time an annual quota for the admission of immigrants but insisted that all foreigners must adhere to the values of the German *Leitkultur* ("guiding culture"). The Bavarian wing of the party (CSU) went even further in its independent position paper, concluding that foreigners living in Germany should embrace "values rooted in Christianity, the Enlightenment, and humanism" (Cohen 2001; *Migration News* 2000b). As Dietrich Thränhardt notes, "in the competitive German political system, party conflict about migration has become an everyday experience" (2000:166).

This political scapegoating of foreigners, coupled with the anti-asylum-seeker riots in cities such as Rostock, Hoyerswerda, and Mannheim in

1991 and 1992, reinforced Muslims' alienation from German society and made them increasingly fearful. Muslims themselves were victimized in a November 23, 1992 firebombing in Mölln, which killed two Turkish girls and a Turkish grandmother (Bundesverfassungsschutz 1993:74–5; Karapin 2000:330–5).

For many Muslims, the reaction to these events was to place an even greater emphasis on religion as a key part of their identity (Karakasoğlu 1996:158; Stowasser 2002:60). Second- and third-generation immigrant Muslims became more interested in rediscovering their religious heritage and living in accordance with Islamic teaching. As Tariq Ramadan notes, this religious revival was an attempt to understand the genuine teachings of the faith "purified from the accidents of its traditional reading" (1999b:114). For many young Muslims in Germany, the goal became not to assimilate themselves into the secular values of the West, but instead to adopt a true Islamic identity while living in the West. In many ways, German citizenship and settlement policies were ill prepared to facilitate this goal. However, Germany's church–state structure provided some institutional openings for Muslims to maintain their religious values.

Institutional and Social Context

Multiple Establishment

The German church–state system strikes a middle ground between Britain's established church and France's *laïcité*. The German Basic Law establishes a formal separation between church and state, but at the same time the constitution secures cooperation between the two institutions in such areas as education and social welfare (Davie 2000:5–23; de Galembert 2001; Deutscher Bundestag 1998; Robbers 1996). This cooperation with the state is particularly strong for the historically dominant and state-supported Roman Catholic and *Evangelische* churches, which together represent over 90 percent of Germany's religious population. The reason for this unusual arrangement has much to do with Germany's unique church–state history.

Political conflict around religion was particularly strong in Germany in the years after the Protestant Reformation, as the Catholic Church and various Protestant churches fought for political control of the state. The 1648 Peace of Westphalia, which ended the devastating Thirty Years' War, established the practice of *cuius regio, eius religio* ("the religion of the ruler is the religion of the state"). The princes of the German principalities determined whether their subjects would be Catholic, Lutheran, or Calvinist. As a result, whole areas were created that were almost totally committed to one of these religious traditions within Christianity (Koch 1978:43–8; Philpott 2001). Even today, traces of this pattern remain, with certain areas of Germany still being predominantly Roman Catholic or *Evangelische*. *Cuius regio, eius religio* also established a strong link between church and state, as political and religious leaders saw themselves united in a common purpose (Monsma and Soper 1997:158–60; Robbers 1996).

The development of the German national state in the second half of the nineteenth century threatened the political system that allowed religious diversity among the various German-speaking states. Led by the overwhelmingly Protestant Prussia, German unification resulted in Roman Catholics becoming a minority and Protestants a majority in the resultant nation-state. The most significant religious policy in the new united Germany was the *Kulturkampf*, the state-led attack on the institutional power of the Roman Catholic Church and its influence over its adherents. Thus, the government abolished the Catholic section of the Prussian Ministry of Ecclesiastical Affairs and Education in 1871, dissolved the Jesuit order in 1872, and imposed government supervision over Catholic education in 1873. By 1876, every bishop in Germany was either in prison or in exile (Gould 1999:81; Holborn 1969:261–6; Kalyvas 1996:179). Far from weakening the power of the Catholic Church, however, the *Kulturkampf* unintentionally had quite the opposite effect; the state's political persecution resulted in Catholics uniting and creating the *Zentrum*, the Catholic Center Party, to defend Catholic interests. By the century's end, it became apparent that the *Kulturkampf* had failed, and the state repealed most of its anti-Catholic measures (Gabriel 1995; Gould 1999; Hofmann 1993:156–65; Kalyvas 1996; Schmidt-Volkmar 1962).

The German *Kulturkampf* also did little to strengthen liberal political voices or lead to a marked secularization of the German state. The secular political movement that dominated French politics was not nearly so prominent in Germany. The German state did gradually liberalize under the Weimar Constitution after the First World War, but the Weimar Republic did so without a direct assault on the churches. For example, the Weimar Constitution adopted the principle of church–state separation, affirming in Article 137 that "there shall be no state church." Article 136 likewise provided that "civil and political rights and duties shall be neither dependent on nor restricted by the exercise of religious freedom." Despite these liberal clauses, the Weimar Constitution nevertheless retained various subsidies and privileges for the Catholic and *Evangelische* churches. The

Constitution thus codified religious free exercise rights while maintaining cooperative relations between church and state alongside the development of a dual ecclesiastical systems – Catholic and Protestant – that continued to work closely with the German state on social welfare and education issues (Deutscher Bundestag 1998:91–2; Hofmann 1993:109–87; Kolb 2000:12, 19). Though abandoned during the Third Reich, these Weimar-era church–state provisions later served as the model for the post–World War II constitution.

Given Adolph Hitler's efforts to concentrate all power in the Nazi state, the two major churches represented a potential challenge to the regime. Most *Evangelische* churches came to accommodate themselves to National Socialist rule and provided little active opposition to the persecution of religious minorities such as the Jews (Shirer 1960). Some Protestant clergy, known as the "Confessing Church," nonetheless opposed Nazi racial theories and pseudoreligious doctrines. During the Nazi era, the party imprisoned or executed thousands of such dissident pastors and laity, including the noted theologian Dietrich Bonhoeffer (Bonhoeffer 1990; Meier 1992; Shirer 1960:324–33). The Third Reich's relationship with the Catholic Church was more complex. The Vatican negotiated a concordat with Hitler in 1933 that supposedly preserved Catholic schools, protected the Church's right to publicize its doctrines, and allowed some autonomy for Church institutions. By 1937, however, Pope Pius XI vigorously protested the Nazi's flagrant violations of this agreement. This break with Hitler renewed the conflict between Catholics and the German state and led to the persecution of many priests (Holborn 1969:739–44; Meier 1992:197–224).

After the Second World War, the allied powers drafted a new constitution for West Germany that reaffirmed the historical pattern of church–state cooperation. Article 140 of the Basic Law *(Grundgesetz)* reinstated several articles from the old Weimar Constitution, which had established a close partnership between church and state in various policy areas. While the *Grundgesetz* affirms that Germany is to have no state church, the document nonetheless recognizes as public corporations *(Körperschaft des öffentlichen Rechts)* those religious communities that previously had that status in the Weimar Republic. Public corporation status helps ensure the legal autonomy of these religious bodies. In particular, a religious "public corporation" is entitled to have the government collect money from church or synagogue members on its behalf *(Kirchensteuer)*. This tax amounts to 8–10 percent of what is owed the federal government in income taxes and is used for the religious, social welfare, and educational work of the churches. In 2000, the church tax raised around 8 billion euros for Protestant and Roman Catholic churches (Deutscher Bundestag 1998:88, 91–2; Evangelische Kirche in Deutschland 2003; Robbers 2000).

Article 140 also set out a procedure for granting public corporation status to other religious entities: "Other religious communities shall be granted like rights upon application where their constitution and the number of their members offer an assurance of their permanency" (Deutscher Bundestag 1998:91). In the German federal system, each *Land*'s government determines the eligibility of those religious groups in that jurisdiction. According to the German government's official report on Islam in Germany, this procedure generally requires, among other things, that the group formally submit an application in a given *Land*, that the group has existed for at least thirty years, that its members comprise at least one-one thousandth of the total *Land* population, and that the group respect the law (Bundesregierung 2000:33–7; see also Lemmen 2001:183–92). While various Christian and Jewish groups have received this public corporation status in one or more *Länder*, no Muslim group has yet received equivalent recognition (KIGST 2003).

Officially, Muslims' applications have been rejected because they did not meet at least one of the requirements of Article 140. Some organizations had insufficient members. Others failed the "permanency" test, while still other groups are viewed as unrepresentative or undemocratic (Robbers 2000; von Schroeter 2001; Wanzura and Rips 1981:11–16). Many German Muslims, however, see a bias against Islam behind the continued lack of formal recognition and resent what they perceive as unequal treatment. The leader of a major Muslim umbrella organization expresses it as follows:

> In contrast with the other religious groups..., we receive next to no [governmental] support for our institutions.... The other religious groups receive – quite apart from their *Kirchensteuer*, which the state collects for them – public money for their hospitals, for the [Catholic social service organization] Caritas, for the [*Evangelische* social welfare group] Diakonisches Werk.... They receive 100 percent funding from the state for all of these social programs. But for us, even though we pay our taxes, our tax money goes somewhere else [than to Muslim-run social agencies] (Totakhyl 2001).

Besides the financial benefits from official recognition, achieving public corporation status would also represent a symbolic affirmation by the state that Islam has become part of the everyday religious landscape in Germany (Lemmen 2001:183; Wanzura and Rips 1981:18).

Given that Germany has ultimately granted public corporation status to religious groups other than the "big two" in the past, we find it hard to believe that the more than 3 million German Muslims will be forever shut out of this system. A particular *Land* government is nonetheless reticent about being the first to grant a Muslim group this status because doing so would create a precedent for other *Länder*. As Henning von Schroeter (2001; see also Lemmen 2001:184) notes, "the various *Länder* have [agreed] to coordinate with each other on granting public corporation status because a positive decision made in [the *Land* capitals of] Hamburg or Berlin has an influence on Munich and Düsseldorf." But regardless of when Muslims ultimately obtain public corporation status, they have been content to work within the inherited church–state structure to become part of the multiple establishment themselves.

Religious Free-Exercise Rights

Although Muslims in Germany have yet to obtain equal standing with other religious groups as recipients of state aid, the German Constitution broadly protects individuals' religious free-exercise rights. Article 4 of the Basic Law declares that "freedom of faith and conscience as well as freedom of creed, whether religious or ideological, are inviolable" (Deutscher Bundestag 1989:13). In general, Muslims do not allege violations of this right. Ghulam Dastagir Totakhyl (2001) emphasizes that "at the individual level, there are no restrictions on Muslims' religious freedom." Of course, the former German Democratic Republic brutally suppressed religious freedom until 1989 (Fulbrook 1997:87–125), but the situation in eastern Germany has improved dramatically since reunification.

The *Grundgesetz*, however, protects not only a person's right to believe but also her or his right to put those religious views into practice. Article 4 guarantees "the undisturbed practice of religion," while Article 140 forbids the state from restricting one's civil liberties based on the "exercise of religious freedom." The Basic Law even goes so far as to protect the right not to work on Sundays and publicly recognized religious holidays (Article 140) and the right to decline military service based on personal conscience (Deutscher Bundestag 1998:13, 88, 91–2). In various cases, the German Constitutional Court has likewise recognized this positive notion of religious freedom (Monsma and Soper 1997:164–71). Muslims, however, are more likely to complain about violations of this expansive understanding of religious liberty. Muslim practices often conflict with German policies in such areas as family law, burial regulations, the slaughter of animals, and public recognition of religious holidays (Heine 1997:137–285; Khoury, Heine, and Oebbecke 2000; Rohe 2001; Spuler-Stegemann 1998:161–212). While Muslims recognize that the Basic Law is rooted in a Christian world-view (Elyas 2001), the Constitution nonetheless provides opportunities for them to argue for state recognition of their religious practices as well.

Secularization

As in Britain and France, the weakening of ties to organized religion significantly influences Muslims' incorporation into the preexisting church–state system. On the one hand, practicing Muslims have become more prevalent in Germany and have pressed for closer links between religion and the state. On the other hand, most Germans no longer attend church, many have abandoned traditional religious beliefs, and some have instead adopted a more secular worldview that is in many respects hostile to close church–state relations.

Since the early 1960s, the number of Muslims living in Germany has mushroomed. While the *Stuttgarter Zeitung* posited at least 50,000 Muslims in 1962, seven years later an official *Evangelische* research institute estimated the Muslim population at over 250,000. Muslim scholar Muhammad Salim Abdullah (1981:70–7; 2002) put the figure at 1.7 million for 1981 and at almost 3.5 million for 2002 (see also Karakasoğlu 1996:159; Robbers 1996:57; Spuler-Stegemann 2002:14). About three-quarters of these Muslims, moreover, claim to worship in a mosque or prayer hall with any degree of regularity and feel that their religious beliefs are an important part of their identity (Abdullah 2002).

In contrast, while a certain form of cultural Christianity prevails in Germany, traditional religious practices and belief have waned. True, official church statistics for 2003 count nearly 27 million Roman Catholics and just over 26 million *Evangelische* (REMID 2003). Yet while in 1967 one-quarter of the German population went to church "every or almost every" Sunday, only 10 percent did so in 1992 (Shand 1998). Western German data from the Politbarometer (a German public opinion poll) show a similar retrenchment of religious practice, falling from 10.6 percent weekly church attendance in 1977 to 8.2 percent by 1995. The proportion of effectively secular western German respondents correspondingly rose from 18.3 percent in 1977 to 28.0 percent in 1995 (Forschungsgruppe Wahlen 1996). Finally, belief in traditional Christian doctrines has fallen. In 1967, 42 percent of West Germans affirmed that "Jesus was the Son of God," but only 29 percent agreed with this statement in 1992 (Shand 1998).

As German society secularizes, many practicing Muslims fear that policy makers, who might be comfortable with privatized religion, will become increasingly hostile to the public expression of Muslims' faith. In fact, some Muslim leaders are more troubled by this secular ethos than any supposed clash with active Christians. Nadeem Elyas (2001; see also Akkent and Franger 1987:154–77), president of the umbrella organization Zentralrat der Muslime in Deutschland, for example, suggests that many Germans are "shocked" to see Muslims pray or wear the *ḥijāb* in public. Such believers are not necessarily trying to proselytize for Islam, he maintains, but merely following the dictates of their faith. A less public expression of their faith is simply not possible for orthodox Muslims because they are obligated, for example, to pray at five predetermined times of the day regardless of where these believers find themselves.

In pressing for state accommodation of their religious practices, then, German Muslims are advantaged by a preexisting church–state structure that allows for substantial state support for religion. The increasingly secular German society, however, militates against Muslims' acting out their faith in public or receiving state funding for their religious practices and institutions.

Major Areas of Religious Accommodation

Religious Activities in State Schools

The most contested educational issue for German Muslim parents is probably the teaching of religion to the estimated seven hundred thousand Muslims in public schools (Knubbertz 2000). As in Britain, state schools provide formal religious instruction *(Religionsunterricht)* as part of the core curriculum. In Germany, this commitment is regulated above all by Article 7 of the Basic Law:

> Religious instruction shall form part of the regular curriculum ... in state schools. Without prejudice to the state's right of supervision, religious instruction shall be given in accordance with the doctrine of the religious community concerned (Deutscher Bundestag 1998:14; Lemmen 2001:159).

German school authorities see themselves more as helping the churches teach their own doctrines rather than as taking an official position on theological matters. Thus, churches themselves usually select appropriate teachers and textbooks (Monsma and Soper 1997:176–84; Pfaff 2000). Parents generally choose whether to send their children to the *Evangelische* or Roman Catholic religion class, or parents may choose to withdraw their children entirely from religion courses (Lemmen 2001:159).

Not only *Evangelische* and Catholic parents but also many Muslims very much want their children to receive suitable religious instruction in public schools. Delivery of this instruction is far from assured for Muslims, however. One Egyptian-born German Muslim lamented the dearth of such classes:

> I want my children to be educated in the Islamic faith, but the schools in Germany don't have a class for Islam. I found that my children were becoming worse because they lacked any religious teaching. So I asked that they be taught in one of the Christian religion classes. I told myself, "their learning about some religion is better than about none at all" (Kusbah 1997:71).

Since no Muslim group has yet achieved public corporation status, *Land* school officials do not feel obligated to provide Islamic instruction or to consult formally with Muslim leaders on the content of any such classes.

In all but one *Land*, moreover, Muslims only receive *Religiöse Unterweisung* or *Religionskunde* (religious studies), not true *Religionsunterricht*. The distinction between *Religiöse Unterweisung* and *Regl/igionsunterricht* has important legal, practical, and philosophical implications. Ulrich Pfaff (2000), the official responsible for overseeing religious education in North Rhine-Westphalia, defines the distinction as follows:

> At its core, *Religionsunterricht* does not aim simply to convey facts. Rather, it is guided by the conviction that the religious doctrines being taught are true. It uses denominationally specific arguments and gives students a self-conscious and goal-oriented belief system. . . . [In contrast, *Religiöse Unterweisung*] describes the content of a religion, its culture and history, and its religious practices. It refrains from promulgating [religious] beliefs but instead highlights [objective] understanding and knowledge about religion.

The distinction, in short, is between something akin to state-funded Sunday school versus a comparative religion course.

That educational policy is the responsibility of *Land* governments further complicates Muslims' efforts to obtain Islamic instruction for their children. Even federal constitutional law governing religious instruction varies across *Länder*.[1] This federal system, not surprisingly, leads to large differences in how or whether public schools provide Islamic instruction.

---

[1] Under the so-called "Bremen clause" (Article 141 of the Basic Law), Article 7's requirement that religious instruction be part of the regular curriculum in state schools does not apply in those *Länder* where different *Land*-level provisions were in place on January 1, 1949 (Deutscher Bundestag 1998:88).

In Bremen, for example, Muslim students receive neither Islamic *Religionsunterricht* nor the more objective *Religiöse Unterweisung*. Instead, under the so-called "Bremen clause" of the Basic Law (Article 140), state schools are supposed to teach "Biblical history in a Christian context" (Deutscher Bundestag 1998:88). Efforts also to include material on the history and tradition of Islam have thus far born no fruit (Algan 2001; Bundesregierung 2000:43). One city official argued that Muslims have a difficult time obtaining their own religious instruction since even the Christians complain that the current classes are too watered-down (Hafner 2001). Bremen does have Turkish language and culture classes that often include some treatment of Islam. However, these courses are not part of the official curriculum, are only open to Turkish citizens, and are taught by employees of the secularly oriented, Turkish Diyanet (Heine 1997:183; Karakasoğlu 1996:164–5).

Hamburg, in turn, has opted for a more comparative religion approach, teaching students of all faiths together in the same class instead of allowing different religious communities to offer religious instruction to coreligionists. Beginning with the traditional separate classes for Catholics and *Evangelische*, public school officials soon realized that the student population was much more religiously diverse. As Halima Krausen (2001), a theologian from the Islamisches Zentrum Hamburg, recalls:

> In Hamburg we had Protestant religious instruction, but we had no Protestants. There were schools where you had 60 percent Turks, Greek Orthodox, Russian Orthodox, atheists, a Hindu, a Buddhist, and maybe two or three Protestants.

In response, teachers began to advocate interreligious education, and Hamburg's education officials worked with religious leaders from the various traditions to formulate the resulting religious education class (Krausen 2001; Weiße 2000).

North Rhine-Westphalia has arguably been the most pioneering in its efforts to provide religious instruction to Muslims under the same conditions it offers such classes to the publicly recognized religious communities. Because this *Land* has not yet granted public corporation status to any Muslim groups, the people who would be entitled to run *Religionsunterricht* courses for Muslim students are not available (Pfaff 2000; 2001). Moreover, state educational officials technically may not provide such faith-oriented instruction on their own. *Land* school authorities have tried to resolve this dilemma by offering, on an experimental basis, courses that are billed as objective religious studies (*Religiöse Unterweisung*) but which, especially at the elementary school level, look very much like the more spiritually grounded

Religionsunterricht. Textbooks published by the official Landesinstitut für Schule und Weiterbildung (State Institute for Schools and Continuing Education), for example, are clearly intended for believing Muslims. The cover of the grade school textbook features an Arabic version of the first half of the Muslim statement of faith, "There is no God but Allah," and the first inside page opens with the *bismillah*, the standard Arabic invocation translated as "in the name of Allah, the most compassionate, the most merciful" (Landesinstitut für Schule und Weiterbildung 1986). The textbook for sixth-graders expects them to learn that the *qur'ān* is the "direct word of Allah" and that in the *qur'ān*, Allah "speaks to us" (Landesinstitut für Schule und Weiterbildung 1991:3, 124). As with established *Religionsunterricht* courses, this Islamic *Unterweisung* is taught by coreligionists. Pfaff sees such a compromise as "a pragmatic way to offer Muslims any kind of [religious] instruction at all" (2000).

Land authorities also view the course as an opportunity to expose Muslim students to a version of Islam that is compatible with the form of liberal democracy practiced in the Federal Republic and to ease their incorporation into mainstream German society. Citing the well-known *qur'ānic* passage, "There is no compulsion in religion" (sura 2:256), a lesson for tenth-graders suggests that it is impossible to develop a system of government based on the *sharī'ah* (Landesinstitut für Schule und Weiterbildung 1996:165–70). Another unit in the grade school textbook acknowledges the tensions that Muslims might experience in living in the non-Muslim German culture, but urges students to "respect the law … in Germany," and to "strive to be good neighbors to non-Muslims [*Andersgläubige*]" (Landesinstitut für Schule und Weiterbildung 1986:184–93).

The architect of this curriculum, Klaus Gebauer (2001) of North Rhine-Westphalia's Landesinstitut, openly acknowledges that the program intends to teach a form of Islam that supports democracy. He would likewise "welcome the democratization of Islam spreading out [to the Muslim world] from Germany." Contrasting the situation in North Rhine-Westphalia with that in France, he argues that it is far better to "bring [Muslim] students into the [public] schools" to learn about Islam than for such pupils to get their "Islamic education" elsewhere, from "dreadful organizations."

The city and *Land* of Berlin offer yet another example of how differently individual federal states manage Islamic instruction. Technically also under the constitutional "Bremen clause," Berlin adopted a 1947 school code affirming that religion classes were voluntary, not part of the core curriculum, and were to be administered directly by the various churches or philosophical societies. While Turkish language and culture classes have for many years covered Islam, among other topics, Berlin public schools did not until recently allow full-fledged Islamic *Religionsunterricht* because no Muslim group had been formally recognized to administer it. Beginning in 1980, however, the Islamische Föderation Berlin (IFB) pressed Berlin school authorities to recognize the group as entitled to run Muslim *Religionsunterricht*. After many legal battles, the Federal Administrative Court *(Bundesverwaltungsgericht)* ultimately ruled in 2000 that Berlin had to recognize the IFB as a "religious society" within the meaning of the Berlin school code (Knubbertz 2000; Lemmen 2001:172–4; Rohe 2001:161–2). Two years later, the IFB was administering such classes to more than one thousand students in sixteen public schools. Following this precedent, Berlin school officials have likewise allowed Alevite Muslims to offer their own religion classes (am Orde 2002). While many Muslims welcomed this opening for religious pluralism (Kesici 2001), other observers were dismayed that the IFB, which they accuse of having Islamist tendencies, is now free to "proselytize" and "pressure" students to conform to its version of Muslim practice (Woltersdorf 2003).

Despite the raging controversy in France over students wearing the *ḥijāb*, German school authorities have almost universally accommodated Muslim girls who wish to wear this headcovering. Under German law, forbidding a student to wear the *ḥijāb* would violate her right to practice her religion (Heine 1997:171; Lemmen 2001:149; Rohe 2001:140–1). The situation for *teachers*, however, is more complicated. Though some instructors in such *Länder* as Hamburg and Brandenburg are free to wear the *ḥijāb*, federal states such as Baden-Württemberg and Lower Saxony forbid this practice as a violation of the state's duty to be neutral toward all religions. Some German policy makers fear that a teacher wearing the *ḥijāb* gives the impression that the German state endorses Islam (Lemmen 2001:148–52; Rohe 2001:145).

Probably the most celebrated case of such a conflict was that of Fereshta Ludin, an Afghan-born German Muslim from Schwäbisch Gmünd, a small town in Baden-Württemberg (Spuler-Stegemann 2002:202). Although Ludin, who wears the *ḥijāb*, experienced no serious difficulties as a university student or teaching intern, in 1998 the *Land*'s culture minister determined that because of her *ḥijāb*, she could not be hired as an official teacher (Lemmen 2001:150–2). In 2002, the Federal Administrative Court confirmed the minister's decision. The court opined that the only way Ludin, as a public employee, could fulfill her duty to be religiously neutral was to remove her *ḥijāb* during class (*Suddeutsche Zeitung* 2002). This ruling came despite the presence of crucifixes on the walls of many public school classrooms in the *Land*. Responding to the court's argument, Ludin (2001) contends that the state's neutrality claim is hollow when any number of Christian symbols and activities are allowed in public schools:

> What does "neutral" mean? When you have two standards, then you can openly say, "for us Christians it's okay, but for everyone else, it's not." ... The Christian communities [in Baden-Württemberg] have great freedom of expression, but all the other [religious groups] don't.

In September 2003, the Federal Constitutional Court *(Bundesverfassungsgericht)* issued its opinion on Ludin's appeal of the lower court's ruling from 2002. The court ruled that absent a *Land* law specifically barring a teacher from wearing the *ḥijāb*, Ludin should be allowed to teach in the public schools (Landler 2003). While awaiting the outcome of her case, however, Ludin left her home region of Swabia and accepted a teaching position at the private Islamic school in Berlin. She also suffered from the media's invasion into her personal life and her being uprooted from southern Germany (Ludin 2001). Despite the apparently pro-*ḥijāb* outcome of this case, the issue is likely to remain politicized as each individual *Land* is free to set its own policy on the question.

As in Britain and France, German Muslim parents have raised such concerns as the provision of *ḥalāl* meat in school cafeterias, mixed-gender sports classes, overnight field trips, and absences for Muslim holidays. While *Länder* differ somewhat in how accommodating they are to such concerns, local school authorities generally try to work out pragmatic compromises with Muslims. In Cologne, for example, Muslim girls were allowed to take swimming classes from women instructors in an all-female pool chosen specifically because it was not visible from the street (Heine 1997:156–82; Konya 2001; Lemmen 2001:146–8; Rohe 2001:134–54).

Public Funding for Islamic Schools

Article 7, section 4 of the German Basic Law establishes the right to operate private schools, although they do need to receive the approval of the particular *Land* government (Deutscher Bundestag 1998:15). Only about 4 percent of German school children attend private schools, which is a much smaller fraction than in Britain or France (German Information Service 1996:450–2). This low percentage of private schools perhaps stems from the more extensive denominational influence allowed in the public schools.

Although German Muslims appear less eager to obtain public funding for private schools than are their British coreligionists, *Land* governments have approved two Muslim elementary schools in Munich and Berlin. Opened in 1981 by the Islamisches Zentrum München, the Deutsch-Islamische Schule offers instruction in German and Arabic to about one hundred students in grades one through five. Though most students originate in Arabic-speaking countries, a few ethnic Turks attend as well. Under the school regulations of the *Land* of Bavaria, government funding for this school can cover as much as 80 percent of its expenses. According to Abdel Sattar Hasanein (2001), the school's principal, the institution's value added is that it encourages the students' Arabic and Islamic identity: "Here, the student doesn't feel different. In most public schools, he or she is viewed as a for-eigner, which has a psychological impact." Such psychological well-being, he argues, will ultimately facilitate the pupil's healthy incorporation into the larger German society (Deutsch-Islamische Schule, n.d.; Hasanein 2001; Lemmen 2001:163; von Denffer 1995:57–8).

The Islamische Grundschule Berlin first opened its doors in 1989 as a privately financed, German-language elementary school for Muslim stu-dents. In 1995, however, the Berlin Senate officially recognized the school and agreed to pay virtually all of its expenses. Among the student body of about 140 first- through sixth-graders, pupils from a Turkish background predominate. Besides teaching Berlin's normal core curriculum, the school offers classes in Islam and the Arabic language. Biology classes cover both Darwinist and creationist versions of the origins of life. Though some teachers are lifelong or converted Muslims, others are socialist-oriented atheists or nominal Christians. As does Hasanein, Principal Renate Nadja Abed (2001) emphasizes her school's ability to foster better integration of Muslim students into the broader, non-Muslim German environment. Muslim parents choose the school more for academic than religious rea-sons, she notes (Abed 2001; Lemmen 2001:164; Mohr 2000:59–61; Spuler-Stegemann 1998:236).

Mosque Building

The permanent settlement of Muslims in Germany led to their search for appropriate places of worship. While some Muslims had to content them-selves with no more than a "prayer room" set aside in an apartment, more fortunate coreligionists obtained the permission and resources to construct a mosque. From around seven hundred mosques or prayer rooms in 1981, the Muslim presence had expanded to about twenty-four hundred such places of worship in 2002 (Abdullah 1981:78; 2002). Given an estimated Muslim population of 3.5 million, Germany still has only one mosque or prayer room for every 1,458 Muslims, which is a slightly higher average than that in Britain and a slightly lower one than that in France.

As in these two other countries, local governments have the primary responsibility for regulating the construction of mosques. In Germany, the local politics of mosque building varies tremendously, yet overall the situation is neither so benign as in England nor so contentious as in France. Some local Muslims have successfully built large, traditionally styled mosques in such major German cities as Berlin, Cologne, and Frankfurt (Spuler-Stegemann 1998:150–3). Often, however, local political and economic realities necessitate that large mosques be located in lower-income residential areas near industrial parks (such as those in Bremen and Munich).

The construction of the Yavuz Sultan Selim Mosque in Mannheim is probably as close as one can get to a best-case scenario in Germany. In 1984, Muslim leaders from the Islamischer Bund Mannheim began talks with the city government about constructing a purpose-built mosque in the city center. As the Muslims' plans reached the public, many residents began to campaign against the project because they feared the mosque would attract even more Muslim immigrants to the already predominantly Turkish area. Over the next six to seven years, Muslims formed alliances with local Catholic and *Evangelische* churches along with Mannheim's Office of Foreigner Affairs *(Ausländerbeauftragter)*. Even Martin Wetzel (2001), the Catholic priest whose church was directly across from the proposed mosque site, helped found and lead the Christlich-Islamische Gesellschaft Mannheim, an interfaith group that tried to calm the public's fears about the mosque. In 1993, the city gave its final approval, and the 2,500-person, traditionally styled mosque was completed in 1995. Since its opening, both Muslims and Mannheim city officials hold it up as an example of how a mosque can contribute to social order and educate Germans about Islam. Specially designed as an open, transparent mosque, the structure contains a multitude of small windows symbolizing the congregation's commitment to peaceful interaction with the community. The mosque's Institute for German-Turkish Integration Studies and Interreligious Activity annually hosts school groups, civic organizations, and public officials, explaining the basics of Muslims' faith and practice (Albert, Kamran, and Alboğa 1995; Alboğa n.d., 2001; IDTIA 1999; Schmitt 2001; Spuler-Stegemann 1998: 17–27; but see Albert 2001a; 2001b:ch. 4).

Stuttgart, on the other hand, illustrates what can go wrong when Muslims try to open a mosque. In 1999, VIKZ-affiliated Muslims purchased a former factory building in the Heslach neighborhood, planning to convert it into a mosque and Islamic boarding school. The project immediately encountered both popular and official opposition. Local residents, organized into such antimosque lobbies as Pro Heslach and the Bürger- und Gartenbauvereins Heslach, tried to persuade government officials to deny VIKZ permission to renovate the building (Kaufmann 2001; *Stuttgarter Zeitung* 2001). Besides voicing concern about increased traffic and noise, some potential neighbors feared being "overrun" by Muslims (Rupp 2000; Seifert 2000). Some even envisioned the mosque being used to train Islamist cadres (Mack and Hohnecker 2000). The issue polarized local parties: The Christian Democrats and the Republikaner opposed the plan, the Greens and the Free Democrats unequivocally supported the mosque, and the Social Democrats conditionally favored it (Oßwald 2001a; 2001b). The Turkish Consul General in Stuttgart, meanwhile, did not support the project, opining that the city already had "a sufficient number of facilities for the religious needs of the Turks" (Pazarkaya 2000). City administrators and politicians eventually blocked plans for the Heslach site, but in May of 2003 were trying to convince the VIKZ group to build a mosque elsewhere in greater Stuttgart (Oßwald 2003; Per 2001; Regierungspräsidium Stuttgart 2001). This failure suggests the importance of eliciting the support of key political and religious leaders early on and perhaps also of being perceived as religiously moderate.

Similarly, German Muslims have sometimes faced difficulties obtaining approval to build tall, traditional minarets as part of their mosques and have almost always been forbidden to use loudspeakers to broadcast the Muslim call to prayer *(adhān)* from such structures. Neighbors contend that the call to prayer would disturb public order, and a few even base their opposition on theological grounds. Some Muslims, on the other hand, find the ubiquitous Christian church bells equally disturbing, and note that the ringing of bells is generally not regulated so strictly (Bundesregierung 2000:15–16; de Galembert 1994; Heine 1997:250–1; Lemmen 2001:136–41; Mazyek 2001; Spuler-Stegemann 2002:160–1).

Testing the Theories

Our review of religious instruction in state schools, state aid to Muslim schools, and mosque building suggests that overall, the German state is less accommodating than the British but more so than the French. In each instance, the German state has not consistently opposed Muslim efforts, as has sometimes been the case in France, nor has the state consistently worked to incorporate Muslim perspectives in public policy, as has most often been true in Britain. What explains the curious middle ground staked out thus far by Germany?

Resource Mobilization

One theory that often is used to explain the outcome of state policy is resource mobilization. According to this theory, the concessions that German Muslims have won from the state are a function of the various resources at their disposal, while those instances where the state has been less accommodating point to the absence of some key assets. In comparative terms, the theory would predict that German Muslims have more politically useful resources than Muslims in France have, but fewer than British Muslims have.

Perhaps the most important asset that can be measured is the organizational strength of German Muslims. As was the case in Britain and France, German Muslims have formed various social, religious, and political organizations. According to a 1995 estimate (Karakaşoğlu 1996:168–9), Germany had more than two thousand Turkish-Islamic organizations with a membership of half a million. Later membership estimates are significantly higher (Abdullah 2000; Spuler-Stegemann 2002:98–100). While probably only a minority of these groups are politically oriented, they nonetheless have brought Muslims together in ways that facilitate their political mobilization.

That most German Muslims initially came from Turkey might in itself make it easier for them to be organized than for British or French Muslims, who originated from a wider array of countries. DİTİB certainly sees itself as the representative organization for Turkish-German Muslims, and it has functioned as the official liaison between the Turkish and German governments. However, as various commentators have noted, DİTİB hardly speaks for a supposedly unified Turkish-German community (Amiraux 1996:37; Doomernik 1995:60; Joppke 1999:212; Karakaşoğlu and Nonneman 1996:257–8). Instead, alternative groups have formed that reject DİTİB's laicist ideology and its coordination with the Turkish government. Chief among them are Milli Görüş and VIKZ. Furthermore, the much more theologically and politically liberal Alevite Muslims have organized themselves into the Föderation der Aleviten Gemeinden in Deutschland, which certainly does not support the Turkish state (Gülçiçek 1996; Kaplan 2001).

Finally, other German Muslims claim, quite rightly, that a self-described Turkish-German group – whatever its ideological or religious appeal – hardly speaks to the interests of non-Turkish Muslims. Discussing whether

DİTİB effectively represents Muslims in Hamburg, Krausen (2001) notes, "there are a lot of Iranians, Arabs, and Pakistanis [in Hamburg], and they definitely don't agree with anything that comes from the Turkish government." Instead, Muslims with different national origins have organized themselves into such groups as the Arabic-oriented Islamische Gemeinschaft in Deutschland, the Vereinigung Islamischer Gemeinden der Bosniaken in Deutschland, and the Union der Islamisch Albanischen Zentren in Deutschland (Lemmen 2001:100, 108–9).

In short, various groups in Germany aspire to represent Muslim interests before the government, but no single umbrella organization speaks effectively for the entire Muslim community. The multiplicity of groups has very real consequences for Muslims who want the state to recognize their interests. Von Schroeter (2001) comments that "up until now, Muslim groups have been very splintered and have had very different interests." Whatever success German Muslims have had in Germany, therefore, is not a function of the community's organizational strength and unity.

Nor are German Muslims' resources consistently strong in other significant ways. Until the 2000 changes in German nationality law, only a small percentage (possibly one-sixth) of Muslims in Germany had become citizens, which obviously limited the kind of electoral pressure that they could bring to bear through conventional political channels. Only one Muslim, Green Party member Cem Özdemir, has served recently in the Bundestag (Özdemir 1999; 2002). And until the 2000 change, none of the major parties had specifically selected Muslims as party candidates. Historically, the Social Democrats, Greens, and Party of Democratic Socialism have been more likely to support the rights of immigrants but have largely ignored these predominantly Muslim immigrants' religious needs and rights. Totakhyl (2001) describes the party situation in this way:

> [Which party is pro- or anti-Islam] varies quite a lot from *Land* to *Land*. In those *Länder* where the SPD is in opposition, for example, in Bavaria or Baden-Württemberg, the SPD advocates the teaching of Islam in the schools and fights for the rights of the Muslim community. But where this same party is in power, for example, in North Rhine-Westphalia, Lower Saxony, Hamburg, or Bremen, it doesn't do so. And the opposite is also true: Where the CDU is in opposition . . . it supports Muslims' political demands.

Party support for Muslims, in short, appears to have been strategic and selective; the SPD and CDU appeal to Muslims when they are out of power to try to win their votes. When these same parties are in power, however, they generally dismiss those voters and their concerns. Given the change in nationality law, however, more and more Muslim immigrants will become voters. Totakhyl notes that German Muslims could determine the outcome of a highly contested future election similar to that between Helmut Kohl and Rudolf Scharping in 1994. Overall, a majority of Muslims appear to support parties of the left, such as SPD and the Green Party (Abdullah 2000).

Resources do seem to be a significant factor explaining mosque building in Germany, although even on this issue church–state institutions are vitally important. A key reason for the success of the building of the Mannheim mosque, as well as the failure of the proposed project in Stuttgart, was the support of key religious and political elites. Early in the project, Muslims in Mannheim secured the aid of city leaders, which in turn defused the controversy that the construction of the mosque inspired. In Stuttgart, by contrast, Muslim leaders were politically naive; they purchased the building to be renovated without considering how difficult it would be to gain approval to convert it into a mosque. They failed to build a political coalition in support of their efforts, the local controversy intensified, and the city eventually denied permission for the project. It is nevertheless important to emphasize the vital role that church leaders and institutions played in the two cases. In Mannheim, a Catholic priest helped mobilize support among religious leaders for the mosque by forming an interfaith organization to defuse the opposition of local residents – including those in his own church (Wetzel 2001). A comparable, pro-mosque alliance of religious leaders was absent in Stuttgart.

German Muslims are somewhere between their coreligionists in Britain and those in France in winning policy concessions from the state. Resource mobilization theory would therefore expect that Muslims in Germany would have more resources than Muslims in France, but fewer resources than those in Britain. The data, however, do not support this assumption. In these three countries, it is, ironically, French Muslims who are the most formally unified through the Conseil Français du Culte Musulman. British Muslims, on the other hand, seem the least cohesive. Nor does the theory adequately explain Muslims' electoral impact. British Muslims are most likely to influence party politics and gain national political office, which is consistent with resource theory's prediction of their greater policy impact. French Muslims have more electoral strength than do German Muslims, yet the French state is much less likely to accommodate Muslims' religious needs than is the German government.

The point of the comparison is not to suggest that resources have been wholly irrelevant to Muslim efforts to win state accommodation for their political demands in the three states. Instead, we argue there is no one-to-one correspondence between the resources available to Muslims in Britain, France, and Germany and how each state has treated Islam.

Political Opportunity Structures

Political opportunity structure theory provides an alternative explanation for the accommodation of Muslims' religious needs. This theory posits that a state's political institutions – including its legal and political systems, party structure, the media, and interest groups – can all affect how or whether a given state makes room for Muslims' religious practices. Policy outcomes are a function not of resources, according to political opportunity structure theory, but result from how amenable preexisting institutions are to a group's political demands.

While no scholar has specifically used a political opportunity structure theory to explain public accommodation of Muslim religious practices in Germany, some writers have employed this approach to analyze immigration politics. In discussing the political impact of immigrant groups in Germany, for example, Virginie Guiraudon (1998:277) argues that "the structure of political opportunity in Germany makes it difficult for them [immigrants] to participate." Christian Joppke (1999:283) similarly comments on the "pivotal importance of the legal process" in Germany to explain policy outcomes on immigration-related issues.

Germany's political structure does appear amenable to Muslims' political activism. Theoretically, Germany's federal polity provides more opportunities for meaningful political participation and impact by Muslims than does France's more unitary structure. The fact that policy on religious instruction in state schools is a *Land* prerogative might empower Muslim groups to have a dramatic impact at the local level. In both Berlin and North Rhine-Westphalia, Muslims receive religious instruction in the public schools that is nearly equal to that for Christians. Political opportunity structure theory would thus seize on these cases as evidence that Muslims took advantage of the preexisting federal structure and extracted policy concessions at the *Land* level.

A closer analysis of the issue, however, indicates that religious instruction was not something that Muslims secured for themselves by mobilizing at the local level. We found no evidence that the officials responsible for overseeing religious education in North Rhine-Westphalia, for example, felt compelled to offer Islamic religious instruction because of the political pressure brought to bear by the Muslim community. Instead, civil servants were accustomed to working closely with religious leaders to find appropriate textbooks and teachers for the state schools. The "problem" with the Muslim community was that they did not have an organizational structure similar to that of the Catholic and *Evangelische* communities to facilitate such collaborative efforts. In the absence of such a structure, educational officials – instead of the religious community's acknowledged leaders – assumed responsibility for the religious curriculum for Muslim schoolchildren and trained teachers to teach it. Project leader Klaus Gebauer (2001) describes the process:

> On December 11, [1979,] a memorandum from the Ministry [of Education] was sent to the Landesinstitut, asking [us] to develop a curriculum for Islamic religious instruction.... Consulting with the Muslim community in accordance with Article 7, paragraph 3 of the Basic Law ... was not feasible then because there was no organization that could claim to speak for all the Muslims in North Rhine-Westphalia.... So it became clear that if we were not going to let the project fail, we would have to complete it without them [Muslim groups].

Thus, the rationale for including Muslims in the system of religious instruction had nothing to do with the mobilization opportunities that Germany's federal structure offered Muslims. Instead, *Land* policy makers seem to have felt obligated under Germany's Basic Law to make some effort to provide appropriate religious instruction for Muslims as well as Christians (Pfaff 2001).

The potential importance of federalism can also be ascertained in an analysis of local politics. Frankfurt, for example, has a higher proportion of foreign residents than any other city in Germany. The political power of this constituency is at least partly reflected in the handful of Muslims who sit on the Frankfurt city council (Dal 2001; Yüksel 2001). Given the very large foreign population, especially before the 2000 citizenship reforms, the City of Frankfurt also created the Local Foreigners' Representative Board (KAV) in 1991 (Nirumand 2001). This elected body is mandated to "represent the interests of the foreign inhabitants ... and to advise the executive bodies of the community on all matters concerning foreign inhabitants" (KAV 1998:12). By definition, the board is a political structure that enables Muslims without German citizenship to express their political interests. The formation of the KAV, however, follows the pattern for religious instruction: It was not something for which foreigners as a bloc successfully advocated, but was instead created for them on their behalf.

A similar argument applies to granting Muslims public corporation status. One interpretation for how Muslims might gain this privilege would focus on their mobilizing effectively at the local level to take advantage of a federal structure giving *Länder* the power to make this decision. More important than federalism, however, is the existence of public corporation status itself. After all, the Constitution mandates this status for religious groups and outlines the requirements for gaining this right. What seems more plausible is that German-born, university-educated Muslims will become deft at working this preexisting system to their advantage and thereby win public corporation status (von Schroeter 2001). But the larger point is that they will still be operating within the inherited church–state structure.

A political opportunity structure theory is correct to highlight the ways in which existing arrangements frame the political debate and influence a policy outcome. However, on issues related to accommodation of Muslim religious practices, this theory has largely dismissed church–state practices, which we consider the most salient institution of all.

Ideology

A third way to explain state accommodation of Muslim religious practices in Germany is to focus on ideology. According to ideological accounts, preexisting ideas about citizenship, nationality, and the assimilation of foreigners better explain how and why Germany responded to Muslim religious needs than do political resources or state structures. Several analysts have documented, for example, that the guestworker model was built on the idea that Germany was not a country of immigration (Joppke 1998:271; Leggewie 1994; Nielsen 1992:25). Germany's traditional citizenship policy, based as it was on ethnic descent (*jus sanguinis*) rather than place of birth (*jus soli*), not only made it more difficult for foreigners to become German citizens, but reinforced the ideological assumptions of the guestworker regime (Brubaker 1992; Peach and Glebe 1995:42; Stowasser 2002:52–3).

A focus on ideology can also be used to explain how the state initially accommodated Muslim religious practices. For decades, the German government relied on the Turkish government, through DİTİB, to provide for the religious needs of the large Turkish population in Germany. The classes that DİTİB offered, however, focused on Turkish language and culture, which reinforced the idea that the guestworkers were eventually going back "home." The German government, in short, did accommodate some Muslim religious practices in the public schools, for example, but only within the confines of an ideology that insisted that foreigners were not and never would become Germans.

This ideological theory has several limitations, however. First, as we have already noted, Germany has loosened its citizenship policy; nationality is no longer based on ethnic descent, but rather on place of birth. Moreover, few mainstream political leaders continue to insist that Germany is not a country of immigration or claim that public policy should encourage the "return" of its *Gastarbeiter* population (Joppke 1998:287). While ideas about citizenship and guestworkers might have historically driven German policy on how the state would accommodate Muslim religious needs, this ideology no longer does so in the same way.

As with political opportunity structure theory, our claim is not that ideas are, or were, unimportant in explaining German policy. We suggest, instead, that analysts have given insufficient attention to how ideas about church–state practices have influenced the politics of state accommodation of Muslims' religious needs. A key determinant of the policies that have developed in Germany is a legal tradition where the state works with religious communities on various issues. The public corporation status provided in the Basic Law ensures a close working relationship between church and state, as does the constitutional provision mandating religious instruction in public schools. These legal requirements reinforce the ideology that political institutions should look for ways to encourage religious practices. Such a worldview not only sustains state support for Christian religious practices, but also provides a framework for Muslims as they press the state to recognize the legitimacy of their claims. Notions of equity, justice, and equal treatment permeate Muslim claims that the state should provide them the same opportunities for religious expression that it offers Christian believers. It is these ideas about the relationship between church and state, we contend, that drive the politics of state accommodation of Muslim religious practices.

Church–State Institutions

We believe that inherited church–state institutions, as well as the attendant practices and ideology, best explain how Germany has accommodated Muslim religious practices. Theories that highlight political resources, state structures, or ideology are not so much wrong as deficient in failing to consider systematically the importance of church–state relations. In this section, we expand on how these relations have been instrumental in the politics of state recognition of Muslims' religious needs.

Germany's inherited church–state institutions and practices have structured the political agenda for Muslims. That the German state had a long tradition of working closely with the churches on such issues as religious instruction in public schools and the granting of public corporation status to recognized churches – both of which are mandated in the Constitution – helps to explain why those policies have been at the forefront of Muslims' activism. In contrast with Britain, where the dominant issue among Muslims is state funding for private Islamic schools, there is little activism in Germany on that issue. Two Islamic schools in Germany do receive state aid, but the absence of an extensive system of publicly financed Christian schools helps to explain why this topic is not particularly salient for German Muslims.

What is similar in Germany and Britain is that Muslims expect the state to accommodate them in the same manner that the state treats Christian religious groups. The Islamrat's Totakhyl (2001), for example, frames his argument about the absence of Islamic religious instruction in the public schools of many *Länder* by referring both to the Constitution and to the treatment that other religious groups receive:

> Under Article 7 of the Basic Law of the Federal Republic of Germany, the state must provide religious instruction in agreement with the particular religious community. But some states up till now have refused to provide such religious instruction for Muslims, even though they have for the *Evangelische*, Catholics, and Jews.

Totakhyl's comment illustrates how Germany's policy tradition of church–state accommodation on religious instruction in public schools creates an expectation for new religious groups, such as Muslims, that the state should similarly work closely with them to provide appropriate instruction for their children.

Inherited church–state institutions also help elucidate the places where the state has fully, or nearly fully, accommodated Muslims. As we have noted previously, for example, the public schools in North Rhine-Westphalia and Berlin do offer some form of Islamic religion instruction. These *Länder* appear to have done so because the institutional framework obliges educational officials to work with church leaders on the issue. They seem to have concluded that they have a similar obligation to make religious instruction available to Muslim schoolchildren. Again, what is vital is that in Germany, existing church–state institutions make the government and the Christian churches partners in various endeavors, which makes possible a similar collaborative relationship between the state and Muslim groups.

Because they play such a key policy role on various issues, *Evangelische* and Catholic churches have developed organizations that are well positioned to lobby the government on behalf of their interests. The political clout of Christian churches is important for Muslims because the major recognized churches have, by and large, supported policy that would accommodate Muslims. The Evangelische Kirche in Deutschland (1999), for example, has officially endorsed the right to equal treatment of Muslims' religious needs:

> The religious liberty [provisions] of the Basic Law are not limited to Christian/Western religions. The government of the Federal Republic of Germany guarantees the right of religious practice to all citizens of this state – even if they belong to religions rooted in different cultures. . . . Many of the . . . pedagogical and theological reasons for having cooperative but nonetheless confessional Christian religious instruction are also reasons to institute religious instruction for Muslim students in accordance with Article 7, section 3 of the Basic Law.

A possible reason for this support is that the churches understand that the extension of privileges to other religious communities is not only consistent with constitutional principles, but, more importantly, protects from separationist voices the state institutions that actively aid religion. As Catholic priest Martin Wetzel (2001) points out:

> There are movements to do away with government-run religion classes or to take religious instruction out of the [public] schools altogether. I can see how lobbying for Islamic religious instruction would, in the end, help Christians ensure the long-term survival of their own religious instruction. If religious instruction is denied to one group, then religious instruction for all groups is up for grabs.

Whether out of principle or self-interest, Christians are more likely to fight for state accommodation of Muslims' religious practices in Germany, where church and state work together on various issues, than in France, where the institutions are rigidly separated.

Church–state institutions are also important in those instances where Muslims have failed to receive equal treatment from the state. On public corporation status, for example, Muslims have been disadvantaged because their organizational structure is not hierarchical like that of the major Christian churches. The established mechanism for deciding to grant this status, however, assumes such a hierarchy. Observing that Islam has no "Pope or archbishop," von Schroeter (2001) laments, "We don't have just one, two, three applications from Muslim groups [for public corporation status], but a huge stack of them.... Whom do we talk to?" Despite Muslims' current lack of public corporation status, the existence of this church–state institution channels their activism and perhaps will lead to their ultimate success in obtaining official recognition and public acceptance.

Conclusion

Overall, Germany has thus been less accommodating to the religious needs of its Muslim population than has Britain, but has been more generous than France. German policy continues to disadvantage Muslims in some ways. No Muslim group has yet received the public corporation status that would secure various privileges for the community and, even more importantly, demonstrate the state's symbolic acceptance of the Muslim presence in Germany. Moreover, only a few *Länder* provide Muslim schoolchildren with the religious instruction offered to most Christian students, and no *Land* formally works with Muslim leaders on the curriculum as the authorities typically do with Christian officials. In these regards, German policy is less accommodating to Muslims than is British policy.

However, as Germany has recognized that it has a significant Muslim population, that these Muslims are not somehow going to "return" to their country of origin, and that Muslims have religious needs that are habitually not being met, the state is gradually accommodating Muslims' religious practices. The state now funds a few Islamic schools under the same conditions that apply to Christian schools, and some *Länder* have introduced Islamic religious instruction in public schools. In general, the German state is therefore far more accommodating to Muslim needs than is the French state; no German mayor has yet had a mosque bulldozed, and German society is not convulsed over *ḥijāb*-wearing teenagers the way France is.

The data from the German case therefore seem to support our church–state theory more than the other three previous explanations. Key factors often overlooked in explaining Germany's accommodation of Muslims' religious needs are the inherited church–state institutions. These institutions, and the policy traditions that have developed from them, shape the politics of recognition for religious newcomers, who can reasonably argue that the state should accommodate and work with them in the same way that it is formally linked with the churches.

5

Public Attitudes toward State Accommodation of Muslims' Religious Practices

May I suggest that the last thing our society needs at this moment is more schools segregated by religion? Before 11 September, it looked like a bad idea; it now looks like a mad idea.

Tony Wright (2001)

My country, France, my fatherland, is once again being invaded, with the blessing of our successive governments, by an excessive influx of foreigners, notably Muslims, to which we are giving our allegiance. . . . From year to year we see mosques sprout up pretty much everywhere in France, while church bells are becoming silent because of a lack of priests.

French actress and animal-rights advocate
Brigitte Bardot (Agence France Presse 1996)

How family, friends, neighbors, and colleagues react to the announcement "Praise God, I'm a Muslim!" depends on their educational level and kindheartedness, but above all else [also] on their own religiosity.

Murad Wilfried Hofmann (1996:185),
German diplomat and convert to Islam

Introduction

THE PREVIOUS CHAPTERS have analyzed the conditions under which the British, French, and German states have accommodated the religious needs of Muslims. Our focus has been on how the inherited church–state model unique to each country has structured public policy. In this chapter, we turn our attention from political institutions and their impact on policy to an analysis of mass-level public attitudes toward state accommodation of Muslim religious practices.

In functioning democracies such as those studied in this book, elites ignore mass opinion at their electoral peril. The political appeal of such anti-immigrant – or even anti-Muslim – political parties as the British National Party, the French Front National, and the Dutch List Pim Fortuyn appears to have led governing parties to adopt harsher measures toward immigrants, most of whom are Muslims. Rather than be thrown out of office by anti-Muslim voters, mainstream politicians prefer to adopt moderate versions of the anti-immigrant or anti-Muslim platforms advocated by the extreme right (Geddes 2002). Determining the extent of opposition to state accommodation of Muslim religious practices and isolating the causes of such hostility have thus become all the more critical to West European politics.

Many scholars have studied Europeans' attitudes toward immigration policy (e.g., Fetzer 2000; Hoskin 1991). Very few microlevel data on public views of Muslims' religious rights even exist, however, and methodologically sophisticated, crossnational analysis of masslevel attitudes toward Muslims is virtually nonexistent. Following a brief description of overall European attitudes toward state accommodation of Muslim practices, we therefore intend to close this gap in the literature by conducting a mulitivariate analysis of our privately commissioned poll on Muslim rights and of several related surveys.

Descriptive Statistics

To measure public support for state accommodation of Muslims' religious practices, respondents in our three-nation survey (Roper Europe 2001, 2002) were asked policy questions specific to their country. In Britain, participants were surveyed about whether the government should 1) approve funding for more Islamic schools ("expand"), 2) limit its approval to those currently permitted ("status quo"), or 3) cancel its approval ("restrict"). French interviewees indicated whether 1) wearing the *ḥijāb* should always be allowed in state schools ("expand"), 2) should only be allowed during school breaks and other recreational times ("status quo"), or 3) should never be allowed ("restrict"). In Germany, finally, respondents stated that state schools should 1) provide instruction in Islam for every Muslim student who wishes to have it ("expand"), 2) provide such instruction only where

Muslim students make up a large proportion of the school ("status quo"), or 3) never provide such classes ("restrict").

Ideally, we would have used a common question in the three countries to make the responses perfectly comparable. However, as our country chapters have indicated, policy debate on state accommodation of Muslims' religious rights varies in the three nations. The issue at the forefront of debate in Britain, state aid to separate Islamic schools, is not even on the political agenda in France. On the other hand, a very controversial issue in France, students' wearing of the *ḥijāb* in public schools, has been settled in Britain and Germany with little fanfare. It is also important to note that the status quo position in the three countries is not equal. Arguably, Germany, where some *Länder* provide public instruction in Islam, has gone farther to recognize and accommodate Muslim religious practices than has France, where many state schools do not allow Muslim students to wear the *ḥijāb* in class.

As Figure 5.1 indicates, there are significant differences in public attitudes toward state accommodation of Muslim religious practices in the three countries. French respondents are far less likely to support an expansive policy (17 percent) than are their British (32 percent) or German counterparts (62 percent). It is also interesting to note that in none of the countries did a majority of the respondents support the policy status quo, which further indicates that issues surrounding Muslims' religious rights are both unsettled and contentious in each of the countries.

Three other relevant polls generally mirror our results. A November 2001 Market and Opinion Research International (MORI) poll on "Public Perceptions of Faith Schools" in Britain contained two questions on popular attitudes toward religious schools (MORI 2001a). Almost half (46 percent) of those surveyed indicated support for publicly funded religious schools in general, while 25 percent were opposed. When specifically asked about the government's recent policy that expanded funding to Muslim, Sikh, and Greek Orthodox schools, however, respondents became less enthusiastic (25 percent supportive, 43 percent opposed). The 1995 SOFRES (Société française d'études statistiques) French National Election Study likewise included an item on whether it was "normal" for "Muslims living in France" to have "mosques to practice their religion" (Boy and Mayer 1997:Annexe 4). Nearly half (43 percent) of the respondents disagreed with this statement. Finally, the 1996 German Social Survey (ALLBUS 1996) asked respondents their views about including Islam in religion classes in the state schools. A plurality (40.3 percent) of western German interviewees believed that such instruction should be provided, 33.3 percent held that only Christianity should be taught, and 26.5 percent maintained that religion classes should be abolished altogether.

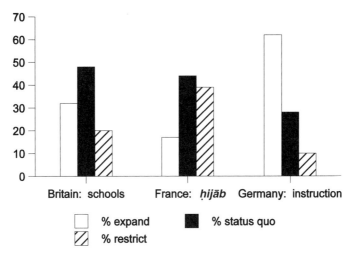

Figure 5.1. Public support for Islam in the schools in Britain, France, and Germany. *Source:* Roper Europe (2001).

Explanations of Opposition to the Political Accommodation of Muslim Religious Practices

No one theory specifically attempts to explain public attitudes toward state accommodation of Muslim religious practices. However, a number of more general theories of political behavior can be applied to our inquiry.

Status as Religious Majority/Minority

One theory that seems particularly relevant to our study is that developed by Seymour Martin Lipset and Stein Rokkan (1967). Lipset and Rokkan proposed that religious cleavages were the basis for party division in modern Europe. Historically, the majority religion, often with the support of the state, subjected minority religions to various types of social and political discrimination. Minority groups responded by forming movements of religious defense, thereby bringing religious cleavages to the center of partisanship and political debate. In the early twentieth century, a freezing of the party system occurred that extended the early impact of religion into the contemporary political era.

As noted in the previous chapters, there are various ways in which state policy in Britain, France, and Germany advantages some churches and disadvantages Muslims and some other religious minorities. It is possible that mass public attitudes toward state accommodation of Muslim religious practices reflect those policy choices. If this theory is correct, a person's religious identification should determine her or his attitude toward the political question of whether the state should accommodate Muslim religious practices. Religious minorities would favor an extension of state benefits to include Muslims, while members of the religious majority would oppose any further accommodation of Muslims' religious practices. The theory would also predict that respondents who identify with the mainstream political party most closely affiliated with the religious majority would likewise be more opposed to accommodation.

Duncan Macpherson (1997:110) has similarly hypothesized about a mobilization among religious minorities in Britain. He suggests that the situation in which British Muslims found themselves at the end of the twentieth century is in many ways analogous to the social and political position of Roman Catholics in the last three-quarters of the nineteenth century. Given that they share "analogous experiences of exclusion and discrimination, of popular hostility and of intellectual disdain," it is quite possible that Muslims and Roman Catholics in Britain would join forces for political purposes.

As Table 5.1 indicates, the religious majorities in the three countries are Church of England in Britain, Roman Catholic in France, and Lutheran

Table 5.1. Religious Identification in Britain, France, and Germany (in Percentages)

	Britain	France	Germany
Church of England	51.9		
Catholic	10.8	66.5	32.6
Lutheran or Reformed Protestant	2.2	1.9	39.8
Evangelical, Born-Again, or Free-Church Protestant	2.5		0.2
Methodist	3.1		
Baptist	1.3		
Muslim	2.3	3.5	0.8
Jewish	1.0	0.6	
Hindu	1.2		
Buddhist		0.2	
Other	4.7	1.4	1.5
No religion	19.0	26.1	25.1
n	872	976	959

NOTE: Data weighted by demographic characteristics. Smaller religious groups (such as Muslims and Jews in Germany) may have been underrepresented in this sample.

Source: Roper Europe (2001).

or Reformed Protestant *(Evangelische)* in Germany. Prominent religious minorities, on the other hand, include Jews, Hindus, Muslims, Buddhists, Baptists, Methodists, British and German Catholics, French Protestants, and British evangelical or German "free-church" Protestants.

Comparison of these 2001 Roper data on the percentage of Muslims with parallel statistics in Chapters 2 to 4 suggests that Roper significantly under-sampled Muslims and/or that Muslim respondents denied their religious identity. It might have been more difficult to reach potential Muslim interviewees by telephone, and even before the current "War on Terrorism," Europeans hardly increased their popularity by embracing Islam.

As Table 5.2 suggests, public opinion data do not generally support this religious-majority/minority theory. With the obvious exception of Muslims, religious minorities did not usually support the expansion of Islam in the schools. Conversely, our results do not confirm the hypothesis that the religious majority is significantly more hostile to such expansion.

The German sample in Table 5.3 echoes our results in Table 5.2; religious minorities showed no more support for Islamic instruction in state schools than did the majority.[1] In France, by contrast, Jews (b = 1.784, p < .10) and members of "other religions" (b = 1.373, p < .05) did support Muslims' right to build mosques.

Perhaps this slight difference in results between Tables 5.2 and 5.3 stems from the different policies proposed. State funding for Islamic schools, Islamic instruction in state schools, or even sanctioning of the wearing of the *ḥijāb* in public schools may all be plausibly viewed as state support for religion. Permission to build a mosque, on the other hand, does not imply state sponsorship of Islam. Religious minorities may be more likely to exhibit solidarity with one another on questions of religious liberty than on policies requiring explicit state encouragement.

Unfortunately, none of the Roper surveys contains an item on partisanship. In only one of the remaining three polls, however, did preference for the "religious-majority" party appear to increase opposition to Islam. While the variable for this partisanship (as opposed to that for the dominant opposition party) had no statistically significant effect in the British MORI and German ALLBUS samples (the full regression table is not shown), identifying with the Gaullist RPR (Rassemblement Pour la

---

[1] Although the independent variable "other religion" is statistically significant and strongly pro-expansion (b = 2.072), this classification likely includes a majority of Muslims. Unfortunately, the 1996 ALLBUS survey grouped all non-Christian religions into a single category.

Table 5.2. Determinants of Support for Islam in the Schools in Britain, France, and Germany

	Britain	France	Germany
Catholic	.229		.104
Lutheran or Reformed Protestant		.058	
Evangelical, Born-Again, or Free-Church Protestant	.865*		−.537
Baptist, Methodist, or Other Protestant	−.094		
Muslim	2.537*	.833**	.107
Hindu, Jewish, Buddhist, or Other Religion	−.242	−.202	−.397
No religion	−.047	.126	−.030
Low support for church–state structure	−.771**	−.134	.151
Medium support for church–state structure	−.459*	−.871	.150
Female	.393	.168	.204
Class			
A (upper middle)	−.176	−.529*	.476
B (middle)	.044	−.414	−.130
C1 (lower middle)	−.074	−.297	.192
C2 (skilled working)	−.341	−.124	.737
D (working)			
Income		.048	.065
Bac/Abitur		.120	.429**
Higher university degree		.386*	.039
Age	.017**	.023**	.027**
Children	−.071	−.067	−.317
Constant, restrict Islam in schools	−2.591**	−1.737**	−2.929**
Constant, maintain status quo of Islam in schools	−.254	.440	−1.105
n	695	811	738
Pseudo R^2	.111	.065	.086
χ^2	70.612**	47.097**	54.720**
df.	16	16	17

NOTE: Estimates are ordered logit coefficients. Data weighted by demographic characteristics.

* = p < .10. ** = p < .05.

Source: Roper Europe (2001).

Table 5.3. Determinants of Support for Muslim Religious Practices in
Britain, France, and Germany

	Britain	*France*	*Germany*
Catholic			
Active		.484**	.066
Nominal			.192
Protestant		.089	
Active			−.342
Free-Church Protestant			−.545
Other Christian			−.590
Muslim	1.388**	6.225	
Jewish		1.784*	
Other religion		1.373**	2.072**
No religion		.252**	.463**
Female	.199**	−.123*	.441**
Professional/managerial	.276*	.215	.420**
Manual laborer	−.100	−.166	.140
Nonpaid worker	.157	.003	.067
Income		.068**	.038
A-Level/*Bac*/*Abitur*	.107	.730**	.354
Higher university degree	−.058	.851**	−.104
Age	−.011**	.011**	−.021**
Constant		−.963**	.103
Constant, strongly oppose	−1.159**		
Constant, tend to oppose	−.529**		
Constant, neither	.757**		
Constant, tend to support	2.739**		
n	1607	3617	1305
Pseudo R^2	.024	.123	.122
χ^2	37.5**	346.5**	125.1**
df.	8	14	15

NOTE: Estimates are ordered (Britain) or dichotomous (France and Germany) logit
coefficients. British and French data are weighted by demographic characteristics.

* = p < .10. ** = p < .05.

Source: For Britain, MORI 2001a; for France, SOFRES 1995; for Germany, ALLBUS 1996.

République) party does seem to have boosted French respondents' opposition to mosques (b = −.344, p < .01). Overall, then, centrist partisanship
does not appear to have much impact on mass attitudes toward Muslims'
religious practices.

Solidarity of the Religious

Several other theories examine the effects of secularization on political behavior. Theories of culture wars (Hunter 1991), value conflict (Leege and

Kellstedt 1993), and culture shift (Inglehart 1990) similarly claim that secularization undermines the political role of religion and poses a threat to religious groups who advocate religiously based public policy. The electoral impact has been a shift from political cleavages based on class to those based on lifestyle concerns. The result, particularly in the United States, has been political conflict around such cultural issues as abortion, gay rights, and the place of religion in public schools. The religious and political divide is not, however, between majority and minority faiths but rather between orthodox religionists of various traditions, who are culturally conservative, and secularists or religious liberals, who are culturally liberal (Wuthnow 1988).

Given that large percentages of the population in each of the three countries in our survey claim to have no religion (19 percent in England, 26 percent in France, and 25 percent in Germany), secularism has clearly had an impact on the region. Religiously orthodox elites are becoming increasingly aware that secularism threatens their social and political identities. Tariq Modood, a British Muslim, notes that "the real division of opinion is not between a conservative element in the Church of England versus the rest of the country, but between those who think religion has a place in secular public culture and those who think not" (1994:72). Similarly, Leslie Newbigin, a British Christian, asserts "in our present situation in Britain where Christians and Muslims share a common position as minority faiths in a society dominated by the naturalistic ideology, we share a common duty to challenge this ideology" (Newbigin et al. 1998:22).

If these theories are correct, the data should show a political coalition of secularists on the one hand, and orthodox religionists on the other. Arguing that religion should be purely private, secularists should oppose the state accommodating Muslim religious practices. Religionists, on the other hand, ought to support Muslims out of a common conviction that the state should make room for the public expression of religious values.

The results for secularists ("no religion") in Tables 5.2 and 5.3 fail to support this theory, however. Nowhere were secularists more likely than the majority religious group to oppose state accommodation of Muslims' religious practices. In none of the three countries in our survey did the "no religion" variable achieve statistical significance (see Table 5.2). In Table 5.3, moreover, being a secularist appears to have *increased* support for Muslims' practices (b = .252, p < .05 for France; b = .463, p < .05 for Germany).

Data from practicing or orthodox religionists, on the other hand, provide mixed support for this theory. In Britain, born-again Protestants, who are very likely to be religiously orthodox, did disproportionately agree with the expansion of faith-based schools to include Muslims (b = .865, p < .10; see Table 5.2). Practicing Catholics in France likewise defended Muslims' right to build mosques (b = .484, p < .05; see Table 5.3). In Germany, by contrast, Catholics or *Evangelische* Protestants who regularly attend religious services, and Free-Church Protestants, who are likely orthodox, all failed to produce statistically significant results.

The data, in short, do tend to confirm the view that orthodox religionists have joined forces. It is too early to tell if this centripetal tendency represents the beginnings of the kind of political coalition of religious defense that Europe has seen in the past (Gould 1999; Kalyvas 1996). Secularists, however, do not appear to be joining forces against Islam. Perhaps they do not view orthodox religion as enough of a political threat against which to mobilize.

Gender

Gender is another factor that might help to explain public attitudes toward state accommodation of Muslim religious practices in Western Europe. From the standpoint of some feminists, the Islamic faith oppresses women in various ways. They claim that certain passages from the *qur'ān* teach the inferiority of women; that Islamic laws of inheritance, marriage, and divorce favor males over females; that practices in some Muslim countries oppress women; and that patriarchal pressures and assumptions force Islamic women in Western countries into traditional gender roles. While French feminist Elizabeth Altschull, for example, believes that "all religions have their oppressive aspects toward women," she nevertheless concludes that "none [but Islam] has gone so far, is as systematic, or is as explicit about the inferior status of women, [a status] willed and created by God" (1995:200). German scholar Ursula Spuler-Stegemann likewise labels the *shī'ah* practice of "temporary marriage" *(mut'ah)* as "religiously legitimated prostitution" (1998:193–4). Sallah Eddine Ben Abid acknowledges that there has indeed been a revival in the practice of such marriages "in certain Muslim communities which have immigrated into Europe" (2000:13; see also Heine 1997:204–5). What is beyond dispute is that the role of women in Islam is a highly contested issue in Western Europe.

According to gender theory, public accommodation of Islam reinforces sexist models about the proper role of women. To the extent that Islam oppresses women, they would claim, the state should not actively promote this faith by encouraging separate Islamic schools (Britain), allowing Muslim girls to wear the *ḥijāb* (France), or teaching about the faith in state schools (Germany). If this theory holds, women – especially educated ones – should disproportionately oppose these policies.

The data do not generally support this theory. No female variable in Table 5.2 achieves statistical significance, and in the British MORI and German ALLBUS samples (see Table 5.3), women are significantly *more* supportive of Islamic schools or instruction (b = .199, p < .05 for Britain; b = .441, p < .05 for Germany). The only result confirming gender theory is that for women in the French National Election Study, who are more likely to oppose mosque building (b = −.123, p <.10).

All possible interaction terms between education and gender, moreover, failed to achieve statistical significance in a parallel set of regression equations for our Roper surveys and for the 1996 German ALLBUS survey; these French and German data (the English poll contained no education measure) suggest that even being a highly educated women did not increase one's opposition to accommodation. In the British MORI survey, being a highly educated female *increases* support for accommodation (b = .483, p < .10 for the interaction term between female and A-level education; b = .603, p < .05 for female and postgraduate degree). Only in the French National Election Study did being a *bac*-holding woman make one more likely to oppose state efforts to accommodate Muslims (b = −.371, p < .05). In this parallel French regression, however, neither the variable simply for being female nor the interaction term with having a postgraduate degree achieved statistical significance.

What explains the fact that women usually are no more likely than men to oppose state accommodation of Muslims' religious practices? One set of explanations comes from some practicing Muslim women, who argue that the *qur'ān* preaches the spiritual equality of women and men and that Islam is no more inherently patriarchal than other religious traditions. In a study of Islamic women in the West, Anne Sofie Roald notes that "as in Christianity, where interpretations of biblical verses pertaining to women have been undergoing a process of change recently, in Islam a similar movement seems to be in progress" (2001:296).

Similarly, many Muslim women argue that the wearing of the *ḥijāb* is a symbol of cultural identity, not a sign of women's oppression at the hands of men. While noting that "the early feminist lifting of the face-veil was about emancipation from exclusion," Fadwa El Guindi asserts that "the voluntary wearing of the *ḥijāb* since the mid-1970s is about liberation from imposed, imported identities, consumerist behaviors, and resisting . . . Western dominance" (1999:184; see also Akkent and Franger 1987). That women in these three countries do not generally oppose state accommodation of Islam might suggest that they are just as likely to accept the claims of many Muslim women as they are to believe non-Muslim feminists about the effects of those policies on gender rights.

Social-Class Theory

An alternative theory focuses on social class. Scholars of immigration politics have demonstrated that members of the lower- and lower-middle classes disproportionately oppose immigration and immigrant rights (Fetzer 2000:116–17; Simon and Alexander 1993:39–40), perhaps out of fear of economic competition with working-class immigrants. Because large percentages of migrants to Western Europe are Muslim, lower- and lower-middle-class respondents might plausibly oppose the accommodation of Muslim religious practices. Making life too comfortable for Muslim immigrants, such interviewees might argue, would encourage even greater numbers of Muslims to settle in Europe and compete economically with natives.

The data that we analyze produce conflicting results. Among respondents in our survey (see Table 5.2), only professionals or managers from France produced a statistically significant estimate. This estimated effect, however, is in the direction opposite that predicted by social-class theory (b = −.529, p < .10). Rather than disproportionately supporting state accommodation of Islam, French professionals were more likely to oppose this policy. No occupation variable in the French National Election Study achieved statistical significance (see Table 5.3). In the British MORI and German ALLBUS polls, in contrast, professionals and managers were more supportive of Islamic instruction (b = .276, p < .10 for Britain; b = .420, p < .05 for Germany), thus tending to confirm social-class theory.

These results for attitudes toward state accommodation of Muslim religious practices diverge slightly from the findings of some studies of public opinion on immigration policy, which seem more likely to find class effects. It is possible that lower- or lower-middle-class respondents want to restrict immigration but do not necessarily make the connection between stopping further migration and making it more difficult for immigrants already in Europe to practice their religion. If so, this view is consistent with the policies of many states in the region, which are simultaneously acknowledging Muslims' religious rights but also drastically increasing the barriers to immigration by asylum seekers or economic migrants (Lyall 2002).

Education

A number of studies have suggested that education has a liberalizing effect on political opinions (Alwin, Cohen, and Newcomb 1992; Erickson, Luttbeg, and Tedin 1991:154–9; Jennings and Niemi 1981). Arguably, the liberal political position is for the state to accommodate Muslims' religious practices. Some scholars have advocated multicultural education in West European countries on the ground that learning about other faiths would make people more tolerant and understanding of religious diversity (Nielsen 1999; Parekh 2000). If this theory holds, those with more education should be more likely to support Muslims' religious rights.

In almost all polls for which we have education data, our analysis confirms this explanation. In the French and German samples of our survey (see Table 5.2), respondents with higher levels of education demonstrate greater support for allowing Muslim practices in the schools. In Table 5.3, French holders of both the *baccalauréat* (b = .730, p < .05) and such advanced university degrees as the *maîtrise* (b = .851, p < .05) were substantially more sympathetic to Muslims' religious needs. In the ALLBUS, the effect of passing the German *Abitur* just misses reaching traditional levels of statistical significance (p – .108). Only in the British MORI poll did education fail to produce any effect at all.

Views on Church–State Arrangements

The next theory looks at the relationship between mass attitudes toward the church–state arrangements in a particular country (that is, an established church in Britain, *laïcité* in France, and a multiple religious establishment in Germany) and popular support for the state accommodating Muslims' religious practices. We hypothesize that these different institutional church–state models socialize individuals to expect the state to accommodate religious groups in particular ways. Those citizens who favor the existing models in Britain and Germany may value state recognition of religion and may therefore be more likely to see the benefits of extending that system to include Muslims. The French, by contrast, might oppose the wearing of the *ḥijāb* in public schools because of a strong preference for institutional *laïcité* and a strict separation of religion and public life.

To measure public support for existing church–state arrangements, respondents in the three countries in our survey were asked about the institutional model unique to each country. In Britain, the questionnaire asked about the Church of England's gradual accommodation of religious groups in areas such as education and membership in the House of Lords. French respondents indicated their level of support for the strict separation of religion and state *(laïcité)*. In Germany, finally, interviewees voiced their agreement or disagreement with the system by which the state collects funds for churches that are publicly recognized *(Kirchensteuer)*.

At least in France and Germany, however, the data provide no support for the mass-level version of our church–state structure theory. French dévotés of *laïcité* were no more likely to oppose the wearing of the *ḥijāb* than were those who rejected French separatism. German respondents likewise showed no propensity to link support for *Kirchensteuer* to sympathy for Islamic instruction in public schools. In Britain, on the other hand, opposing the Church of England's policy on nonestablished religious groups does appear to have increased hostility to the expansion of Islamic schools (b = −.771, p < .05).

The September 11 Attacks

The final theory is that the September 2001 terrorist attacks in New York and Washington affected Europeans' attitudes toward state accommodation of Muslims' religious practices. In the aftermath of the attacks, West European governments became aware that many of the terrorists had lived in Europe, and that other radical Islamists were still in their midst (Waldman 2002). In response, England, France, and Germany passed laws to crack down on domestic terrorists and further to restrict immigration and political asylum (Daley 2001).

In addition, the European Monitoring Center on Racism and Xenophobia reported that Muslims across Western Europe had suffered increased hostility and physical attacks since September 11 (Watson 2002). In Britain alone, more than three hundred assaults on Muslims were reported after the terrorist attacks (*Guardian* 2002). Finally, a British public opinion poll taken shortly after September 11 found that 26 percent of the population felt that Islam was a threat to Western values (Travis 2001).

If this theory is correct, public support for state accommodation of Muslims' religious practices in the schools should have decreased. Perhaps British MORI respondents' relatively high opposition to the government's funding of Islamic schools (43 percent) resulted from the survey being conducted a mere two months after the attacks. To test this explanation, we had the identical policy questions from our July 2001 survey (Roper Europe 2001) added to a poll conducted in April 2002 (Roper 2002).

The data reported in Table 5.4 partially confirm this theory. In Britain, support for abolishing state funding of Islamic schools increased from 19.9 percent to 25.6 percent, a statistically significant change. In Germany, support for always providing Islamic instruction fell from 61.6 percent to 55.8 percent, which is also statistically significant. The percentage of French respondents who advocated banning the *ḥijāb* in public schools also rose

Table 5.4. Support for Islam in the Schools before and after September 11

	Britain		France		Germany	
	Pre-	Post-	Pre-	Post-	Pre-	Post-
Expand (%)	31.8	28.0	16.7	14.4	61.6	55.8*
Status quo (%)	48.4	46.4	44.5	44.4	27.9	32.4*
Restrict (%)	19.9	25.6*	38.8	41.2	10.5	11.8
n	756	777	951	1014	950	928
Muslim (%)	2.3	0.8*	3.5	3.0	0.8	0.2
n	872	896	976	1031	959	956

NOTE: Data weighted by demographic characteristics. * = statistical test for independence of pre- and postwaves significant at the .05 level (see Wonnacott and Wonnacott 1985:242).

Source: Roper Europe (2001, 2002).

from 38.8 percent to 41.2 percent, though this difference fails traditional tests of statistical significance.

It is also intriguing that the percentage of respondents who identified themselves as Muslims fell in all three countries. Only in Britain was this difference statistically significant, however. Given the increase in anti-Muslim hate crimes and the intense public attention paid to Islamist radicals in the West, this apparent reluctance to acknowledge being Muslim is not surprising.

Discussion

According to our analysis, the variables that best explain Europeans' support for the public accommodation of Muslim religious practices are education and religious practice. On the other hand, the data in this chapter do not generally support explanations based on social class, gender, and status as a religious minority. Exposure to a liberal arts–style education (for example, in the German *Gymnasium* or French *lycée*) seems to increase support for public accommodation of Muslim religious practices. Students who have reached this educational level have likely learned about cultures other than that dominant in a particular country. Perhaps those who favor pro-accommodation policies, as we do, therefore ought to advocate multicultural education throughout the curriculum.

Our analysis also confirms that religiously active respondents do show solidarity with practicing Muslims. As Modood and others have argued, religionists perceive secularism as a common threat to their values. On the other hand, the data in this chapter do not support the second half of the solidarity-of-the-religious theory; secularists tend disproportionately to *support* state accommodation of Muslim religious practices. Our findings parallel those by Gordon W. Allport (1979:449–53) on the curvilinear relationship between religiosity and racial or religious prejudice. In a predominantly post-Christian Western Europe, secularists may not feel threatened by a few orthodox religionists. Despite the apparent philosophical similarities between practicing Muslims and Christians, Muslims might be better served to join political forces with the large number of pro-multicultural secularists than with the small band of orthodox Christians.

The events of September 11, 2001, have affected popular attitudes toward European Muslims. In all three countries in our before-and-after surveys, respondents were less likely after September 11 to support the accommodation of Islam in state-run schools. In France, however, this decline in support did not achieve statistical significance. Nonetheless, interviewees even in Britain and Germany did not become markedly anti-Islamic, only changing their propensity to oppose accommodation by a few percentage points. Moreover, respondents in Britain and Germany seem far more tolerant toward Islam than reports in the popular press might suggest. Even with the knowledge that some of the 9/11 terrorists lived in Germany and Britain, German respondents remain overwhelmingly supportive of Islamic instruction in state schools, while most British interviewees continue to endorse state funding of Islamic schools. At least in Germany and Britain, politicians might thus consider policies that recognize the genuine religious pluralism in the region without having to worry about widespread public hostility to such programs.

Finally, our data do not seem to confirm a micro version of our church–state theory. At a popular level, the church–state structures that are so important for shaping elite attitudes and public policy in these three countries do not appear to determine individuals' views on state accommodation of Muslim religious practices. Perhaps as Philip E. Converse (1964) might suggest, the Islam-related attitudes of European elites – who are more likely to strive for ideological consistency – are much more constrained by their country's particular church–state arrangement than are the views of ordinary citizens.

6

Integration and Muslim Practice

Those who believe, and suffer exile and strive with might and main, in the cause of Allah, with their goods and their persons, have the highest rank in the sight of Allah: they are the people who will achieve [salvation].

qur'ān 9:20

It is ridiculous for any person to profess himself to be a Mahometan only in his religion, but in everything else a faithful subject to a Christian magistrate, whilst at the same time he acknowledges himself bound to yield blind obedience to the Mufti of Constantinople, who himself is entirely obedient to the Ottoman Emperor and frames the feigned oracles of that religion according to his pleasure.

John Locke (1990 [1689]), *A Letter Concerning Toleration*

The same questions which were put to the Jews for decades, if not centuries, have arisen among Muslims as to the authenticity of their belonging. Are they members of the *umma* whose order they are completely bound by or rather true citizens of the state in which they live, bound, as all other citizens, by its constitutions and laws? What are they first: Muslim or British, French, German, or Spanish? In such a situation, the point is plain: are the so-called European-Muslims trustworthy?

Muslim theologian Tariq Ramadan (1999b:162)

Determinants of State Accommodation for Muslims

OUR COUNTRY COMPARISONS suggest that states follow no single model in accommodating Muslims' religious practices, but that church–state

Table 6.1. Summary of Theoretical Findings

	Accommodation	Resources	Structures	Ideology	Church–state
Britain	High	Low	High	High	High
France	Low	High	Low	Low	Low
Germany	Medium	Medium	High	Low	Medium

Notes:

"Accommodation" = dependent variable, or degree of state accommodation of Muslims' religious practices.

"Resources" = first independent variable, or amount of effective political resources for Muslims' mobilization.

"Structures" = second independent variable, or degree to which the political-opportunity structure facilitates the mobilization of religious groups.

"Ideology" = third independent variable, or degree to which the dominant political ideology encourages accommodation of religious minorities' practices.

"Church–state" = fourth independent variable, or level of support that inherited church-state institutions provide to the practices of religious newcomers.

institutions in each nation significantly structure the political debate. Britain's established church, France's *laïcité*, and Germany's multiple religious establishment shape the politics of religious accommodation in various ways. In each country, Muslims inherited a web of church–state interactions based on constitutional principles, legal practice, historical precedent, and foundational conceptions of the appropriate relationship between church and state. This combination of factors eventually determined how each state accommodated Muslims on the issues of religion in public schools, state aid to private Islamic schools, and, in part, mosque building.

Table 6.1 sets out the empirical findings from the country chapters (Chapters 2–4) for each of the four major explanations for state accommodation of Muslims' religious practices. The first column of this table, labeled "Accommodation," indicates the relative level of state accommodation of Muslims' religious practices in each of the three countries. Overall, Britain is more accommodating than Germany, which in turn is more accommodating than France. We are not, of course, suggesting that British Muslims are fully accommodated in Britain, merely that they enjoy more opportunities fully to practice their religion than do their coreligionists in Germany and especially France.

Of the four explanations of state accommodation, resource mobilization performed the worst. Evidence from our country chapters provides little support for the theory that states accommodated Muslims in response to their political resources. Muslims appeared comparably mobilized in all three countries. Where Muslims were most organizationally unified (France), moreover, the state was least responsive to their demands. Conversely, where they were the least effectively unified (Britain), the government was the most willing to accommodate them.

An alternative organizational hypothesis would suggest that the level of Muslim mobilization is a function, rather than a cause, of how much opposition Muslims face from the state. Muslims in France, on this reading, are more organized precisely because they face the most intense opposition from the state. Given the state's relatively poor treatment of its Muslim population, French Muslims have a stronger incentive to commit time and resources to political mobilization than their coreligionists in Britain and Germany, where the political environment is more supportive of Muslim demands. It is possible, therefore, that the greater need for collective political action explains the more effective formation of interest groups among French Muslims.

There are at least two limitations with this particular reading of a resource based theory. First, while the state has treated Muslims better in Britain and Germany than in France, this hardly means that they have no legitimate grievances with state policy that would warrant their mobilization. It took decades for British Muslims to gain state aid for their schools, their schools that are funded are still few, and Muslims have failed to win statutory protection against religious discrimination. In Germany, it remains an open question when, or if, *Länder* will grant public corporation status to Muslim organizations. British and German Muslims, in short, have plenty of incentive for political mobilization, but they have failed to mobilize systematically.

A second and related problem with this alternative resource theory is that it presumes that a group's grievances are a sufficient condition for political mobilization, and that such groups will be better mobilized than those with fewer complaints with state policy. However, political scientists have long noted that groups do not form automatically on the basis of their grievances with the state; incentives for mobilization, even if they are strong ones, are not a sufficient condition for group formation (Berry 1997). Nor is the political effectiveness of a group a function of its size or its "objective" complaints with state policy. In Britain, for example, the small Jewish community has a relatively strong political influence through the Board of Deputies of British Jews, while the much larger Muslim community, whose grievances with state policy are as great or greater than their Jewish colleagues, are not well organized at all.

The data we collected do provide more support for the political opportunity structure theory. Germany's federal polity does appear to have allowed local Muslims to have a greater impact on public policy than French Muslims have been able to achieve in their country's more unitary structure. While Britain is technically not a federal system, local educational authorities have significant control over the issues about which Muslims care deeply. This local autonomy also seems to have given British Muslims a more effective political voice.

Ideological theories also found some confirmation in our data. British pragmatism appears to have allowed the state greater room to change public policy to Muslims' benefit. Also consistent with this theory, French republicanism limits the state's ability to accommodate the needs of specific ethnic or religious groups. Germany's pre-2000 "not-a-country-of-immigration" ideology, finally, would be hostile to efforts to accommodate non-ethnic German Muslims fully. However, this ideology seems not to have particularly impeded German officials' pre-2000 practice of making room for Muslims' religious needs.

The weakness of political opportunity structure and ideology theories, we argue, is that they fail systematically to consider the church–state aspects of their frameworks. Such church–state institutions as public corporation status in Germany and House of Lords' seats reserved for Anglican leaders impact policy on Muslims just as much as federalism does. The ideology of French *laïcité* likewise influences Islam-related policy even more directly than does ideological republicanism. Ideology and political opportunity structures are therefore important, but often in ways not considered by theorists using these models.

The four major explanations in Table 6.1 focus primarily on *elite* behavior and public policy. Chapter 5, however, examines mass-level attitudes toward similar issues. This chapter suggests that Europeans' support for the accommodation of Muslims' religious practices primarily stems from their level of education and degree of religious involvement. The events of September 11, 2001, also appear to have made many Europeans slightly less willing to support the accommodation of Muslims in state-run schools.

The Politics of Accommodation and Integration

The question of state accommodation of Muslims' religious practices has led to considerable, ongoing controversy about how best to ensure the successful incorporation of Muslims into the values of a liberal democracy

(Kymlicka 1995; see also König 2000). Debate over the compatibility of Islam and liberal democracy was heightened by the announcement of the 1998 *fatwa* "Jihad against Jews and Crusaders" in London; the realization that some of the Islamist terrorists involved in the attacks of September 11, 2001, had lived and trained in Europe; and the subsequent arrest of al Qaeda operatives in Britain, France, and Germany (Benjamin and Simon 2003; Erlanger and Hedges 2001). More generally, a number of people have raised questions about how far a liberal state can go to accommodate group identities in public policy (Ackerman 1980; Macedo 1990; McDonough and Feinberg 2003). The basic tension that these theorists highlight is between a liberal state's commitment to the protection of religious rights for their citizens, on the one hand, with the need to promote liberal values (individual autonomy, choice, tolerance) as a way of integrating individuals and groups into democratic society, on the other. There are several points that we think are important for states to consider as they pursue these twin goals as they relate to Muslims.

First, the Muslim experience in Western Europe suggests that their integration to the values of the West will not follow the logic of assimilation as many have understood it. The unstated claim of some is that Muslim integration means their adoption of the religious – or even secular – values of the West. As Ramadan notes, this implies that Muslims should "be *Muslim without Islam*, for there exists a widespread suspicion that to be too much a Muslim means not to be really and completely integrated into the Western way of life and its values" (1999b:184–5). Far from abandoning their Islamic faith, however, many second- and third-generation Muslims in Europe are embracing it, even as they attain economic and educational mobility. Few of these practicing Muslims are interested in a privatized faith as it is experienced by most West Europeans and sometimes advanced as a model for Muslims (Lewis 1993:174–86; Roy 1999:89–103). Instead, the emergent Islam that many second- and third-generation Muslims are constructing in Europe and that will shape their lives will vary from the purely privatized faith of the West, on the one hand, and the sometimes culturally determined and theologically narrow brand of Islam of some first-generation believers (see Lamchichi 1999:78–9). The laudable and realizable aim, as Ramadan urges, is for Muslims in the West to "find partners who will, like them, be determined to select in what Western culture produces in order to promote its positive contributions and to resist its destructive deviations both on the human and environmental level" (1999b:149).

Second, we do recognize that there are legitimate questions about how far states should go to recognize the rights of religious groups to practice their faith. Ayelet Shachar argues that a negative consequence of state policies that accommodate group rights – including religious rights and practices – is that they can unwittingly "leave members of minority groups vulnerable to severe injustice within the group and may ... reinforce some of the most hierarchical elements of a culture" (2001:3). Bassam Tibi like-wise warns that "tolerance ... does not mean surrender. ... We must protect tolerance. But after September 11, 2001, we must no longer allow it to be exploited by Islamists and their supporters" (2002:226, 229; see also Foblets 1999). A very small number of European Muslims do threaten the state by supporting or encouraging the use of terrorism and violence. Few would object to such extremists being arrested or having their religious liberty rights curtailed. Other religious/cultural practices, such as female genital mutilation and the *Shī'ah* practice of "temporary marriage" *(mut'ah)*, are so contrary to human rights that the claims of religious freedom must yield to the welfare of the broader society. These are, however, extremely isolated cases, and they are relatively easy to resolve.

Third, the more difficult cases are when Muslims, or any other group, wish to promote a style of life or a set of values and practices that is inconsistent – or apparently inconsistent – with the dominant values of the broader liberal society. This is particularly true with the issue of state funding for religious schools. What should be done, in short, when ap-parently illiberal groups seek recognition by the liberal state? Is the state bound to support separate Muslim schools if the educational practices of those schools are somehow inconsistent with those of the dominant culture?

In responding to this question, it is important to be very clear about what are essential liberal values that the state absolutely must promote, and which are cases where the state can comfortably tolerate a certain degree of values diversity. For example, there is some debate in Britain now on public funding for private Christian fundamentalist schools sponsored by the Vardy Foundation on the ground that those schools promote – or in the words of some critics, "indoctrinate" – students with biblical creationism. Many Muslims similarly reject Darwinian evolution on the ground that Allah is the sole creator and master of the universe (Keller 1999). Ironically, this criticism of fundamentalist schools has come despite the fact that those schools consistently outperform their state-run counterparts in test scores, and that the schools' biggest supporters are parents of present and former pupils, some of whom are Muslim (Norfolk 2003). While we might not choose to educate our children in schools with such an emphasis in their science curriculum, it seems unreasonable to suggest that the teaching of Darwinian evolution is such an essential liberal value that the state may not accommodate those religious schools that would choose to teach science in some different way. So long as such schools are required to follow a national curriculum and their students are tested to meet basic science skills requirements, the state should grant the schools the autonomy to meet the demands as they see fit.

The tension comes from the fact that a religious school's worldview necessarily varies from its state-run counterparts (Halstead 2003; Macedo 2003). Among the purposes of a state school are the development of autonomous individuals and the formation of citizens. Religious schools share those concerns, but their primary focus is to strengthen the student's commitment to the community of faith and to preserve the group's religious identity, values, and practices. In seeking equal treatment from the state, Muslim schools are often criticized because many people do not share their values. This is particularly the case on gender issues.

Susan Okin (2003) has suggested that any patriarchal religious group – including Roman Catholics, Orthodox Jews, and Muslims – should be denied tax exempt status because they discriminate against women. Okin and others have similarly argued that Muslim conceptions of gender equality are incompatible with liberal values (Okin 1999; Reich 2003; but see El Guindi 1999). There may be some Muslim schools that systematically deny educational opportunities to girls that they provide to boys; in such cases, the state may legitimately choose not to finance them. However, such cases would, in our view, be unusual. What is more common is that Muslim schools, along with those of other religious groups, have an ethos that violates liberal values on gender, but they do not systematically deny women the opportunity for academic success. For example, a Muslim school might separate the sexes for physical education classes and even segregate boys and girls for public worship, but this does not mean that such a school is denying to girls educational opportunities open to boys.

A subtler issue that some have raised is that state accommodation of diverse religious practices might undermine a polity's need to promote consensual civic values. An example of this argument was a report by the British Home Office on the causes of that country's race riots in the summer of 2001. The report, *Community Cohesion*, recommended the establishment of a "meaningful conception of citizenship" that would recognize "the contributions of many cultures to this Nation's development throughout its history, but establish a clear primary loyalty to this nation" (Home Office 2001:20). The document concluded that common elements of British citizenship would include a universal acceptance of the English language and a formal statement of allegiance to the United Kingdom for new citizens.

Many British Muslims argued that the report implicitly questioned whether Muslims could be good citizens (Islamic Human Rights Commission 2001).

As with any religious community that is faithful to its tenets, tensions inevitably arise between Muslims' commitment to practicing their faith authentically and being faithful citizens of their respective nation-states. Muslims, no less than orthodox Jews, Christians, Sikhs, and Hindus, identify themselves more in terms of their distinctive faith and practices than their nationality. This necessarily invites struggle with the moral limits of a secular polity (Hauerwas 1981).

Unlike Christians and Jews in the West, however, Muslims have not had several centuries to work out the implications of their multiple allegiances in Western Europe. There are, nonetheless, resources within Islam, as well as historical precedents of Muslim communities living as a religious minority, upon which European Muslims can and will draw as they seek to maintain a healthy balance between the demands of their faith and their polity (Siddiqui 2002:32). For example, the Islamic theological concept of *tawḥīd*, the oneness of God, can provide the foundation for limiting the political reach of the state. If God is truly sovereign, then theoretically the state's powers can and must be limited. Moreover, God's sovereignty implicitly means that human hierarchies are not possible since humans are essentially equal before God. Such a notion can provide the foundation for both political democracy and individual rights (Esposito and Voll 1996). Moreover, as Ramadan (1999b) makes abundantly clear, Islam is not a static faith, but one that believers have interpreted throughout the centuries. This does not mean that interpretations of the faith by Muslims in the West must necessarily lead to an embrace of political democracy and individual rights, but that they can.

Because so few ethnic Europeans are religiously orthodox, there has in recent decades rarely been tension between an individual believer's faithfulness to God and her or his allegiance to the state. In such a circumstance, we believe it to be imperative for European states to take religious beliefs and practices seriously. Otherwise, the state is implicitly imposing a secular theological view on its citizens, thereby violating their religious liberty. The state, above all, should avoid forcing citizens to choose between obeying their conscience or obeying the law.

Fourth, people's involvement in religious organizations can facilitate their integration into their respective societies. In their study of community engagement in the United States, Sidney Verba and his colleagues demonstrated that religious institutions played a key role in helping to develop citizens' leadership, organizational, and participatory skills, which lay the foundation for a strong civil society. Verba also noted that such participation can facilitate public governance and enhance a citizen's support for democratic values (Verba et al. 1995).

The development of myriad Muslim organizations throughout Western Europe suggests that they are active within their communities, but we know of no data to test systematically the extent or quality of Muslims' civic engagement. It is possible that Muslim organizations have thus far focused mainly on "bonding" activities that strengthen the ties within their religious community, but that they have been less involved in "bridging" activities that would put them into more frequent contact with groups outside their religious community. As Mark Warren notes, bonding activities can strengthen local communities, but such communities can be "isolated, inward looking, even antidemocratic." What is more important over time is for citizens to be involved in bridging activities that bring people together "in order to develop broader identities and a shared commitment to the common good" (2001:25).

The story of the expansion of the East London Central Mosque, however, suggests that Muslims at the local level are involved in bonding and bridging activities (Malik 2000). In response to overcrowded conditions at the nearly century-old East London Central Mosque, leaders of the mosque proposed an expansion by purchasing the land adjacent to the mosque. While they were able to offer more than half a million pounds to buy the land, the owner sold it for considerably more to a private developer. In response, mosque leaders joined forces with The East London Communities Organization (TELCO), a broad-based community group that was active in the neighborhood. TELCO helped Muslim leaders of the mosque to mobilize civic, business, and religious leaders throughout the community and eventually succeeded in convincing the developer to sell the land to the mosque for approximately what the group had originally offered. A political effort that began as a bonding activity within the Muslim community, in short, quickly developed into a bridging event that was more politically effective and that brought Muslims into direct contact with their non-Muslim neighbors. The point of the story is that there is every reason to believe that Muslims will engage in such bridging activities to improve the communities in which they live.

Nor is integration simply a matter of Muslims' embracing the values of the West, but also of "natives'" treating Muslims decently. One response to the 9/11 terrorist attacks was a significant increase in anti-Muslim hate crimes throughout Western Europe. A report by the European Monitoring Centre on Racism and Xenophobia noted a "significant rise in attacks on Muslims across a wide range of media in the immediate aftermath of September 11" (Allen and Nielsen 2002:19). This backlash against Muslims included physical assaults, verbal abuse, and property damage to mosques and Muslim-owned businesses. As this violence demonstrates, "successful integration" needs to be a two-way street.

Finally, our analysis suggests that in looking for policies to incorporate Muslims successfully, states must seek resources within their inherited church–state structures. Our country chapters suggest two broad approaches to these concerns: *laïcité* and a single or multiple establishment. The first model, from France, is some form of church–state separation. One form of such separation ("strict" or "militant" *laïcité*) can be hostile to religion in general, and Islam in particular. This reading of *laïcité* suggests that the state should protect only the purely private expressions of faith. Born of a belief that the public expression of religion is inherently divisive or even hostile to particular notions of human rights, this model implies that the state should not accommodate Muslims by allowing the *ḥijāb* in public schools or funding private Islamic schools. To do so, these *laïcards* claim, would be to violate the principles of French-style church–state separation.

French Muslims experience this type of *laïcité* as a direct attack on their religious faith and on their efforts to transmit their religious beliefs to the next generation. They contend that state protection of purely private expressions of faith does not, in fact, offer much protection for Islam at all. Very few "private" areas of an individual's life remain unaffected by the administrative states of Western Europe, and particularly of France. It is not clear, therefore, what it means for the state to guarantee the freedom of "private" religious expression. To suggest that religiously inspired political views or practices are out of bounds because they are public expressions of religious beliefs is profoundly antidemocratic and badly misunderstands the nature of religion (Greenawalt 1988).

In our view, this reading of *laïcité* is disastrous for Muslim integration in France. It is not hard to understand why Muslims would express hostility to a French state that has been unwilling to allow such unproblematic practices as young women wearing the *ḥijāb* in school or males and females attending separate swimming classes. From a Muslim standpoint, such policies are not neutral toward religion, but instead hostile, and explicitly preference a secular over a religious worldview. These *laïcard* attitudes breed a hostility among Muslims toward French culture and society, and thus propel already disaffected and ghettoized communities further from the political mainstream and into the arms of radical Islamists.

We do not, however, suggest that France can or should abandon its historical commitment to church–state separation. Legal, historical, and constitutional patterns of church–state relations are the framework through which these issues are resolved. What we do argue, however, is that not all forms of *laïcité* are equal. A more benign reading of this tradition ("soft" or "open" *laïcité*) finds some support in French constitutional history and, more importantly, is consistent with the ultimate, successful integration of Muslims into French society. According to this reading, *laïcité* requires government neutrality among religions and between religion in general and secularism. While "soft" *laïcité* does prohibit governmental establishment of religion, it does not require the suppression of individuals' religious practice in public institutions. Read in this light, *laïcité* would not require French schools to expel girls for wearing the *ḥijāb* and would allow the state to fund private Islamic schools just as it does Catholic ones. By the same token, *laïcité* would prohibit the state from paying imams to lead Friday prayers in the local mosque or to teach Muslim theology in French public schools. Allowing Muslims to practice their religious faith would not only send the message that the state is not hostile to Islam, but also would encourage Muslims to put down roots and establish an indigenous form of Islam.

The second model, a single or multiple establishment, is found in Britain and Germany. In these countries, the issue is not so much whether the state will actively promote religious practice; Britain and Germany have a long history of state aid to religion. The question, instead, is whether Muslims will be included in the benefits that the state accords to religious groups. As with *laïcité*, this establishment model has "strict" and "soft" forms.

A "strict" reading would suggest that the British and German states should promote only those religious groups that were a part of the original establishment. In Britain, this reading would mean that in the House of Lords, for example, only Anglican clerics would have automatic seats. In Germany, similarly, a strict reading would make it very difficult, if not impossible, for religious newcomers to be granted public corporation status.

A "softer" interpretation of religious establishment would not be so hostile to Muslims and other religious minorities in Britain or Germany. This reading would contend that the state may aid all religious groups, not simply those that were a part of the original religious establishment. While it is unrealistic to think that Britain or Germany would abandon their well-established church–state regimes, for the most part these countries have understood that a religious establishment may include, rather than exclude, Muslims in the benefits that the state provides to religion.

On the surface, the religious establishments of Britain and Germany preference particular religions. Ironically, however, these two states accommodate the religious practices of Muslims, who are formally excluded from the religious establishment, to a much greater extent than does France, which is officially neutral among religions. While Britain and Germany have not completely solved the "problem" of Muslims' integration, the chief advantage of these nations' establishment model is that they have experienced less conflict around religious questions than has France.

Paradoxically, it took the immigration and eventual settlement of large numbers of Muslims in Britain, France, and Germany over the past several decades to highlight just how important the inherited church–state structures unique to each state were. The presence of Muslims raised questions about which religious groups the state would accommodate, whether or not Muslims would be given the same privileges enjoyed by other religious communities, and whether those states would work to incorporate Muslims into the existing legal and constitutional structure. In all three countries, these issues raised political tensions. A final irony of this story is that Muslims put forward public policy questions about church–state relations at the same time that secular ideas and policy models were becoming predominant in Britain, France, and Germany. Muslims challenged each state's capacity to be equitable in its treatment among different religious groups, but followers of Islam also accentuated tensions between secular and religious worldviews. Church–state matters that West European states seemed to have settled long ago and that appeared to be politically peripheral were suddenly thrust to the center of political and policy debate by Muslim efforts.

Survey Characteristics

2001 and 2002 Roper Europe Religion and the State I and II Surveys

Conducted by RoperASW (London) and its affiliates in France and Germany, this two-wave telephone survey selected respondents via random-digit dialing with quotas on major demographic characteristics. In the first wave, the response rate for the German sample was 61 percent. Other responses rates are not available. Roper targeted all respondents age sixteen and over living in all of France and Germany but only the English and Welsh parts of the United Kingdom. The field dates for the first wave (2001) were July 13–15 (Britain), July 21–2 (France), and July 9–12 (Germany). The second wave (2002) was conducted on April 19–21 (Britain), on April 17–18 (France), and in the second half of April (Germany). Questions Q. 1 and Q. 3 appeared in both waves, but Q. 2 was only included in the 2001 wave. Each country's wave contains around nine hundred respondents.

The original question wording in the three countries follows:

Britain

Q. 1 What is your religion, if any?

1. Baptist

2. Catholic

3. Church of England

4. Church of Scotland

5. Hindu

6. Jewish

7. Methodist

8. Muslim

9. Born-again Christian (no specific denomination)

10. Protestant (no specific denomination)

11. Other

12. None, I am not a religious person

13. Refused/no answer

Q. 2 I would like you to think about the Church of England's gradual accommodation of other religious groups in areas such as education, membership of the House of Lords, etc. Using a scale from 1 to 5, tell me how strongly you agree or disagree with such a proposition. A score of 1 means you disagree strongly, while a score of 5 means you agree strongly.

1. Disagree strongly

2. Disagree slightly

3. Neither agree nor disagree

4. Agree slightly

5. Agree strongly

Q. 3 I am going to read out a few statements that some people have made about government funding for Islamic schools. I would like you to tell me which statement best describes your personal opinion.

1. The government should cancel its approval of the current Islamic schools.

2. The government should limit its approval only to the Islamic schools currently permitted.

3. The government should approve more Islamic schools.

France

Q. 1 Quelle est votre religion si vous en avez une?

1. Bouddhiste

2. Catholique

3. Juive

4. Musulmane

5. Protestante évangélique

6. Protestante reformé ou luthérienne

7. Autre

8. Aucune, je ne suis pas une personne religieuse,

9. Refuse de répondre

Q. 2 Je voudrais que vous pensiez à la laïcité de l'état (séparation stricte entre la religion et l'état). En utilisant une échelle de 1 à 5, dites moi dans quelle mesure êtes-vous d'accord ou pas d'accord avec un tel système. "1" signifie que vous n'êtes pas du tout d'accord, tandis que "5" signifie que vous êtes tout à fait d'accord.

1. Pas du tout d'accord

2. Plutôt pas d'accord

3. Ni d'accord, ni pas d'accord

4. Plutôt d'accord

5. Tout à fait d'accord

Q. 3 Je vais vous lire 3 phrases que des gens ont dit sur les élèves qui portaient le Hijab à l'école publique. Le Hijab est un foulard ou voile islamique qui couvre le cou, la gorge et la tête des musulmanes. Dites-moi la phase qui correspond le mieux à votre opinion personnelle.

1. Porter le Hijab ne devrait pas être permis

2. Porter le Hijab devrait être permis hors de la classe, durant les récréations mais pas pendant les cours

3. Porter le Hijab devrait être toujours permis

Germany

Q. 1 Welcher Religion/Glaubensgemeinschaft gehören Sie an?

1. Katholisch

2. Jüdisch

3. Lutherisch

4. Muslimisch

5. Freie Kirche

6. Andere

7. Keine, bin nicht religiös

8. Keine Angabe/ weiß nicht

Q. 2 Denken Sie bitte einmal an die Kirchensteuer, womit der Staat Geld für religiöse Gruppen die öffentlich anerkannt sind sammelt. Sagen Sie mir bitte anhand der Skala, die von 1 "stimme überhaupt nicht zu" bis 5 "stimme voll und ganz zu" reicht, wie Sie dazu stehen. Mit den Werten dazwischen können Sie Ihre Meinung abstufen.

1	2	3	4	5
stimme überhaupt nicht zu				stimme voll und ganz zu

Q. 3 Ich lese Ihnen jetzt einige Aussagen vor, die Personen über den Islamunterricht in Schulen gegeben haben. Bitte sagen Sie mir, nachdem ich alle Aussagen vorgelesen habe, welche am besten auf Sie persönlich zutrifft.

1. Islamunterricht sollte nicht angeboten werden

2. Islamunterricht sollte nur dort angeboten werden, wo muslimische Schüler einen Großteil der Schule ausmachen

3. Jedem muslimischen Schüler sollte die Möglichkeit gegeben werden, auf Wunsch, Islamunterricht besuchen zu können

2001 MORI Faith Schools Survey

The London-based Market and Opinion Research International (MORI) polling organization conducted its survey on "Public Perceptions of Faith Schools" on November 8–13. Apparently using random-digit dialing and telephone interviews, MORI obtained responses from about two thousand adult residents of Great Britain (Garner 2001; Hayes 2001).

1995 SOFRES French National Election Study

Under the guidance of principal investigators Michael S. Lewis-Beck, Nonna Mayer, and Daniel Boy, SOFRES (Société française d'études statistiques) conducted its French National Election Study from May 8–23, 1995, just after the second round of the 1995 French presidential election. This poll targeted all French citizens age eighteen and over living in France (excluding Corsica and the overseas territories and *départements*) and registered on the electoral lists. From this population, SOFRES used quota sampling (by age, sex, and occupation of head of household) and regional stratification to select 4,078 individuals for the extensive in-person interviews (Boy and Mayer 1997:347–9).

1996 ALLBUS/German Social Survey

Data for the 3,518 adult respondents in the 1996 version of this periodic survey came from a combination of in-person interviews and dropped-off paper questionnaires. Infratest Burke of Munich conducted the poll from March to July. Respondents were selected via two-stage random sampling of all individuals living in households and born before 1978.

Glossary of Non-English Terms

Abitur (Ger.) Highly competitive entrance exam for German universities.

Ausländer (Ger.) Literally "out-lander," or foreigner. Often used to describe immigrants.

bac/baccalauréat (Fr.) Highly competitive entrance exam for French universities.

beur (Fr.) Arab (slang). Generally refers to French-born ethnic North Africans.

citoyens (Fr.) French citizens in the model of the French Revolution.

collège (Fr.) French secondary school roughly equivalent to a U.S. junior high school.

Conseil d'État (Fr.) Supreme administrative court in France.

département (Fr.) Subnational governmental division in France. It is about the same size as a U.S. county but serves a political role similar to a U.S. state.

école laïque (Fr.) French ideal of a public school operating according to the separationist principle of *laïcité*.

Evangelische (Ger.) Members of the largest, state-supported Protestant denomination in Germany. Similar to U.S. Lutherans or Reformed believers.

français de souche (Fr.) French person whose ancestry is "ethnically French" back through recorded time.

Gastarbeiter (Ger.) Guestworkers in Germany, many of whom have lived in the country since the 1950s or 1960s.

Grundgesetz (Ger.) German Basic Law, or de facto constitution.

Gymnasium (Ger.) Elite German secondary school. Roughly equivalent to a combined U.S. high school and junior college.

ḥalāl (Arab.) Literally "permitted." Often used to describe food prepared according to orthodox Muslim specifications.

harkis (Arab.) Ethnically Arabic or Berber Algerians who sided with the French government during the Algerian War and fled to France after the French defeat.

ḥijāb (Arab.) Scarflike headcovering worn by orthodox Muslim women.

ʿid al-fiṭr (Arab.) Muslim celebration of the end of the holy month of *ramadān*.

jus sanguinis (Lat.) Literally "law of the blood." System under which one becomes a citizen by being born to someone of the ethnic group dominant in a certain country (for example, being born to ethnic Germans in pre-2000 Germany).

jus soli (Lat.) Literally "law of the soil." System under which one becomes a citizen by being born within the boundaries of a certain country (for example, being born in the United States regardless of one's ethnicity).

Kirchensteuer (Ger.) Tax collected from members of established religious bodies by the German government.

Körperschaft des öffentlichen Rechts (Ger.) Public corporation status granted to certain religious groups in Germany.

Kulturkampf (Ger.) Literally "cultural struggle." Anti-Catholic campaign waged by German Chancellor Otto von Bismarck in late nineteenth century.

laïcards (Fr.) Strong supporters of the French separationist concept of *laïcité*. Has a slightly pejorative connotation.

laïcité (Fr.) French concept of religion–state separationism.

laïque (Fr.) Characterized by the French separationist concept of *laïcité*.

Land/Länder (Ger.) Subnational governmental division(s) in Germany. About the same size as a U.S. county but serves a political role similar to a U.S. state under federalism.

lycée (Fr.) Elite French secondary school. Roughly equivalent to a combined U.S. high school and junior college.

Maghrébins (Fr.) Ethnically Arab or Berber immigrants from former French colonies in North Africa.

métropole (Fr.) Metropolitan, or European, France.

miḥrāb (Arab.) Alcove or niche in the wall of a traditional mosque. Indicates the direction of Mecca.

minbar (Arab.) In a mosque, the set of stairs from which the sermon is delivered.

pieds-noirs (Fr.) Literally "black feet." Ethnically European colonists in Algeria who fled to France after the French defeat in the Algerian War.

proviseur (Fr.) Administrative head of a French *lycée*, or elite secondary school.

qur'ān (Arab.) Holy book believed by Muslims to have been divinely revealed to the Prophet Muḥammad.

ramadān (Arab.) Lunar month holy to Muslims, who are obliged to fast during daylight hours of this period.

Religionsunterricht (Ger.) Constitutionally guaranteed religious instruction in German public schools.

sharī'ah (Arab.) Islamic law. Similar to canon law of the Roman Catholic Church.

Shī'ah (Arab.) Adjective used to denote the branch of Muslims who believe the supreme religious leader must descend from Muḥammad's daughter Fāṭimah and her husband 'Ali. Opposed to the Sunnis. This branch is common in Iran and part of Iraq.

'ummah (Arab.) Community of all Muslim believers in the world.

Wirtschaftswunder (Ger.) "Economic Miracle," or dramatic economic recovery, of post–World War II Germany.

Bibliography

Data Sources

ALLBUS [Allgemeine Bevölkerungsumfrage der Sozialwissenschaften]. 1996. German social survey. Cologne: Zentralarchiv für empirische Sozialforschung.

Forschungsgruppe Wahlen. 1996. *20 Jahre Politbarometer der Forschungsgruppe Wahlen e.V. Mannheim.* Machine-readable data set on CD. Cologne: Zentralarchiv für empirische Sozialforschung.

MORI [Market and Opinion Research International]. 2001a. "Public Perceptions of Faith Schools." Survey conducted November 8–13. London: MORI.

Roper Europe. 2001. "Religion and the State I." Surrey, UK: RoperASW Europe Ltd. Publicly available from the Paul B. Henry Institute at Calvin College, 3201 Burton SE, Grand Rapids, MI 49546.

Roper Europe. 2002. "Religion and the State II." Surrey, UK: RoperASW Europe Ltd. Publicly available from the Paul B. Henry Institute at Calvin College, 3201 Burton SE, Grand Rapids, MI 49546.

SOFRES (Société française d'études statistiques). 1995. "French National Election Study/Enquête postélectorale – CEVIPOF." May 8–23. BDSP no. Q0891.

Interviews

Abdullah, Muhammad Salim [director, Islam-Archiv-Deutschland]. 2001. Interview with Joel Fetzer, February 21, Soest.

Abed, Renate Nadia [principal, Islamische Grundschule Berlin]. 2001. Interview with Joel Fetzer, May 7, Berlin-Kreuzberg.

Afzal, Muhammad [councilman and racial equalities commissioner, Birmingham City Council]. 2001. Interview with J. Christopher Soper and Joel Fetzer, April 9, Birmingham.

Aïnouche, Azzedine [director, Institut Méditerranéen d'Études Musulmanes]. 2001. Interview with Joel Fetzer, May 29, Marseille.

Albert, Reiner [former co-director, Institut für deutsch-türkische Integrationsstudien of the Yavuz Sultan Selim Mosque; Wissenschaftlicher Mitarbeiter, Department of Catholic Theology, University of Mannheim]. 2001a. Interview with Joel Fetzer, March 27, Mannheim.

Alboğa, Bekir [Geschäftsführer and Islamwissenschaftlicher Leiter, Institut für deutsch-türkische Integrationsstudien und interreligiöse Arbeit; Vorsitzender, Mannheim City Migrationsbeirat]. 2001. Interview with Joel Fetzer, February 22, Mannheim.

Algan, Yusuf [member, Fatih Moschee Bremen]. 2001. Interview with Joel Fetzer, February 9, Bremen.

Amer, Dr. Fatma [head of education and interfaith relations, Islamic Cultural Centre, London Central Mosque]. 2001. Interview with J. Christopher Soper, April 11, London.

Barlow, Anne [director of School Workforce Unit, Department for Education and Skills]. 2001. Interview with J. Christopher Soper, April 18, London.

Barrette, Gilles [Catholic priest, member of the White Fathers Order, and instructor at the Institut de Science et de Théologie des Religions]. 2001. Interview with Joel Fetzer, June 7, Marseille.

Bendelac, Alberto [chef d'établissement, Collège l'Estaque]. 2001. Interview with Joel Fetzer, May 21, Marseille.

Berguin, Francis [secrétaire national, Action juridique, Syndicat National des Enseignements de Second degré]. 2001. Interview with Joel Fetzer, July 5, Paris.

Blanc, Jackie [conseiller régional, Région Provence-Alpes-Côte d'Azur and Secrétaire Départemental for Front National]. 2001. Interview with Joel Fetzer, May 21, Marseille.

Browning, David. [registrar, Oxford Centre for Islamic Studies]. 2001. Interview with Joel Fetzer, August 3, Oxford.

Butt, K. S. [chair, Islamic Resource Centre]. 2001. Interview with J. Christopher Soper and Joel Fetzer, April 9, Birmingham.

Buttner, Yann [staff attorney, service juridique, Rectorat, Académie d'Aix-Marseille]. 2001. Interview with Joel Fetzer, May 22, Aix-en-Provence.

Chaudhary, Dr. Zahoor Anwar [interethnic relations director, Birmingham Local Education Authority]. 2001. Interview with Joel Fetzer, July 17, Birmingham.

Dal, Yalçin [member, Frankfurt a.M. City Council]. 2001. Interview with Joel Fetzer, April 5, Frankfurt a.M.

Dallali, Kamel [président, Centre Essalam]. 2001. Interview with Joel Fetzer, July 2, Le Havre.

Diwan, Mohammed Kassim [moulana, Old Trafford Muslim Society, Masjid-e-Noor Mosque]. 2001. Interview with Joel Fetzer, July 26, Manchester.

Djoufelkit, Youssef [organizational manager affiliated with the Southern Region of Jeunes Musulmans de France]. 2001. Interview with Joel Fetzer, June 9, Avignon.

Douai, Fouad [gérant, Société Civile Immobilière, Grande Mosquée de Strasbourg]. 2001. Interview with Joel Fetzer, July 10, Strasbourg.

Durand, Georges [pseudonym for French educational leader who wishes to remain anonymous]. 2001. Interview with Joel Fetzer, summer, France.

El-Essawy, Doctor Hesham [director, Islamic Society for the Promotion of Religious Tolerance]. 2001. Interview with J. Christopher Soper and Joel Fetzer, April 10, London.

Elyas, Nadeem [vorsitzender, Zentralrat der Muslime in Deutschland]. 2001. Interview with Joel Fetzer, February 15, Cologne.

Fındık, Hicabi [president, Association islamique culturelle turque]. 2001. Interview with Joel Fetzer, June 5, Marignane.

Gebauer, Klaus [Leiter des Referates Sozialwissenschaften, Geschichte, Religionslehre, Erdkunde of North Rhine-Westphalia's Landesinstitut für Schule und Weiterbildung]. 2001. Interview with Joel Fetzer, April 23, Soest.

Granier, Nicole [vice president, Fédération des Conseils de Parents d'Élèves de l'Enseignement Public, region 13]. 2001. Interview with Joel Fetzer, Aix-en-Provence, June 5.

Griffiths, Gill [deputy headteacher, Ladypool Primary School]. 2001. Interview with Joel Fetzer, July 11, Birmingham.

Hafner, Helmut [Religionsbeauftrachter, mayor's office for the City of Bremen]. 2001. Interview with Joel Fetzer, April 2, Bremen.

Hall, Canon John [general secretary, Church of England Board of Education]. 2001. Interview with J. Christopher Soper, April 11, London.

Hasanein, Abdel Sattar [principal, Deutsch-Islamische Schule]. 2001. Interview with Joel Fetzer, March 12, Munich.

Hewitt, Ibrahim [headmaster, Al-Aqsa School]. 2001. Interview with J. Christopher Soper, April 12, Leicester.

Hmito, Abdellatif [member, Centre Essalam, and math teacher in a public junior high school]. 2001. Interview with Joel Fetzer, July 2, Le Havre.

Hussain, Shafaq [national coordinator, People's Justice Party]. 2001. Interview with Joel Fetzer, July 19, Birmingham.

Kabtane, Kamel [director, Grande Mosquée de Lyon]. 2001. Interview with Joel Fetzer, May 30, Lyon.

Kada, Saïda [president, Femmes Françaises et Musulmanes Engagées]. 2001. Interview with Joel Fetzer, July 11, Lyon.

Kaplan, Ismail [education director, Föderation der Aleviten Gemeinden in Deutschland]. 2001. Interview with Joel Fetzer, February 28, Cologne.

Kechat, Larbi [recteur, Mosquée Ada'wa]. 2001. Interview with Joel Fetzer, July 3, Paris.

Kesici, Burhan [Verwaltungsratsvorzitzender, Islamische Föderation Berlin]. 2001. Interview with Joel Fetzer, May 7, Berlin.

Khoirul, Muhammad [project director, School Links Project]. 2001. Interview with J. Christopher Soper, April 11, London.

Konya, Pervin [teacher, Muttersprachliche Unterweisung, Gesamtschule Schinkel, Osnabrück]. 2001. Interview with Joel Fetzer, April 23, Osnabrück.

Krausen, Halima [theologian and representative to the German-speaking community, Islamisches Zentrum Hamburg]. 2001. Interview with Joel Fetzer, February 8, Hamburg.

Le Carpentier, Philippe [chef du Bureau Central des Cultes, Ministère de l'Intérieur]. 2001. Interview with Joel Fetzer, July 4, Paris.

Ludin, Fereshta [English teacher, Islamische Grundschule Berlin]. 2001. Interview with Joel Fetzer, May 7, Berlin.

Malik, Nadeem [research fellow, Islamic Foundation]. 2001. Interview with J. Christopher Soper, April 12, Leicester.

Mammeri, Youcef [biology teacher at Collège Versailles, member of Conseil Administratif de l'Institut Méditerranéen d'Études Musulmanes, and Mosquée Islah's delegate to the Ministère de l'Intérieur's Consultation with French Muslims]. 2001. Interview with Joel Fetzer, June 6, Marseille.

Martinez, Louis [pied-noir, novelist, and professor emeritus of Russian Literature and Language, Université de Provence]. 2001. Interview with Joel Fetzer, May 31, Aix-en-Provence.

Martino, Jean-Louis [proviseur vie scolaire, Rectorat, Académie Aix-Marseille]. 2001. Interview with Joel Fetzer, May 28, Aix-en-Provence.

Maurin, André [chef du service juridique, Rectorat, Académie d'Aix-Marseille]. 2001. Interview with Joel Fetzer, May 22, Aix-en-Provence.

Mazyek, Hildegard [Vorstandsmitglied, Islamisches Zentrum Aachen]. 2001. Interview with Joel Fetzer, March 15, Aachen.

Merroun, Khalil [recteur, Centre Culturel Islamique d'Évry–Courcouronnes]. 2001. Interview with Joel Fetzer, June 29, Évry.

Molla, Osman [president, Grande Mosquée de Saint Denis, Réunion]. 2001. Interview with Joel Fetzer, July 3, Paris-St. Denis.

Muslimah, Fatima [pseudonym for a French Muslim who is cited anonymously to protect her from retaliation]. 2001. Interview with Joel Fetzer, summer, France.

Nielsen, Jørgen [director, Centre for the Study of Islam-Christian Relations]. 2001. Interview with J. Christopher Soper and Joel Fetzer, April 9, Birmingham.

Nirumand, Bahman [Leiter der Geschäftsstelle Komunale Ausländer– und Ausländerinnenvertretung, City of Frankfurt a.M.]. 2001. Interview with Joel Fetzer, April 5, Frankfurt a.M.

Panafieu, Bernard [Catholic archbishop of Marseille, and president, Comité épiscopal des relations interreligieuses]. 2001. Interview with Joel Fetzer, June 1, Marseille.

Parwez, Ahmed [committee member, Islamic Resource Centre of Birmingham]. 2001. Interview with J. Christopher Soper and Joel Fetzer, April 9, Birmingham.

Per, Kazim [general secretary for Baden-Württemberg, Verband der Islamischen Kulturzentren]. 2001. Interview with Joel Fetzer, March 27, Stuttgart.

Pfaff, Ulrich [Ministerialrat, Ministerium für Schule, Jugend und Kinder des Landes Nordrhein-Westfalen]. 2001. Interview with Joel Fetzer, March 23, Düsseldorf.

Qureshi, Mahmooda [vice president, Sister Section of the Young Muslims of the UK]. 2001. Interview with Joel Fetzer, July 18, Birmingham.

Raja, Akhtar [founding partner of the Quist (a firm of lawyers) and Governor of Islamia Primary School]. 2001. Interview with Joel Fetzer, August 2, London.

Schmitt, Helmut [Beauftragter für ausländische Einwohner, City of Mannheim]. 2001. Interview with Joel Fetzer, February 14, Mannheim.

Shaikh, Shuja [councillor and deputy leader, Conservative Group, London Borough of Hackney] 2001. Interview with J. Christopher Soper, April 11, London.

Sicard, Jean [secrétaire général de la Région Aix-Marseille, Syndicat Général de l'Education Nationale]. 2001. Interview with Joel Fetzer, May 29, Marseille.

Siddiqui, Ataullah [head of the Interfaith Unit of the Islamic Foundation]. 2001. Interview with J. Christopher Soper, April 12, Leicester.

Stevens, Philip [project director, Human Rights Unit, Home Office]. 2001. Interview with J. Christopher Soper, April 18, London.

Sunay, Attila [consul general, General Consulate of Turkey in Marseille]. 2001. Interview with Joel Fetzer, May 23, Marseille.

Toihiri, Ali [participant at the Mosqueé al-Shafi'i, and secretary general, Association culturelle comorienne]. 2001. Interview with Joel Fetzer, June 1, Marseille.

Totakhyl, Ghulam Dastagir [general secretary, Islamrat für die Bundesrepublik Deutschland]. 2001. Interview with Joel Fetzer, February 5, Bonn.

Tribalat, Michèle [immigration scholar, Institut national d'études démographiques]. 2001. Interview with Joel Fetzer, June 28, Paris.

von Schroeter, Henning [Ministerialrat, Staatskanzlei von Nordrhein-Westfalen]. 2001. Interview with Joel Fetzer, Düsseldorf, April 6.

Wetzel, Martin [Catholic priest, now in Offenburg but formerly in Mannheim]. 2001. Interview with Joel Fetzer, February 22, Offenburg.

Yüksel, Turgut [member, Frankfurt a.M. City Council, and Referent, Frankfurter Jugendring]. 2001. Interview with Joel Fetzer, April 5, Frankfurt a.M.

Zaki, Yaqub [deputy director, Muslim Institute]. 2001. Interview with J. Christopher Soper and Joel Fetzer, April 10, London.

Print, Media, and Internet Sources

Abdullah, Dr. 1995. *Le foulard islamique et la République française: Mode d'emploi.* Bobigny, France: Éditions Intégrité.

Abdullah, Muhammad S. 1981. *Geschichte des Islams in Deutschland.* Cologne: Verlag Styria.

———. 2000. "Neue Daten und Fakten über die islamischen Großverbände in der Bundesrepublik Deutschland." *Moslemische Revue* [publication of the Zentralinstitut Islam-Archiv-Deutschland Stiftung, Soest], 23(2/April–June): 112–20.

————. 2002. "Fast 3,5 Millionen Moslems in der Bundesrepublik Deutschland: Auszug aus der Frühlingsumfrage des ZIIAD 'Neue Daten und Fakten über den Islam in Deutschland'." *Moslemische Revue*, 23(2/April–June):106–14.

Achi, Raberh. 2001. "L'exception en France: La Medersa ta'lim oul-islam de Saint-Denis de la Réunion." *La Médina* 9(July–August):26.

Ackerman, Bruce. 1980. *Social Justice in the Liberal State*. New Haven, CT: Yale University Press.

Ad-Darsh, Dr. Syed Mutawalli. 1997. "What You Ought to Know." *Q News* 275 (September):24.

Adolino, Jessica, R. 1998. *Ethnic Minorities, Electoral Politics and Political Integration in Britain*. London: Printer.

ADRI [Agence pour le développement des relations interculturelles]. 2000. *L'islam en France*. Paris: La documentation française.

Agence France Presse. 1996. "Brigitte Bardot dénonce le 'débordement islamique' en France." Wire service "informations générales." April 26.

Aït-Hamadouche, Rabah. 2003. 'Pourquoi vouloir calquer le modèle chrétien?': La nouvelle instance, dont on ignore souvent le fonctionnement, est un sujet qui fâche parmi les fidèles." *Le Figaro*, April 5, p. 11.

Akhtar, Shabbir. 1993. *The Muslim Parent's Handbook*. London: Ta-Ha Publishers.

Akkent, Meral, and Gaby Franger. 1987. *Das Kopftuch: Ein Stückchen Stoff in Geschichte und Gegenwart/Başörtü: Geçmişte ve Günümüzde Bir Parça Kumaş*. Frankfurt a.M.: Dağyeli Verlag.

Albert, Reiner. 2001b. "Auf der Suche nach dem Angemessenen in der politischen Planung: Eine Antwort der historisch-philosophischen Hermeneutik auf die Konfrontation von Politik und Wissenschaft mit der multikulturellen Pluralität von Weltbildern in der Postmoderne am Beispiel der Konzipierung des Integrationsprozesses türkischer Sunniten in Deutschland." Habilitationsschrift. Mannheim: University of Mannheim.

Albert, Reiner, Talat Kamran, and Bekir Alboğa. 1995. "Die Neue Moschee in Mannheim: Ihre Einrichtung und Ihre Ziele." Pamphlet. Mannheim: Institut für deutsch-türkische Integrationsstudien.

Alboğa, Bekir. No date. "Der Streit um die Moscheen: Das Mannheimer Beispiel." Unpublished manuscript. Mannheim: Institut für deutsch-türkische Integrationsstudien und interreligiöse Arbeit.

al istichara. 2000. "28 janvier 2000: une date importante dans l'histoire de l'islam de France." *al istichara: Le Journal de la Consultation des musulmans de France*. 1(March):1.

Allen, Christopher and Jørgen S. Nielsen. 2002. *Summary Report on Islamophobia in the EU after 11 September 2001*. Vienna: European Monitoring Centre on Racism and Xenophobia.

Allport, Gordon W. 1979. *The Nature of Prejudice*. Reading, MA: Addison-Wesley.

Altschull, Elizabeth. 1995. *Le voile contre l'école*. Paris: Éditions du Seuil.

Alwin, Duane F., Ronald L. Cohen, and Theodore M. Newcomb. 1992. *Political Attitudes over the Life Span: The Bennington Women after Fifty Years*. Madison, WI: University of Wisconsin Press.

Amalou, Florence. 2001. "Le gouvernement s'attaque aux publicités sexistes." *Le Monde*, July 12, p. 13.

Amiraux, Valérie. 1996. "Turkish Islam in Germany: Between Political Overdetermination and Cultural Affirmation." Pp. 36–52 in W. A. R. Shadid and P. S. van Koningsveld, eds., *Political Participation and Identities of Muslims in Non-Muslim States*. Kampen, Netherlands: Kok Pharos.

am Orde, Sabine. 2002. "Andrang auf Islamunterricht; Die Islamische Föderation will mehr als tausend Kindern an 16 Schulen ihre Sicht auf den Koran beibringen. Erstmals bieten auch die Aleviten Religionsunterricht an. Aber nur für 36 Schüler." *TAZ*, August 17, section Berlin Aktuell, p. 25.

Anwar, Muhammad. 1992. "Muslims in Western Europe." Pp. 71–93 in Jørgen S. Nielsen, ed., *Religion and Citizenship in Europe and the Arab World*. London: Grey Seal.

———. 1995. "Muslims in Britain." Pp. 37–49 in Syed A. Abedin and Ziauddin Sardar, eds., *Muslim Minorities in the West*. London: Grey Seal.

Associated Press. 1990. "Youths Set Fires in Lyon for Fourth Night of Disturbances." Wire service article, October 9.

———. 2004. "Critics Say Draft of Headscarf Ban in French Schools Is Too Vague." Wire service article, April 22.

Aston, John. 2000. "Judge Rebuffs Protesters in Islamic Centre Row." Associated Press, December 11.

Azam, Nadeem. 1997. "Election Analysis." *Q News* 272 (June):21.

Aziz, Philippe. 1996. *Le paradoxe de Roubaix*. Paris: Plon.

Bachmann, Christian, and Nicole Le Guennec. 1996. *Violences urbaines: Ascension et chute des classes moyennes à travers cinquante ans de politique de la ville*. Paris: Albin Michel.

Bacqué, Raphaëlle. 2003. "Le débat sur le port du foulard islamique à l'école divise la droite." *Le Monde*, May 10, p. 7.

Bade, Klaus J. 1983. *Vom Auswanderungsland zum Einwanderungsland? Deutschland 1880–1980*. Berlin: Colloquium Verlag.

———. 1992. "Einheimische Ausländer: 'Gastarbeiter' – Dauergäste – Einwanderer." Pp. 393–401 in Klaus J. Bade, ed., *Deutsche im Ausland – Fremde in Deutschland: Migration in Geschichte und Gegenwart*. Munich: Verlag C. H. Beck.

———. 2000. "The German Hub: Migration in History and the Present." *Deutschland* 6(December/January):38–43.

Barker, Eileen. 1987. "The British Right to Discriminate." Pp. 269–80 in Thomas Robbins and Roland Robertson, eds., *Church–State Relations: Tensions and Transitions*. New Brunswick, NJ, and Oxford, UK: Transaction Books.

———. 1995. "The Post-War Generation and Establishment Religion in England." Pp. 1–23 in Clark Roof, Jackson W. Carrol, and David A. Roozen, eds., *The Post-War Generation and Establishment Religion*. Boulder, CO: Westview Press.

Baubérot, Jean. 2000. *Histoire de la laïcité française*. Paris: Presses Universitaires de France.

Bebbington, David W. 1989. *Evangelicalism in Modern Britain*. London: Unwin Hyman.

Beckford, James A., and Sophie Gilliat. 1998. *Religion in Prison: Equal Rites in a Multi-Faith Society*. Cambridge, UK: Cambridge University Press.

Ben Abid, Sallah Eddine. 2000. "The Sharia between Particularism and Universality." Pp. 11–30 in Silvio Ferrari and Anthony Bradney, eds., *Islam and European Legal Systems*. Dartmouth, NH: Ashgate.

Benjamin, Daniel, and Steven Simon. 2003. *The Age of Sacred Terror*. New York: Random House.

Ben Jelloun, Tahar. 1999. *French Hospitality: Racism and North African Immigrants*. Translated by Barbara Bray. New York: Columbia University Press.

———. 2002. *L'Islam expliqué aux enfants*. Paris: Seuil.

Berry, Jeffrey M. 1997. *The Interest Group Society*, 3rd ed. New York: Longman.

Biehl, Frauke, and Sevin Kabak, eds. 1999. *Muslimische Frauen in Deutschland erzählen über ihren Glauben*. Gütersloh, Germany: Gütersloher Verlagshaus.

Bistolfi, Robert, and François Zabbal, eds. 1995. *Islams d'Europe: Intégration ou insertion communautaire?* Paris: Éditions de l'aube.

Blair, Tony. 2000. "Faith in Politics." Downloaded from www.labour.org.uk on June 15, 2002.

Blatt, David. 1995. "Towards a Multi-Cultural Political Model in France? The Limits of Immigrant Collective Action, 1968–94." *Nationalism and Ethnic Politics* 1(2):156–77.

Bleich, Erik. 1998. "From International Ideas to Domestic Politics: Educational Multiculturalism in England and France." *Comparative Politics* 31(1):81–100.

Boëldieu, Julien, and Catherine Borrel. 2000. "Recensement de la population 1999: La proportion d'immigrés est stable depuis 25 ans." *INSEE Première* 748 (November):1–4.

Bonhoeffer, Dietrich. 1990. *Widerstand und Ergebung: Briefe und Aufzeichnungen aus der Haft*. Munich: Kaiser.

Bourg, Didier. 2000. "L'union des Surs Musulmanes de Lyon." *Hawwa Magazine* 2 (April):20.

Boy, Daniel, and Nonna Mayer. 1997. *L'électeur a ses raisons*. Paris: Presses de Sciences Po.

Boyé, Jean-François. 1994. *Les principaux éléments juridiques de la laïcité*. Fiches juridiques et practiques, no. 32. Paris: Inter Service Migrants.

Boyer, Alain. 1992. *L'Institut musulman de la mosquée de Paris*. Paris: C.H.E.A.M.

———. 1993. *Le droit des religions en France*. Paris: Presses Universitaires de France.

———. 1998. *L'Islam en France*. Paris: Presses Universitaires de France.

Bozonnet, Jean-Jacques. 1989. "Une école islamique sous contrat avec l'État: L'imam, l'institutrice et le Prophète." *Le Monde*, December 1, in Centre de Ressources Documentaires. *Dossier de presse sur l'affaire du foulard islamique*. Paris: Agence pour le Développement des Relations Interculturelles. Vol. 4, p. 72.

Branche, Raphaëlle. 2001. *La torture et l'armée pendant la guerre d'Algérie, 1954–1962*. Paris: Gallimard.

Brierley, Peter W. 2001. *United Kingdom Christian Handbook: Religious Trends Number 3*. London: Christian Research.

Bronner, Luc. 2002. "Les professeurs d'un lycée de Seine-Saint-Denis en grève 'contre l'islamisme'; La réintégration d'une élève portant un voile islamique, demandée par le rectorat, est vécue comme un 'désaveu'." *Le Monde*, March 25 p. 11.

Brubaker, Rogers. 1992. *Citizenship and Nationhood in France and Germany*. Cambridge, MA: Harvard University Press.

Bruce, Steve. 1995. "The Truth about Religion in Britain." *Journal for the Scientific Study of Religion* 34(4):417–30.

Bruce, Steve, and Chris Wright. 1995. "Law, Social Change, and Religious Toleration." *Journal of Church and State* 37 (Winter):103–20.

Buaras, Elham Asaad. 2003. "Muslim School Tops Bradford A Level League." *Muslim News*, May 30, p. 3.

Bundesregierung. 2000. "Antwort der Bundesregierung auf die Große Anfrage der Abgeordneten Dr. Jürgen Rüttgers, Erwin Marschewski (Recklinghausen), Wolfgang Zeitlmann, weiterer Abgeordneter und der Fraktion der CDU/CSU." Drucksache 14/2301 (Nov. 8). Berlin: Deutscher Bundestag.

Bundesverfassungsschutz. 1993. *Verfassungsschutzbericht 1992*. Bonn: Bundesministerium des Innern.

Buttner, Yann, André Maurin, and Blaise Thouveny. 2002. *Le droit de la vie scolaire: Écoles – Collèges – Lycées*. Paris: Dalloz.

Caldwell, Christopher. 2000. "The Crescent and the Tricolor." *Atlantic Monthly*, November 2000, pp. 20–34.

Camus, Jean-Yves. 1996. "Origine et formation du Front national (1972–1981)." Pp. 17–36 in Nonna Mayer and Pascal Perrineau, eds., *Le Front national à découvert*. Paris: Presses de la Fondation nationale des sciences politiques.

Cassidy, Sarah. 2003. "Rapid Rise in Number of Black Pupils Achieving Good Grades." *Independent*, February 21, p. 7.

Castles, Stephen, and Mark J. Miller. 1993. *The Age of Migration: International Population Movements in the Modern World*. New York: Guilford Press.

Cesari, Jocelyne. 1994. *Être musulman en France: Associations, militants et mosquées*. Aix-en-Provence, France: Karthala-IREMAM.

———. 1997. *Faut-il avoir peur de l'islam?* Paris: Presses de Sciences Po.

———. 2000. "Muslims in the West: New Ambassadors of Democratic Pluralism." *Middle East Affairs Journal* 6 (Fall):217–28.

———. 2002a. "Principaux courants et associations de l'Islam français." *Cahiers d'études sur la méditerranée oriental et le monde turco-iranien* 33(January–June):39–42.

———. 2002b. "Islam in France: The Shaping of a Religious Minority." Pp. 36–51 in Yvonne Yazbeck Haddad, ed., *Muslims in the West: From Sojourners to Citizens*. Oxford, UK: Oxford University Press.

Chapman, Colin. 1998. *Islam and the West: Conflict, Co-existence, or Conversion?* Cornwall, UK: Paternoster Press.

Chapman, Hamed, and Ahmed Versi, 2001. "Over 200 Muslim Councillors." *Muslim News*, May 25, p. 2.

Cherribi, Oussama. 2001. "Imams and Issues: The Politics of Islam in European Public Space." Paper prepared for presentation at the annual meeting of the American Political Science Association, San Francisco.

Chevènment, Jean-Pierre. 1998. *La lutte contre les violences urbaines*. Circulaire no. NOR/INT/C/98/00061/C, March 11. Paris: Ministère de l'Intérieur.

Chirac, Jacques. 2002. "Entretien avec Jacques Chirac." *La Médina*, 14(April):20–1.

Clément, Jean-François. 1990. "L'Islam en France." Pp. 89–98 in Bruno Étienne, ed., *L'Islam en France*. Paris: Éditions du CNRS.

Cohen, Roger. 2001. "How Open to Immigrants Should Germany Be?" *New York Times*, May 13, p. 11.

Cohn-Bendit, Daniel, and Thomas Smid. 1992. *Heimat Babylon: Das Wagnis der multikulturellen Demokratie*. Hamburg: Hoffmann und Campe.

Colio, Jean. 1998. *Le rap: une réponse des banlieues?* Lyon: Aléas.

Collinson, Sarah. 1993. *Beyond Borders: West European Migration Policy Towards the Twenty-First Century*. London: Royal Institute of International Affairs.

Converse, Philip E. 1964. "The Nature of Belief Systems in Mass Publics." Pp. 206–61 in David Apter, ed., *Ideology and Discontent*. New York: Free Press.

Cornevin, Christophe. 2002. "Islam: L'édifice religieux a été maculé de painture; La mosquée de Lyon appelle ses fidèles à garder leur sang-froid." *Le Figaro*, December 30, p. 7.

Couvreur, Gilles. 1998. *Musulmans de France: Diversité, mutations et perspectives de l'islam français*. Paris: Éditions de l'Atelier.

Crewe, Ivor. 2002. "A New Political Hegemony?" Pp. 207–32 in Alan King, ed., *Britain at the Polls, 2001*. New York: Chatham House.

Daley, Suzanne. 2001. "Europe Wary of Wider Doors to Immigrants." *New York Times*, October 20, p. A3.

———. 2002a. "World Briefing Europe: France: Crime on the Rise." *New York Times*, January 29, p. A8.

———. 2002b. "Extreme Rightist Eclipses Socialist to Qualify for Runoff in France." *New York Times*, April 22, p. A1.

Dassetto, Felice. 2000. "The New European Islam." Pp. 31–45 in Silvio Ferrari and Anthony Bradney, eds., *Islam and European Legal Systems*. Dartmouth, NH: Ashgate.

Davie, Grace. 2000. *Religion in Modern Europe: A Memory Mutates*. Oxford, UK: Oxford University Press.

Deakin, Stephen. 1984. "The Churches, Immigration, and Race Relations." *New Community*, 12(1)(Winter):101–15.

Debeusscher, Philippe. 1995. "Rpt avec mention 'prev'." Wire service article. Informations Générales, November 3. Paris: Agence France Presse.

de Galembert, Claire. 1994. "L'état et les religions des immigrés en France et en Allemagne." Pp. 321–44 in Bernard Falga, Catherine Wihtol de Wenden, and

Claus Leggewie, eds., *Au miroire de l'autre: De l'immigration à l'intégration en France et en Allemagne*. Paris: Les éditions du Cerf.

de Galembert, Claire. 2001. "Les Églises en Allemagne: des colosses au pieds d'argile." *Projet* 267(Fall):65–74.

Delorme, Christian. 1998. *Les banlieues de Dieu*. Paris: Bayard Éditions.

Dennis, Guy and Jon, Ungoed-Thomas. 2000. "Oxford rebels over plan for a minaret amid the spires." *Sunday Times (London)*, July 16.

Depagneux, Marie-Annick. 1994. "La deuxième grande mosquée de France ouvre des portes à Lyon." *Les Échos*, September 30, p. 30.

Department for Education. 1994. *Religious Education and Collective Worship, Circular Number One*. London: Department for Education.

Department for Education. Undated publication. *Information Pack for Promoters of New Minority Schools*. London: Department for Education.

Department of Education and Science. 1985. *Education for All (The Swann Report)*. London: HMSO.

Deutscher Bundestag. 1998. *Grundgesetz für die Bundesrepublik Deutschland*. Bonn: Deutscher Bundestag.

Deutsch-Islamische Schule. n.d. "Deutsch-Islamische Schule: Private Grundschule." Pamphlet. Munich: Deutsch-Islamische Schule.

de Wenden, Catherine Wihtol, and Rémy Leveau. 2001. *La beurgeoisie : Les trois âges de la vie associative issue de l'immigration*. Paris: CNRS Éditions.

Didier, Arnaud. 2000. "Monsieur le maire de Charvieu est extrêmement nerveux. Déjà condamné, Dezempte (DVD) mène sa ville à la baguette." *Libération*, January 14, p. 22.

DİTİB. 1987. "Türkisch-Islamische Union der Anstalt für Religion, e.v." Informational pamphlet. Cologne: DİTİB.

Doomernik, Jeroen. 1995. "The Institutionalization of Turkish Islam in Germany and the Netherlands: A Comparison." *Ethnic and Racial Studies* 18(January):46–63.

Droz, Bernard, and Évelyne Lever. 1982. *Histoire de la guerre d'Algérie, 1954–1962*. Paris: Éditions du Seuil.

Ducomte, Jean-Michel. 2000. *Regards sur la laïcité*. Paris: EDIMAF.

Dwyer, Claire, and Astrid Meyer. 1996. "The Establishment of Islamic Schools: A Controversial Phenomenon in Three European Countries." Pp. 218–42 in W. A. R. Shadid and P. S. van Koningsveld, eds., *Muslims in the Margin: Political Responses to the Presence of Islam in Western Europe*. Kampen, Netherlands: Kok Pharos.

El Ghissassi, Hakim. 2001. "Interview, Osman Molla." *La Médina*, 9(July–August):20–2.

———. 2003. "Les secrets de Sarkozy dans la représentativité de l'islam de France." *Islam: revue de société, d'histoire et de théologie* 4(February–April):6–10.

El Guindi, Fadwa. 1999. *Veil: Modesty, Privacy and Resistance*. Oxford, UK: Berg.

Erikson, Robert S., Norman R. Luttbeg, and Kent L. Tedin. 1991. *American Public Opinion*, 4th ed. New York: Macmillan.

Erlanger, Steven, and Chris Hedges. 2001. "Terror Cell Slips through Europe's Grasp." *New York Times*, December 28, p. A1.

Esposito, John L., and John O. Voll. 1996. *Islam and Democracy*. Oxford, UK: Oxford University Press.

Étienne, Bruno. 1989. *La France et L'islam*. Paris: Hachette.

Evangelische Kirche in Deutschland. 1999. "Religionsunterricht für muslimische Schülerinnen und Schüler: Eine Stellungnahme des Kirchenamtes der Evangelischen Kirche in Deutschland." Pamphlet. Hannover: Kirchenamt der Evangelischen Kirche in Deutschland.

――――. 2003. "EKD-Statistik, Kirchensteuer 2000." Available at http://www.ekd. de/statistik/3217_kirchensteueraufkommen.html. Accessed May 5, 2003.

Evans, Peter B., Dietrich Rueschemeyer, and Theda Skocpol, eds. 1985. *Bringing the State Back In*. Cambridge, UK: Cambridge University Press.

Falanga, Olivier, and Isabelle Trouvé. 1992. "Une grande mosquée pour Marseille? Les enjeux locaux d'un débat national." *Esprit* (January) 138–45.

Faraz, Mohammed. 1998. "MCD: Dad's Muslim Army." *Q News* 287 (April):24.

Favell, Adrian. 1998. *Philosophies of Integration: Immigration and the Idea of Citizenship in France and Britain*. London: Macmillan.

FCCM [Forum citoyen des cultures musulmanes]. 2002. *Pour une France juste: 89 propositions du F.C.C.M. aux candidats*. Paris: La Médina Édition.

Ferree, Myra Mae. 1992. "The Political Context of Rationality: Rational Choice Theory and Resource Mobilization." Pp. 29–52 in Aldon D. Morris and Carol McClung Mueller, eds., *Frontiers in Social Movement Theory*. New Haven, CT: Yale University Press.

Fetzer, Joel S. 2000. *Public Attitudes toward Immigration in the United States, France, and Germany*. Cambridge, UK: Cambridge University Press.

Filali, Salim. 2002. "Élections, les musulmans aux urnes: L'appel des sirènes électorales." *La Médina* 14(April):18–9.

Flinthoff, John-Paul. 2003. "Cruel Britannia Britain Has a History of Tolerance towards Immigrants." *Financial Times Weekend Magazine*, May 31, pp. 14–20.

Foblets, Marie-Claire S. F. G. 1999. "Family Disputes Involving Muslim Women in Contemporary Europe: Immigrant Women Caught between Islamic Family Law and Women's Rights." Pp. 167–78 in Courtney W. Howland, ed., *Religious Fundamentalisms and the Human Rights of Women*. New York: Palgrave.

Foreign and Commonwealth Office. 1995. *Muslims in Britain*. London: Foreign and Commonwealth Office.

Fregosi, Franck. 1997. "L'Islam en Terre Concordataire." *Hommes & Migrations* 1209(September–October):29–48.

Frémeaux, Jacques. 1991. *La France et l'islam depuis 1789*. Paris: Presses Universitaires de France.

Friedman, Michel. 1990. "Mosquées en terre de France." *Jeune Afrique Plus* 4 (January–February):55–68.

Frigulietti, James. 1991. "Gilbert Romme and the Making of the French Republican Calendar." In David G. Troyanksky, Alfred Cismaru, and Norwood Andrews, eds., *The French Revolution in Culture and Society*. Westport, CT: Greenwood.

Fulbrook, Mary. 1997. *Anatomy of a Dictatorship: Inside the GDR 1949–1989*. Oxford, UK: Oxford University Press.

Gabriel, Karl. 1995. "The Post-War Generations and Institutional Religion in Germany." Pp. 113–39 in Wade Clark Roof, Jackson W. Carrol, and David A. Roozen, eds., *The Post-War Generation and Establishment Religion*. Boulder, CO: Westview Press.

Gadant, Monique. 1988. *Islam et nationalisme en Algérie d'après 'El Moudjahid,' organe central du FLN de 1956 à 1962*. Paris: Éditions L'Harmattan.

Gamson, William. 1990. *The Strategy of Social Protest*. Belmont, CA: Wadsworth.

Garbaye, Romain. 2000. "Ethnic Minorities, Cities, and Institutions: A Comparison of the Modes of Management of Ethnic Diversity of a French and a British City." Pp. 283–311 in Ruud Koopmans and Paul Statham, eds., *Challenging Immigration and Ethnic Relations Politics*. Oxford, UK: Oxford University Press.

Garner, Richard. 2001. "Faith Schools Expansion Opposed by 43%." *Independent* [London], December 1, p. 2.

Gaspard, Françoise, and Farhad Khosrokhavar. 1995. *Le foulard et la République*. Paris: La Découverte.

Gastaut, Yvan. 2000. *L'immigration et l'opinion en France sous la V ͤ République*. Paris: Seuil.

Gattegno, Hervé, and Erich Inciyan. 1996. "La piste islamiste est priviliée après l'attentat du RER Port-Royal." *Le Monde*, December 5, p. 6.

Gebauer, Klaus, ed. 1986. *Religiöse Unterweisung für Schüler islamischen Glaubens: 24 Unterrichtseinheiten für die Grundschule*. Soest, Germany: Landesinstitut für Schule und Weiterbildung.

Geddes, Andrew. 2002. "The Borders of Absurdity and Fear." *Times Higher Education Supplement*, May 24, p. 17.

Geisser, Vincent. 2002. "Les musulmans de France: Un lobby électoral en marche?" *La Médina* 14(April):26–8.

German Information Service. 1996. *Facts about Germany*. Frankfurt: Societäts-Verlag.

Gildea, Robert. 1997. *France since 1945*. New York and Oxford, UK: Oxford University Press.

Gilroy, Paul. 1991. *There Ain't No Black in the Union Jack: The Cultural Politics of Race and Nation*. Chicago, IL: Chicago University Press.

Giudice, Fausto. 1992. *Arabicides: une chronique française, 1970–1991*. Paris: La Découverte.

Gür, Metin. 1993. *Türkische-islamische Vereinigungen in der Bundesrepublik Deutschland*. Frankfurt a.M.: Brandes & Apsel.

Gold, Richard. 1999. *The Education Act Explained*. London: Stationary Office.

Gonod, Michel. 1989. "La riposte: Pourquoi ce principal de collège s'oppose à l'offensive des religieux." *Paris-Match*, November 9, pp. 60–3.

Gould, Andrew C. 1999. *Origins of Liberal Dominance: State, Church, and Nineteenth Century Europe*. Ann Arbor, MI: University of Michigan Press.

Greenawalt. Kent. 1988. *Religious Convictions and Political Choice*. Oxford, UK: Oxford University Press.

Guardian. 2002. "From Scholarship, Sailors and Sects to the Mills and the Mosques." *Guardian* (London), June 18, p. 6.

Guillaume, Myriam. 2001. "Un accord-cadre pour donner une vraie place à l'Islam." *La Marseillaise*, May 30, p. 8.

Guiraudon, Virginie. 1998. "Citizenship Rights for Non-Citizens: France, Germany, and the Netherlands." Pp. 272–318 in Christian Joppke, ed., *Challenge to the Nation-State: Immigration in Western Europe and the United States*. Oxford, UK: Oxford University Press.

Gülçiçek, Ali Duran. 1996. *Der Weg der Aleviten (Bektaschiten): Menschenliebe, Toleranz, Frieden und Freundschaft*, 2nd ed. Cologne: Gülçiçek-Ethnographia Anatolica-Verlag.

Haarscher, Guy. 1998. *La laïcité*, 2nd ed. Paris: Presses Universitaires de France.

Halstead, J. Mark. 2003. "Schooling and Cultural Maintenance for Religious Minorities in the Liberal State." Pp. 273–98 in Kevin McDonough and Walter Feinberg, eds., *Education and Citizenship in Liberal-Democratic Societies: Teaching for Cosmopolitan Values and Collective Identities*. Oxford, UK: Oxford University Press.

Hargreaves, Alec G. 1995. *Immigration, Race and Ethnicity in Contemporary France*. London: Routledge.

Hasselbach, Ingo. 1995. *Die Abrechnung: Ein Neonazi steigt aus*. Berlin: Aufbau Taschenbuch Verlag.

Hauerwas, Stanley. 1981. *A Community of Character: Toward a Constructive Christian Social Ethic*. Notre Dame, IN: Notre Dame University Press.

Haut Conseil à l'Intégration. 1998. *Lutte contre les discriminations: faire respecter le principe d'égalité*. Rapport au Premier ministre. Paris: La documentation Française.

———. 2001. *L'Islam dan la République*. Rapport au Premier ministre. Paris: La documentation Française.

Hayes, Dominic. 2001. "Belief in Faith Schools Wavering–Poll." *Press Association News*, November 30, section "Home News."

Heine, Peter. 1997. *Halbmond über deutschen Dächern*. Munich: List Verlag.

Heitmeyer, Wilhelm, Joachim Müller, and Helmut Schröder. 1997. *Verlockender Fundamentalismus: Türkische Jugendliche in Deutschland*. Frankfurt a.M.: Suhrkamp.

Hepple, Bob and Tufyal Choudhury. 2001. *Tackling Religious Discrimination: Practical Implications for Policymakers and Legislators*. London: Home Office Research, Development, and Statistics Directorate.

Herbert, Ulrich. 1990. *A History of Foreign Labor in Germany, 1880–1980*. Translated by William Templer. Ann Arbor, MI: University of Michigan Press.

Hervier-Léger, Danièle. 1995. "The Case of French Catholicism." Pp. 151–169 in Wade Clark Roof, Jackson W. Carroll, and David A. Roozen, eds., *The Post-War Generation and Establishment Religion*. Boulder, CO: Westview Press.

Hewitt, Ibrahim. 1998. "Beyond the Holy Grail." *Q News* 285 (February):14.

―――. 2002. "Schools of Good Faith." *Q News* 339–40 (January–February):16–17.

Hoffman, Abdul Hadi. 1996. "Muslims in Germany: The Struggle for Integration." Pp. 41–55 in Tamara Sonn, ed., *Islam and the Question of Minorities*. Atlanta, GA: Scholars Press.

Hofmann, Murad Wilfried. 1996. *Reise nach Mekka: Ein Deutscher lebt den Islam*. Munich: Eugen Dietrichs Verlag.

Hofmann, Robert. 1993. *Geschichte der deutschen Parteien: Von der Kaiserzeit bis zur Gegenwart*. Munich: Piper.

Hoge, Warren. 2002. "New Immigration Plan in Britain Would Restrict Asylum Seekers." *New York Times*, May 31, p. A4.

Holborn, Hajo. 1969. *A History of Modern Germany, 1840–1945*. New York: Alfred A. Knopf.

Hollifield, James F. 1992. *Immigrants, Markets, and States: The Political Economy of Postwar Europe*. Cambridge, MA: Harvard University Press.

Home Office. 2001. *Community Cohesion: A Report of the Independent Review Team Chaired by Ted Cantle*. London: Home Office.

Hoskin, Marilyn. 1991. *New Immigrants and Democratic Society: Minority Integration in Western Democracies*. New York: Praeger.

House for the Future, A. 2000. London: Stationary Office.

Howe, Darcus. 1998. "State Funding for Muslim Schools Is a Victory against Islamophobia and for Common Sense. *New Statesman* 127(January 16):48.

Hunter, James Davison. 1991. *Culture Wars: The Struggle to Define America*. New York: Basic Books.

Hylson-Smith, Kenneth. 1988. *Evangelicals in the Church of England*. Edinburgh, UK: T&T Clark.

IDTIA [Institut für deutsch-türkische Integrationsstudien und interreligiöse Arbeit]. 1999. "Institut für deutsch-türkische Integrationsstudien und interreligiöse Arbeit." Pamphlet. Mannheim: Institut für deutsch-türkische Integrationsstudien.

INED [Institut National d'Études Démographiques]. 1977. *Les immigrés du Maghreb: Études sur l'adaptation en milieu urbain*. Paris: Presses universitaires de France.

Inglehart, Ronald. 1990. *Culture Shift in Advanced Industrial States*. Princeton, NJ: Princeton University Press.

IQRA Trust. 1991. "Participating in SACREs: Advice for Muslims." London: IQRA Trust.

Ireland, Patrick R. 1994. *The Policy Challenge of Ethnic Diversity: Immigrant Politics in France and Switzerland*. Cambridge, MA: Harvard University Press.

Islamic Human Rights Commission. 2000. *Anti-Muslim Discrimination and Hostility in the United Kingdom*. London: Islamic Human Rights Commission.

———. 2001. *The Oldham Riots: Discrmination, Deprivation and Communal Tension in the United Kingdom*. London: Islamic Human Rights Commission.

James, Barry. 2002. "British Debate Deepens on Faith-Based Schools." *International Herald Tribune*, February 12, p. 3.

Jansen, Frank. 1999. "Rassistische Alltagserfahrungen im Osten." Pp. 227–37 in Jens Mecklenburg, ed., *Braune Gefahr: DVU, NPD, REP Geschichte und Zukunft*. Berlin: Elefanten Press.

Jeffries, Stuart. 2000. "France Horrified by Rise of the Teenage Killers: Turf Wars and Macho Culture Fuel Increase in Violent Crime by Juveniles." *Guardian* (London), December 13, p. 15.

Jennings, M. Kent, and Richard G. Niemi. 1981. *Generations and Politics: A Panel Study of Young Adults and their Parents*. Princeton, NJ: Princeton University Press.

Jézéquel, Laurent. 1999. *Liberté de croire, liberté de penser: essai et anthologie*. Paris: Gallimard.

John, Mark. 2002. "France and Germany Push for Tighter Immigration." *Muslim News*, May 27, p. 1.

Joly, Danièle. 1995. *Britannia's Crescent: Making a Place for Muslims in British Society*. Aldershot, UK: Averbury.

Joppke, Christian. 1998. "Why Liberal States Accept Unwanted Immigration." *World Politics* 50(2):266–93.

———. 1999. *Immigration and the Nation-State: The United States, Germany, and Great Britain*. Oxford: Oxford University Press.

Jospin, Lionel. 2002. "Entretien avec Jacques Chirac." *La Médina*, 14(April):22–5.

Kaltenbach, Jeanne-Hélène, and Michèle Tribalat. 2002. *La République et l'islam: Entre crainte et aveuglement*. Paris: Gallimard.

Kalyvas, Stathis N. 1996. *The Rise of Christian Democracy in Europe*. Ithaca, NY, and London: Cornell University Press.

Karakasoğlu, Yasemin. 1996. "Turkish Cultural Orientations in Germany and the Role of Islam." Pp. 157–79 in David Horrocks and Eva Kolinsky, eds., *Turkish Culture in German Society Today*. Providence, RI: Berghahn.

Karakasoğlu, Yasemin, and Gerd Nonneman. 1996. "Muslims in Germany, with Special Reference to the Turkish-Islamic Community." Pp. 241–65 in Gerd Nonneman, Tim Noblock, and Bogdan Szajkowski, eds., *Muslim Communities in the New Europe*. Reading, UK: Ithaca Press.

Karapin, Roger. 2000. "Major Anti-Minority Riots and National Legislation in Britain and Germany." Pp. 312–47 in Ruud Koopmans and Paul Statham, eds., *Challenging Immigration and Ethnic Relations Politics*. Oxford, UK: Oxford University Press.

Kassovitz, Mathieu. 1996. *Hate/La haine*. Videotape. New York: PolyGram Video.

Kaufmann, Horst. 2001. "Großzügig genug: Zum Thema eine Moschee für Stuttgart." Letter to the editor. *Stuttgarter Zeitung*, February 8, p. 29.

KAV [Kommunale Ausländer- und Ausländerinnenvertretung]. 1998. "KAV Local Foreigners' Representative Board, Frankfurt am Main." Pamphlet. Frankfurt a.M.: KAV.

Kaye, Ronald. 1993. "The Politics of Religious Slaughter of Animals: Strategies for Ethno-Religious Political Action." *New Community* 19(2):235–50.

Keene, Michael, and Jan Keene. 1997. *Junior Steps in Religious Education, Year 4*. Cheltenham, UK: Stanley Thornes.

Keller, Nuh Ha Mim. 1999. *Evolution Theory and Islam*. Cambridge, UK: Muslim Academy Trust.

Kepel, Gilles. 1991. *Les banlieues de l'islam: Naissance d'une religion en France*. Paris: Éditions du Seuil.

———. 1997. *Allah in the West: Islamic Movements in America and Europe*. Translated by Susan Milner. Stanford, CA: Stanford University Press.

Kettani, M. Ali. 1996. "Challenges to the Organization of Muslim Communities in Western Europe: The Political Dimension." In W. A. R. Shadid and P. S. Van Koningsfeld, eds., *Political Participation and Identities of Muslims in Non-Muslim States*. Kampen, Netherlands: Kok Pharos.

Khan, Khalida. 1999. "Where's the Muslims in Macpherson's Black and White Britain?" *Q News* 302–3(March):26–7.

Khoury, Adel Theodor, Peter Heine, and Janbernd Oebbecke, eds. 2000. *Handbuch Recht und Kultur des Islams in der deutschen Gesellschaft: Probleme im Alltag – Hintergründe – Antworten*. Gütersloh, Germany: Gütersloher Verlagshaus.

KIGST [Kirchliche Gemeindschaftsstelle für elektronische Datenverarbeitung]. 2003. Available at http://www.kigst.de/gesetze/kirchgesetze/frame.htm. Accessed May 5.

Knubbertz, Angelika. 2000. "Das 'Berliner Modell' oder: Die andere Art, Religionsunterricht zu organisieren." Pp. 18–24 in Beauftragte der Bundesregierung für Ausländerfrage, *Islamisher Religionsunterricht an staatlichen Schulen in Deutschland: Praxis – Konzepte – Perspektiven; Dokumentation eines Fachgespräches*. No. 8 (September). Berlin and Bonn: Beauftragte der Bundesregierung für Ausländerfrage.

Koch, H. W. 1978. *History of Prussia*. New York: Dorset.

Kolb, Eberhard. 2000. *Die Weimarer Republik*. Munich: Oldenbourg.

Kolinsky, Eva. 1996. "Non-German Minorities in German Society." Pp. 71–111 in David Horrocks and Eva Kolinsky, eds., *Turkish Culture in German Society Today*. Providence, RI: Berghahn Books.

König, Matthias. 2000. "Identités nationales et institutions globales: la restructuration des relations entre religion et citoyenneté en Europe." Pp. 211–22 in Jean-Pierre Bastien, Françoise Champion, and Kathy Rousselet, eds., *La globalisation du religieux*. Paris: L'Harmattan.

Koopmans, Ruud, and Paul Statham. 2000. "Migration and Ethnic Relations as a Field of Political Contention: An Opportunity Structure Approach." Pp. 11–56 in Ruud Koopmans and Paul Statham, eds., *Challenging Immigration and Ethnic Relations Politics*. Oxford, UK: Oxford University Press.

Koulberg, André. 1991. *L'Affaire du voile islamique: Comment perdre une bataille symbolique*. Marseille: Fenêtre sur cour.

Krieger-Krynicki, Annie. 1985. *Les musulmans en France*. Paris: Maisonneuve & Larose.

Kugler, Roland. 1993. *Ausländerrecht: Ein Handbuch*. Göttingen, Germany: Lamuv Verlag.

Kusbah, Muafa Disūfī. 1997. *al-Muslimūn fī Almāniyā: usūlun wa hijrāt* [Muslims in Germany: Origins and Migrations]. Cairo: Majallat al-Azhar.

Kymlicka, Will. 1995. *Multicultural Citizenship: A Liberal Theory of Minority Rights*. Oxford, UK: Oxford University Press.

Lamchichi, Abderrahim. 1999. *Islam et musulmans de France: Pluralisme, laïcité et citoyenneté*. Paris: L'Harmattan.

Landesinstitut für Schule und Weiterbildung. 1986. *Religiöse Unterweisung für Schüler islamischen Glaubens: 24 Unterrichtseinheiten für die Grundschule*. Soest, Germany: Landesinstitut für Schule und Weiterbildung.

———.1991. *Religiöse Unterweisung für Schülerinnen und Schüler islamischen Glaubens: 12 Unterrichtseinheiten für die Klassen 5 und 6*. Soest, Germany: Landesinstitut für Schule und Weiterbildung.

———.1996. *Religiöse Unterweisung für Schülerinnen und Schüler islamischen Glaubens: 24 Unterrichtseinheiten für die Jahrgangsstufen 7 bis 10*. Soest, Germany: Landesinstitut für Schule und Weiterbildung.

Landler, Mark. 2003. "A German Court Accepts Teacher's Head Scarf." *New York Times*, September 25, p. A3.

Lebon, André. 2000. *Immigration et présence étrangère en France en 1999: Premiers enseignements du recensement*. Paris: La documentation Française.

Le Breton, Jean-Marie. 1998. *Muslims in France and Britain*. London: Franco-British Council.

Leckie, David, and David Pickersgill. 1999. *The 1998 Human Rights Act Explained*. London: Stationary Office.

Leege, David C., and Lyman A. Kellstedt. 1993. *Rediscovering the Religious Factor in American Politics*. Armonk, NY: M. E. Sharpe.

Leege, David C., Kenneth D. Wald, Brian S. Krueger, and Paul D. Mueller. 2002. *The Politics of Cultural Differences: Social Change and Voter Mobilization Strategies in the Post-New Deal Period*. Princeton, NJ: Princeton University Press.

Leggewie, Claus. 1992. "'Stotz, ein Deutscher zu sein . . .'–die neue Angst vor den Fremden." Pp. 423–30 in Klaus J. Bade, ed., *Deutsche im Ausland, Fremde in Deutschland: Migration in Geschichte und Gegenwart*. Munich: Beck.

———.1994. "Das Ende der Lebenslügen: Plädoyer für eine neue Einwanderungspolitik." Pp. 55–60 in Klaus J. Bade, ed., *Das Manifest der 60: Deutschland und die Einwanderung*. Munich: Beck.

Le Hir, Pierre. 1991. "Deux ans après la déstruction 'accidentelle' de la mosquée, le maire de Charvieu-Chavagneux addresse un ultimatum à l'Association islamique." *Le Monde*, August 17, p. 6.

Le Messager de Marseille. 1839. "Nouvelles de la ville." May 24, p. 1.

Lemmen, Thomas. 2001. *Muslime in Deutschland: Eine Herausforderung für Kirche und Gesellschaft*. Baden-Baden, Germany: Nomos.

Le Moigne, Guy. 1986. *L'immigration en France*, 3ʳᵈ ed. Paris: Presses Universitaires de France.

Le Monde. 1989a. "Il n'existe qu'un seul établissement confessionel subventionné par l'Education nationale." December 1, in Centre de Ressources Documentaires. *Dossier de presse sur l'affaire du foulard islamique*. Paris: Agence pour le Développement des Relations Interculturelles. Vol. 4, p. 73.

———.1989b. "Un musulman français sur deux n'en veut pas." December 1, in Centre de Ressources Documentaires. *Dossier de presse sur l'affaire du foulard islamique*. Paris: Agence pour le Développement des Relations Interculturelles. Vol. 4, p. 73.

———.1991. "Des cocktails Molotov ont été lancés contre la mairie et le centre islamique de Charvieu-Chavagneux." December 21.

———.1992. "Des élus de l'Isère condamnés pour incitation à la haine raciale." December 21.

———.1994. "Inaugurant la nouvelle mosquée de Lyon, Charles Pasqua souhaite que 'l'islam trouve sa place en France'." October 1, p. 26.

———.2003. "Trois associations pronent un 'islam citoyen'." May 21, p. 11.

Le Tourneau, Dominique. 2000. *L'Église et l'État en France*. Paris: Presses Universitaires de France.

Leveau, Rémy, and Dominique Schnapper. 1988. "Religion et politique: Juifs et musulmans maghrébins en France." Pp. 99–140 in Rémy Leveau and Gilles Kepel, eds., *Les musulmans dans la société française*. Paris: Presses de la Fondation nationale des sciences politiques.

Lewis, Bernard. 1993. *Islam and the West*. Oxford, UK: Oxford University Press.

Lewis, H. D. 1985. *The French Education System*. New York: St. Martin's Press.

Lewis, Philip. 1994. *Islamic Britain: Religion, Politics and Identity among British Muslims*. London: I. B. Tauris.

Liederman, Lina Molokotus. 2000. "Pluralism in Education: The Display of Islamic Affiliation in French and British Schools." *Islam and Christian Muslim Relations* 11(1):105–17.

Lipset, Seymour Martin, and Stein Rokkan. 1967. "Cleavage Structures, Party Systems and Voter Alignments." In Seymour Martin Lipset and Stein Rokkan, eds., *Party Structures and Voter Alignments*. Baltimore, MD: Johns Hopkins University Press.

Loch, Dieter. 1995. "Moi, Khaled Kelkal." *Le Monde*, October 7, pp. 10–12.

Locke, John. 1990 [1689]. *A Letter Concerning Toleration*. Amherst, NY: Prometheus.

Loeffel, Laurence. 1999. *Ferdinand Buisson: Apôtre de l'école laïque*. Paris: Hachette Éducation.

Lorcerie, Françoise. 1994. "L'Islam dans les cours de 'langue et culture d'origine': le procès." *Revue Européenne des Migrations Internationales* 10(2):5–43.

Luck, Deborah. 2000. "Smallest Party Hoping for a Big Future." *Birmingham Post*, May 6.

Lyall, Sarah. 2002. "When Asylum Seekers Knock, Europe Is Deaf." *New York Times*, June 20, p. A3.

Macedo, Stephen. 1990. *Liberal Virtues*. Oxford, UK: Oxford University Press.

———.2003. "Liberalism and Group Identity." Pp. 414–36 in Kevin McDonough and Walter Feinberg, eds., *Education and Citizenship in Liberal-Democratic Societies: Teaching for Cosmopolitan Values and Collective Identities*. Oxford, UK: Oxford University Press.

Machen, G. I. T. 1998. *Churches and Social Issues in Twentieth Century Britain*. Oxford, UK: Clarendon Press.

Mack, Daniela, and Martin Hohnecker. 2000. "'Wir sind zum Gespräch und zu Kompromissen bereit': Vertreter des Landesverbandes der Islamischen Kulturzentren: Wir machen uns schon Gedanken über die Ängste der Bevölkerung." *Stuttgarter Zeitung*, March 29.

Macpherson, Duncan. 1997. "Papists Then and Muslims Now." Pp. 109–26 in Alan Jones, ed., *University Lectures in Islamic Studies*. London: Altajir World of Islam Trust.

Malik, Nadeem. 2000. *The East London Central Mosque: Organising in Action*. Leicester, UK: Islamic Foundation.

———. 2001. *Religious Discrimination: Historical and Current Developments in the English Legal System*. Leicester, UK: Islamic Foundation.

Mammeri, Youssef. 2002. "Le Conseil Français du Culte Musulman: Avant l'Assemblée Nationale." *La Médina* 14(April):14.

Marchand, Stephane. 1997. "Patrick Weil remet ce matin son rapport à Lionel Jospin, en vue du débat parlementaire de l'automne." *Le Figaro*, July 31, section "Notre Vie."

Marlowe, Lara. 1998. "Voices of Left Sound Faintly through Uproar on Immigration." *Irish Times*, April 9, city edition, section "World News," p. 14.

Marseille, Jacques, and Jacques Scheibling, eds. 1997. *Histoire Géographie 5e: Programme 1997*. Paris: Nathan.

Mason, Trevor, and Zoe Hughes. 2002. "Asylum Bill Clears Commons." *Press Association Limited*, June 12, p. 2.

McAdam, Doug. 1982. *Political Process and the Development of Black Insurgency, 1930–1970*. Chicago, IL: University of Chicago Press.

McClean, David. 1996. "State and Church in the United Kingdom." Pp. 307–22 in Gerhard Robbers, ed., *State and Church in the European Union*. Baden-Baden, Germany: Nomos.

McDonough, Kevin, and Walter Feinberg, eds. 2003. *Education and Citizenship in Liberal-Democratic Societies: Teaching for Cosmopolitan Values and Collective Identities*. Oxford, UK: Oxford University Press.

McLoughlin, Sean. 2002. "Recognising Muslims: Religion, Ethnicity and Identity Politics in Britain." *Cahiers d'études sur la Méditerranée orientale et le monde turco-iranien* 33(January–June):43–54.

McRoy, Anthony. 2001. "British Muslims and the Elections." *Q News* 330 (April):12.

Meier, Kurt. 1992. *Kreuz und Hakenkreuz: Die evangelische Kirche im Dritten Reich.* Munich: Deutscher Taschenbuch Verlag.

Messina, Anthony M. 1996. "The Not So Silent Revolution: Postwar Migration to Western Europe." *World Politics* 49:130–54.

Messner, Francis. 1998. "L'enseignement de la théologie à l'université publique: L'exemple de la création d'une faculté de théologie musulmane à Strasbourg." Pp. 141–67 in Franck Frégosi, ed., *La Formation des Cadres Religieux Musulmans en France: Approches socio-juridiques.* Paris: L'Harmattan.

———. 2000. "Régime des cultes: Caractères et principes généraux, Police des cultes." *Juris-Classeur*, Alsace-Moselle, Fasc. 230, 8/2000, 10 April, pp. 1–16.

Migration News. 1998. "France: New Law." Migration News [published by the University of California at Davis, Department of Agricultural and Resource Economics, and available at http://migration.ucdavis.edu/mn] 5(5)(May).

———. 2000a. "Germany: Naturalization." 7(1)(January).

———. 2000b. "Germany: Culture, Immigration." 7(12)(December).

———. 2003. "France, Benelux." 10(3)(July).

Ministère de l'intérieur. 1999. *Cultes et associations cultuelles, congrégations et collectivités religieuses.* March 12 edition. Paris: Journaux officiels.

Modood, Tariq. 1994. "Establishment, Multiculturalism and British Citizenship." *Political Quarterly* 65(1):53–73.

Mohr, Irka-Christin. 2000. *Muslime zwischen Herkunft und Zukunft: Islamischer Unterricht in Berlin.* Berlin: Das Arabische Buch.

Monchambert, Sabine. 1993. *L'enseignement privé en France.* Paris: Presses Universitaires de France.

Money, Jeannette, 1999. *Fences and Neighbors: The Political Geography of Immigration Control.* Ithaca, NY: Cornell University Press.

Monin, Jacques. 1989. "Foulards sans drame à Montpellier." *Le Monde*, October 25, in Centre de Ressources Documentaires. *Dossier de presse sur l'affaire du foulard islamique.* Paris: Agence pour le Développement des Relations Interculturelles. Vol. 1, p. 93.

Monsma, Stephen V., and J. Christopher Soper. 1997. *The Challenge of Pluralism: Church and State in Five Western Democracies.* Lanham, MD: Rowman and Littlefield.

MORI [Market and Opinion Research International] 2001b. "Voters Oppose Expansion of Faith Schools." http//:www.mori.com/polls. Accessed on February 28, 2003.

———. 2001c. "Eastern Eye Survey Confirms the Loyalty of British Asians." http//:www.mori.com/polls. Accessed on May 5, 2003.

Morris, Nigel. 2002. "Dobson Leads Labour Revolt on Faith Schools." *Independent* (London), February 2, p. 3.

Morsy, Magali. 1992. "Rester musulman en société étrangère." *Pouvoirs* 62:119–33.

Münz, Rainer, and Ralf Ulrich. 1995. *Changing Patterns of Migration: The Case of Germany, 1945–1994.* Center for German and European Studies Working Paper 4.5. Berkeley, CA: University of California, Berkeley.

Muslim Council of Britain. 2003. "About MCB." http://www.mcb.org.uk. Accessed April 28.

Muslim Directory. 2000. London: Muslim Directory.

Muslim Educational Trust. 1984. *Syllabus and Guidelines for Islamic Teaching*. London: Muslim Educational Trust.

Muslim Liaison Committee. n.d. "Report on the Policy on Meeting the Religious and Cultural Needs of Muslim Pupils." Unpublished manuscript of the Muslim Liaison Committee, City of Birmingham.

Nanji, Azim A. 1996. *The Muslim Almanac*. New York: Gale Research.

Nekkaz, Rachid. 2002. "89 propositions pour la France de demain." *La Médina* 14(April):30–1.

Newbigin, Leslie, Lamin Sanneh, and Jenny Taylor, eds. 1998. *The Secular Myth*. London: SPCK.

Nielsen, Jørgen S. 1992. *Muslims in Western Europe*. Edinburgh, UK: University of Edinburgh Press.

———.1995. *Muslims in Western Europe*, 2nd ed. Edinburgh, UK: Edinburgh University Press.

———.1999. *Toward a European Islam*. London: Macmillan.

Noiriel, Gérard. 1988. *Le creuset français: Histoire de l'immigration, XIXᵉ–XXᵉ siècles*. Paris: Éditions du Seuil.

Norfolk, Andrew. 2003. "Creationists Planning to Open Six New Schools." *Times (London)*, April 28, p. 4.

OECD [Organisation for Economic Co-operation and Development]. 1995. *Secondary Education in France: A Decade of Change*. Paris: OECD.

Office for National Statistics. 2002. *Social Focus in Brief: Children*. http://www.statistics.gov.uk. Accessed May 9.

———. 2003. "Census 2001: Ethnicity and Religion in England and Wales." http://www.statistics.gov.uk. Accessed on June 4.

O'Keefe, Bernadette. 1986. *Faith, Culture, and the Dual System*. London: Falmer Press.

———.1988. *Schools for Tomorrow: Building Walls or Building Bridges?* London: Falmer Press.

Okin, Susan Moller, ed. 1999. *Is Multiculturalism Bad for Women?* Princeton, NJ: Princeton University Press.

———. 2003. "Mistresses of Their Own Destiny: Group Rights, Gender, and Realistic Right of Exit." Pp. 325–50 in Kevin McDonough and Walter Feinberg, eds., *Education and Citizenship in Liberal-Democratic Societies: Teaching for Cosmopolitan Values and Collective Identities*. Oxford, UK: Oxford University Press.

Olivier, Bertrand. 2003. "Un foulard déclenche une grève dans un lycée de Lyon." *Libération*, March 13, p. 18.

O'Neill, Daniel I. 1999. "Multicultural Liberals and the Rushdie Affair: A Cultural Critique of Kymlicka, Taylor, and Walzer." *Review of Politics* 61 (2):219–50.

Oßwald, Hildegund. 2001a. "Streit um Heslacher Moschee geht weiter: Gemein-deratsvotum erst in zwei Wochen – Stadt rechtfertigt Genehmigungsabsicht." *Stuttgarter Zeitung*, January 17, p. 18.

———. 2001b. "Gutachten: Stadt muss Moschee nicht genehmigen." *Stuttgarter Zeitung*, January 26, p. 25.

———. 2003. "Streit ums Geld blockiert Moscheepläne: Gemeinderat soll Ende Juli über Rücklauf des gannschen Areals in Heslach entscheiden." *Stuttgarter Zeitung*, May 22, p. 20.

Özdemir, Cem. 1999. *Currywurst und Döner: Integration in Deutschland*. Bergisch Gladbach, Germany: Gustav Lübbe Verlag.

———. 2002. *(K)eine Frage der Kultur/Sorun Gerçekten Kültür mü?* Freiburg, Germany: Belchen.

Parekh, Bhikhu. 2000. *Rethinking Multiculturalism: Cultural Diversity and Political Theory*. London: Macmillan.

Pazarkaya, Utku. 2000. "Nachgefragt: Duray Polat." *Stuttgarter Nachrichten*, February 11, p. 19.

Peach, Ceri, and Günther Glebe. 1995. "Muslim Minorities in Western Europe." *Ethnic and Racial Studies* 18(1):26–45.

Pena-Ruiz, Henri. 2001. *La laïcité pour l'égalité*. Paris: Mille et une nuits.

Penninx, Rinus, Jeannette Schoorl, and Carlo van Praag. 1993. *The Impact of International Migration on Receiving Countries: The Case of the Netherlands*. Amsterdam: Swets and Zeitlinger.

Pfaff, Ulrich. 2000. "Islamische Unterweisung an den Schulen in Nordrhein-Westfalen." *Epd-Dokumentation*, 2(February):42–4.

———. 2002. "Islamische Underweisung auf Deutsch: Beitrag zur mündlichen Anhörung des Innen- und Rechtsausschusses des Schleswig-Holsteiner Landtags am 05. Juni 2002." Electronic press release (June 3). Düsseldorf: Ministerium für Schule, Wissenschaft und Forschung des Landes Nordrhein-Westfalen.

Philippe, Bernard, and Nathaniel Herzberg. 1997. "Immigration: le gouvernement reste sourd aux critiques émises à gauche; Les projets de loi sur la nationalité et les conditions d'entrée et de séjour des étrangers ont été transmis, lundi 15 septembre, au Conseil d'État. Malgré des voix discordantes dans la majorité, les arbitrages n'ont guère modifié l'équilibre des textes, fondé sur le rapport de Patrick Weil." *Le Monde*, September 16, section "Société," p. 10.

Philpott, Daniel. 2001. *Revolutions in Sovereignty: How Ideas Shaped Modern International Relations*. Princeton, NJ: Princeton University Press.

Poly, Jean-Pierre. 1992. "Les deux France." Pp. 133–55 in Yves Lequin, ed., *Histoire des étrangers et de l'immigration en France*. Paris: Références Larousse.

Poly, Jean-Pierre, and Pierre Riché. 1992. "La fin de l'errance." Pp. 65–80 in Yves Lequin, ed., *Histoire des étrangers et de l'immigration en France*. Paris: Références Larousse.

Power, Carla. 2003. "The War at Home." *New York Times*, March 31, p. 50.

Preißler, Claus [Assistant to Helmut Schmitt, the Beauftrager für ausländische Einwohner of the City of Mannheim]. 2003. Fax to Joel Fetzer, July 7.

Putnam, Robert D. 1993. *Making Democracy Work: Civic Traditions in Modern Italy*. Princeton, NJ: Princeton University Press.

Pyslarou, Elizabeth. 2000. *Exprimer son malaise: le cas des jeunes marginaux en France et aux États-Unis*. M.A. thesis, University of Toledo.

Q News. 1998. "Satire Gets Priest Hot under the Collar." *Q News* 290 (May):16.

———. 2002. "Muslim Council of Britain: Much Ado about Nothing." *Q News* 341–2 (March–April):22–3.

Ramadan, Tariq. 1999a. *Muslims in France: The Way Towards Coexistence*. Leicester, UK: Islamic Foundation.

———.1999b. *To be a European Muslim*. Leicester, UK: Islamic Foundation.

Rath, Jan, Rinnus Pennix, Kees Groendendijk, and Astrid Meyer. 1999. "The Politics of Recognizing Religious Diversity in Europe: Social Reactions to the Institutionalization of Islam in the Netherlands, Belgium, and Great Britain." *Netherlands Journal of Social Sciences* 35(1): 53–70.

———. 2001. *Western Europe and Its Islam*. Leiden, Netherlands: Brill.

Ray, Joe. 2002. "New Flash for a Paris Light Night, and Attack, Add to Mayor's Flair." *Boston Globe*, October 13, p. A22.

Regierungspräsidium Stuttgart. 2001. "Regierungspräsidium weist Widerspruch des Verbands der Islamischen Kulturzentren e.V. zurück." Press release, December 14. Stuttgart, Germany: Regierungspräsidium Stuttgart.

Reich, Rob. 2003. "Multicultural Accommodations in Education." Pp. 299–324 in Kevin McDonough and Walter Feinberg, eds., *Education and Citizenship in Liberal-Democratic Societies: Teaching for Cosmopolitan Values and Collective Identities*. Oxford, UK: Oxford University Press.

REMID [Religionswissenschaftlicher Medien– und Informationsdienst e. V.]. 2003. "Religionen in Deutschland: Mitgliederzahlen." Available at http://www.uni-leipzig.de/ ~religion/remid_info_zahlen.htm. Accessed May 7.

Rémond, René. 1999. *L'anticléricalisme en France: de 1815 à nos jours*, new revised and expanded edition. Paris: Fayard.

Renard, Michel. 1999. "France, Terre de Mosquées?" *Hommes et Migration* 1220 (July–August) 30–41.

Révillion, Bertrand. 1989a. "'Ne faisons pas la guerre aux adolescentes beurs': Le cardinal Lustiger se demande s'il ne s'agit pas d'abord d'un problème d'identité." *La Croix*, October 21, in Centre de Ressources Documentaires. *Dossier de presse sur l'affaire du foulard islamique*. Paris: Agence pour le Développement des Relations Interculturelles. Vol. 1, p. 41.

———.1989b. "Robert Chapuis face à la question du voile: Demain, des écoles islamiques sous contrat?" *La Croix*, October 26, in Centre de Ressources Documentaires. *Dossier de presse sur l'affaire du foulard islamique*. Paris: Agence pour le Développement des Relations Interculturelles. Vol. 1, p. 102.

Roald, Anne Sofie. 2001. *Women in Islam: The Western Experience*. London and New York: Routledge.

Robbers, Gerhard. 1996. "State and Church in Germany." Pp. 54–72 in Gerhard Robbers, ed., *State and Church in the European Union*. Baden-Baden, Germany: Nomos.

_____. 2000. "The Legal Status of Islam in Germany." Pp. 147–154 in Silvio Ferrari and Anthony Bradney, eds., *Islam and European Legal Systems*. Aldershot, UK: Ashgate/Dartmouth.

Rohe, Mathias. 2001. *Der Islam–Alltagskonflikte und Lösungen: Rechtliche Perspektiven*. Freiburg, Germany: Herder.

Rosser-Owen, Daoud. 2001. "Pluralism and the Church–State Link: A View from the Muslim Community." Available at http://www.members.tripod.com/british_muslims_assn/contents.html. Accessed May 3.

Rotman, Charlotte. 2002. "Jurisprudence et médiation, cas d'écoles efficaces." *Libération*, December 4, section "Événement," p. 2.

Roy, Olivier. 1999. *Vers un islam européen*. Paris: Éditions esprit.

Runnymede Trust. 1997. *Islamophobia: A Challenge for Us All*. London: Runnymede Trust.

_____. 2000. *The Future of Multi-Ethnic Britain*. London: Runnymede Trust.

Rupp, Hendrik. 2000. "Heslacher wehren sich gegen eine Moschee: Moslemischer Orden plant Kulturzentrum." *Südwestpresse* (Ulm), February 11.

Sahinoglu, Ahmet. 1986. "Erziehungsrat in der Tükischen Botschaft, Bonn." Pp. 92–5 in Doron Kiesel, Klaus Philipp Seif, and Ulrich O. Sievering, eds., *Islamunterricht an deutschen Schulen?* Frankfurt a.M.: Haag + Herchen.

Salaam Portal. 2003. "Muslim Information Resources." Available at http://www.salaam.co.uk. Accessed June 4.

Samson, Michel. 2002. "À Marseille, les divisions de la communauté freinent le projet de grande mosquée; Le maire a demandé aux musulmans de s'entendre avant le 5 novembre." *Le Monde*, October 6–7, p. 8.

Sanneh, Lamin. 1998. "Islam, Christianity and Public Policy." Pp. 25–74 in Leslie Newbigin, Lamin Sanneh, and Jenny Taylor, eds., *Faith and Power: Christianity and Islam in Secular Britain*. London: SPCK.

Sarwar, Ghulam. 1994. *British Muslims and Schools*. London: Muslim Educational Trust.

Scantlebury, Elizabeth. 1995. "Muslims in Manchester: The Depiction of a Religious Community." *New Community* 21(3):425–35.

Schain, Martin. 1987. "The National Front in France and the Construction of Political Legitimacy." *West European Politics* 10 (2):229–52.

Shachar, Ayelet. 2001. *Multicultural Jurisdictions: Cultural Differences and Women's Rights*. Cambridge, UK: Cambridge University Press.

Schiffauer, Werner. 2000. *Die Gottesmänner: Türkische Islamisten in Deutschland*. Frankfurt a.M.: Suhrkamp.

Schmidt-Volkmar, Erich. 1962. *Der Kulturkampf in Deutschland, 1871–1890*. Göttingen, Germany: Musterschmidt.

Schools: Building on Success. 2001. London: Crown Copyright.

Sciolino, Elaine. 2003a. "A Maze of Identities for the Muslims of France." *New York Times*, April 9, p. A3.

———. 2003b. "French Threaten Expulsions after Islam Radical Victory." *New York Times*, April 16, p. A3.

———. 2003c. "France Envisions a Citizenry of Model Muslims." *New York Times*, May 7, p. A4.

Seifert, Annette. 2000. "Islamisches Zentrum weckt große Ängste: Anwohner und Geschäftsleute in Heslach fürchten Überfremdung–Bürgermeister Murawski will vermitteln." *Stuttgarter Nachrichten*, February 11, p. 19.

Seksig, Alain. 1999. "Les croyants les plus proches de la 'laïcité à la française' sont les musulmans: un entretien avec Soheib Bencheikh, mufti de Marseille." *Hommes et Migrations* 1218(March/April):14–21.

Shadid, Wasif, and Sjoerd van Koningsveld. 1996. "Political Participation: The Muslim Perspective." Pp. 2–13 in W. A. R. Shadid and P. S. van Koningsveld, eds., *Political Participation and Identities of Muslims in non-Muslim States*. Kampen, Netherlands: Kok Pharos.

Shand, Jack D. 1998. "The Decline of Traditional Christian Beliefs in Germany." *Sociology of Religion* 59(2):179–84.

Shatz, Adam. 2002. "The Torture of Algiers." *New York Review of Books*, November 21, pp. 53–7.

Shirer, William L. 1960. *The Rise and Fall of the Third Reich*. New York: Fawcett Crest.

Siddiqui, Ataullah. 2000. "Issues in Co-Existence and Dialogue: Muslims and Christians in Britain." Pp. 183–200 in Jacques Waardenburgh, ed., *Muslim-Christian Perceptions of Dialogue Today*. Sterling, VA: Peeters.

———. 2002. "Believing and Belonging in a Pluralist Society – Exploring Resources in Islamic Traditions." Pp. 23–33 in David A. Hart, ed., *Multi-Faith Britain*. London: O Books.

Siddiqui, Iqbal. 2000. "British Muslims and the Mainstream Political System." *Q News* 324 (October):13–14.

Simon, Rita J., and Susan H. Alexander. 1993. *The Ambivalent Welcome: Print Media, Public Opinion and Immigration*. Westport, CT: Praeger.

Soper, J. Christopher. 1994. *Evangelical Christianity in the United States and Great Britain: Religious Beliefs, Political Choices*. London and New York: Macmillan and New York University Press.

Soper, J. Christopher, and Joel Fetzer. 2002. "Religion and Politics in a Secular Europe: Cutting against the Grain." Pp. 169–91 in Ted Gerard Jelen and Clyde Wilcox, eds., *Religion and Politics in Comparative Perspective: The One, the Few, and the Many*. New York and Cambridge, UK: Cambridge University Press.

Soysal, Yasemin Nuhoglu. 1994. *Limits of Citizenship: Migrants and Postnational Membership in Europe*. Chicago, IL: Chicago University Press.

Spencer, Ian R. G. 1997. *British Immigration Policy Since 1939: The Making of a Multi-Racial Britain*. London: Routledge.

Spuler-Stegemann, Ursula. 1998. *Muslime in Deutschland: Nebeneinander oder Miteinander?* Freiburg, Germany: Herder.

———.2002. *Muslime in Deutschland: Informationen und Klärungen.* Freiburg, Germany: Herder.

Statistics of Education. 2001. *Schools in England.* London: Stationary Office.

Stowasser, Barbara Freyer. 2002. "The Turks in Germany: From Sojourners to Citizens." Pp. 52–69 in Yvonne Yazbeck Haddad, ed., *Muslims in the West: From Sojourners to Citizens.* Oxford, UK: Oxford University Press.

Stuttgarter Zeitung. 2001. "Muslime offen für Alternative: Neue Hoffnung in Heslach." February 13, p. 21.

Suddeutsche Zeitung. 2002. "Lehrerin darf nich mit Kopftuch unterrichten." July 5, p. 6.

Sung, Grace. 2002. "Many in France Are Tired of Living in Fear: The Surging Crime Rate is the Electorate's No. 1 Concern, as Extreme-Right Presidential Candidate Jean-Marie Le Pen Knows Well." *Straits Times* [Singapore], May 5, section "World."

Syal, Roger, and Christopher Morgan. 1997. "Muslims Set to Outnumber Anglicans." *Sunday Times (London)* May 11, p. A1.

Tapinos, Georges. 1975. *L'immigration étrangère en France: 1946–1973.* Paris: Presses universitaires de France.

Tarrow, Sidney G. 1998. *Power in Social Movement: Social Movements and Contentious Politics.* Cambridge, UK: Cambridge University Press.

Ternisien, Xavier. 2003. "À la mairie de Schiltigheim, l'islam de France a choisi ses représentants." *Le Monde*, April 7.

Thränhardt, Dietrich. 2000. "Conflict, Consensus, and Policy Outcomes: Immigration and Integration in Germany and the Netherlands." Pp. 162–86 in Ruud Koopmans and Paul Statham, eds., *Challenging Immigration and Ethnic Relations Politics.* Oxford, UK: Oxford University Press.

Tibi, Bassam. 2000. *Der Islam und Deutschland: Muslime in Deutschland.* Stuttgart, Germany: Deutsche Verlags-Anstalt.

———. 2002. *Islamische Zuwanderung: Die gescheiterte Integration.* Stuttgart, Germany: Deutsche Verlags-Anstalt.

Times (London). 2001. "Home Truths: Blunkett Is Right to Seek a New Approach to Race." December 10, p. 17.

Tolley, Michael C. 2000. "Religion and the State in Great Britain." Paper prepared for delivery at the 2000 annual meeting of the American Political Science Association Meeting, Washington, DC.

Travis, Alan. 2001. "Attack on Afghanistan: ICM Poll." *Guardian* (London), October 12, p. 1.

Tribalat, Michèle, ed. 1991. *Cent ans d'immigration, étrangers d'hier Français d'aujourd'hui: Apport démographique, dynamique familiale et économique de l'immigration étrangère.* Paris: Presses Universitaires de France and Institut National d'Études Démographiques.

————.1995. *Faire France: Une enquête sur les immigrés et leurs enfants*. Paris: Éditions La Découverte.

————.1999. *Dreux: Voyage au cœur du malaise française*. Paris: Syros.

Tristan, Anne. 1987. *Au Front*. Paris: Gallimard.

Turkish Daily News. 1998. "Refah Closure Goes into Effect." *Turkish Daily News* Global News Wire, February 23.

United Press International. 1990. "Two Lyon Suburbs Calm after Third Night of Riots." Wire service article, October 9.

Vallely, Paul. 1997. "Muslims to Offer Voting Advice to the Faithful." *Independent* (London), January 20, p. 4.

VELKD [Vereinigte Evangelisch-Lutherischen Kirche Deutschlands] and EKD [Evangelische Kirche in Deutschland]. 2001. *Was jeder vom Islam wissen muß*, 6th ed. Gütersloh, Germany: Gütersloher Verlagshaus.

Venel, Nancy. 1999. "Le foulard à l'école." *La Médina* 2 (October/November):16–17.

Verba, Sidney, Kay Lehman Schlozman, and Henry E. Brady. 1995. *Voice and Equality: Civic Voluntarism in American Politics*. Cambridge, MA: Harvard University Press.

Vertovek, Steven. 1997. "Muslims, the State, and the Public Sphere in Britain." Pp. 169–85 in Gerd Nonneman, Tim Niblock, and Bogdan Szajkowski, eds., *Muslim Communities in the New Europe*. Reading, UK: Ithaca Press.

————. 2002. "Islamophobia and Muslim Recognition in Britain." Pp. 19–35 in Yvonne Yazbeck Haddad, ed., *Muslims in the West: From Sojourners to Citizens*. Oxford, UK: Oxford University Press.

Vertovek, Steven, and Ceri Peach. 1997. "Islam in Europe and the Politics of Religion and Community." Pp. 3–45 in Steven Vertovek and Ceri Peach, eds., *Islam in Europe:The Politics of Religion and Community*. New York: Saint Martin's Press.

von Denffer, Ahmad. 1995. *Moscheeführer: Islamisches Zentrum München*. Munich: Islamisches Zentrum München.

von Krosigk, Constanze. 2000. *Der Islam in Frankreich: Laizistische Religionspolitik von 1974 bis 1999*. Hamburg: Verlag Dr. Kovač.

Waddington, Robert. 1985. "The Church and Educational Policy." Pp. 221–55 in George Moyser, ed., *Church and Politics Today*. Edinburgh, UK: T & T Clark.

Wald, Kenneth D. 1983. *Crosses on the Ballot*. Princeton, NJ: Princeton University Press.

Waldman, Amy. 2002. "How in a Little British Town Jihad Found Young Converts." *New York Times*, April 24, p. 41.

Walker, David. 2002. "Race and the Workplace: Study Reveals Job Plight of Muslims." *Guardian* (London), February 20, p. 3.

Wallraff, Günter. 1985. *Ganz unten*. Cologne: Kiepenheuer + Witsch.

Wanzura, Werner, and Franz-Georg Rips. 1981. *Der Islam: Körperschaft des öffentlichen Rechts?* Altenberge, Germany: Verlag für Christlich-Islamisches Schrifttum.

Warner, Carolyn. 1999. "Organizing Islam for Politics in Western Europe." Paper prepared for presentation at the annual meeting of the American Political Science Association, Atlanta, GA.

Warren, Mark R. 2001. *Dry Bones Rattling: Community Building to Revitalize American Democracy*. Princeton, NJ: Princeton University Press.

Watson, Rory. 2002. "Terrorism Increases Attacks on Muslims in Europe." *Times* (London), May 24, p. 17.

Webster, Paul. 1993. "Death Paris-Style as Pasqua Applies the Right Stuff: Riot Police Clashed in Paris Last Night with Protesters after a Black Youth Was Shot Dead in Custody." *Guardian* (London), April 8, p. 24.

Weil, Patrick. 1991. *La France et ses étrangers: L'aventure d'une politique de l'immigration de 1938 à nos jours*. Paris: Gallimard.

Weil, Patrick, and John Crowley. 1994. "Integration in Theory and Practice: A Comparison of France and Britain." Pp. 110–26 in Martin Baldwin-Edwards and Martin A. Schain, eds., *The Politics of Immigration in Western Europe*. London: Frank Cass.

Weiße, Wolfram. 2000. "Der Hamburger Weg–Dialogisch orientierter 'Religionsunterricht für alle'." Pp. 25–48 in Beauftragte der Bundesregierung für Ausländerfrage. *Islamisher Religionsunterricht an staatlichen Schulen in Deutschland: Praxis – Konzepte – Perspektiven; Dokumentation eines Fachgespräches*. No. 8 (September). Berlin and Bonn: Beauftragte der Bundesregierung für Ausländerfrage.

Weller, Paul, Alice Feldman, and Kingsley Purdam. 2001. *Religious Discrimination in England and Wales*. London: Home Office Research.

Wihtol de Wenden, Catherine. 1988. *Les immigrés et la politique*. Paris: Presses de la Fondation nationale des sciences politiques.

Wihtol de Wenden, Catherine, and Rémy Leveau. 2001. *La beurgeoisie: Les trois âges de la vie associative issue de l'immigration*. Paris: CNRS Éditions.

Willaime, Jean-Paul. 1998. "Religion and Secular France between Northern and Southern Europe." *Social Compass* 45(1):155–74.

Woltersdorf, Adrienne. 2003. "Die falsche Toleranz; Der Migrationsforscher Ralf Ghadban kritisiert die überholten Grundlagen der Ausländerpolitik in der Stadt. Seit 20 Jahren betreut er Zuwanderer und Flüchtlinge: 'Die Kluft is größer geworden'." *TAZ*, April 2, section Berlin Aktuell, p. 22.

Wonnacott, Ronald J., and Thomas H. Wonnacott. 1985. *Introductory Statistics*. 4th ed. New York: John Wiley and Sons.

Wright, Tony. 2001. Speech to House of Commons, DD, MM. *Parliamentary Debates*, Commons, 5th ser., vol. 375, col. 448.

Wuthnow, Robert. 1988. *The Restructuring of American Religion: Society and Faith since World War Two*. Princeton, NJ: Princeton University Press.

Xinhua News Agency. 1997. "Riot and Robbery Reported on New Year's Eve in France." Wire service article. December 30, item no. 1230252.

Ysmal, Colette. 2002. "Chirac réalise un score que n'avait même pas atteint de Gaulle lors de la consultation de 1958 (79,3%); Un référendum plus qu'une élection présidentielle." *Le Figaro*, May 6, section "politique."

Zald, Mayer N. and John D. McCarthy, eds. 1987. *Social Movements in an Organizational Society*. New Brunswick, NJ: Transaction Books.

Zentralinstitut Islam-Archiv-Deutschland. 2000. "Muslime vor den Landtagswahlen in Nordrhein-Westfalen." Dokumentation Nr. 3/2000 Ergänzungen. Soest: Zentralinstitut Islam-Archiv-Deutschland.

Zolberg, Aristide R., and Long Litt Woon. 1999. "Why Islam Is Like Spanish: Cultural Incorporation in Europe and the United States." *Politics and Society* 27:5–38.

Zouari, Fawzia. 2002. *Le voile islamique: Histoire et actualité, du Coran à l'affaire du foulard*. Lausanne, Switzerland: Favre.

Index